Java EE 7 Development with NetBeans 8

Develop professional enterprise Java EE applications quickly and easily with this popular IDE

David R. Heffelfinger

[PACKT] open source*
PUBLISHING   community experience distilled

BIRMINGHAM - MUMBAI

Java EE 7 Development with NetBeans 8

First published: October 2008

Second edition: June 2011

Third edition: January 2015

Production reference: 1270115

Published by Packt Publishing Ltd.
Livery Place
35 Livery Street
Birmingham B3 2PB, UK.

ISBN 978-1-78398-352-0

www.packtpub.com

Credits

Author
David R. Heffelfinger

Reviewers
Saurabh Chhajed
Halil Karaköse
Mario Pérez Madueño
David Salter
Manjeet Singh Sawhney

Acquisition Editor
Sam Wood

Content Development Editors
Madhuja Chaudhari
Anand Singh

Technical Editor
Pramod Kumavat

Copy Editors
Roshni Banerjee
Neha Karnani

Project Coordinator
Akash Poojary

Proofreaders
Ting Baker
Simran Bhogal
Samuel Redman Birch
Maria Gould
Ameesha Green
Paul Hindle
Bernadette Watkins

Indexer
Tejal Soni

Production Coordinator
Aparna Bhagat

Cover Work
Aparna Bhagat

About the Author

David R. Heffelfinger is the Chief Technology Officer (CTO) at Ensode Technology, LLC, a software consulting firm based in the Greater Washington DC area. He has been architecting, designing, and developing software professionally since 1995. He has been using Java as his primary programming language since 1996. He has worked on many large-scale projects for several clients, including the U.S. Department of Homeland Security, Freddie Mac, Fannie Mae, and the U.S. Department of Defense. He has a master's degree in software engineering from Southern Methodist University, Dallas, Texas. David is the editor-in-chief of Ensode. net (`http://www.ensode.net`), a website on Java, Linux, and other technologies. David is a frequent speaker at Java conferences such as JavaOne. You can follow David on Twitter at `@ensode`.

About the Reviewers

Saurabh Chhajed is a Cloudera Certified Developer for Apache Hadoop and Sun (Oracle) Certified Java/J2EE Programmer with 5 years of professional experience in the enterprise application development life cycle using the latest frameworks, tools, and design patterns. He has extensive experience of working with Agile and Scrum methodologies and enjoys acting as an evangelist for new technologies such as NoSQL and big data and analytics. Saurabh has helped some of the largest U.S. companies to build their product suites from scratch. While not working, he enjoys traveling and sharing his experiences on his blog (`http://saurzcode.in`).

Halil Karaköse is a freelance software architect. He graduated from Işık University in Turkey as a computer engineer in 2005.

He has worked in the telecommunications industry for 10 years, and has worked for Turkcell and Ericsson. In 2014, he quit his job at Ericsson to establish his own software consultancy company, KODFARKI (`http://kodfarki.com`).

His primary focus is Java, Java EE, Spring, and Primefaces. He also likes to give Java trainings. He has a keen interest in Java tools that speed up development, such as NetBeans and IntelliJ IDEA. In his spare time, he likes running, skiing, and playing PES.

Mario Pérez Madueño was born in 1975 in Turin and lives in Barcelona. He graduated in computer engineering from the Open University of Catalonia (UOC), Spain, in 2010. Mario is a Java SE, ME, and EE enthusiast and has been a member of the NetBeans Community Acceptance Testing program (NetCAT) for many years. He was also the technical reviewer of the books, *Java EE 5 Development with NetBeans 6* and *Building SOA-based Composite Applications Using NetBeans IDE 6*, both by Packt Publishing.

I would like to thank my wife, María, for her unconditional help and support in all the projects I get involved in, and Martín and Matías for giving me the strength to go ahead.

David Salter is an enterprise software developer and architect who has been developing software professionally since 1991. His relationship with Java goes back to the beginning, when Java 1.0 was used to write desktop applications and applets for interactive websites. David has been developing enterprise Java applications using both Java EE (and J2EE) and open source solutions since 2001. David wrote the books, *NetBeans IDE 8 Cookbook* and *Seam 2.x Web Development*, both by Packt Publishing. He has also co-authored the book, *Building SOA-Based Composite Application Using NetBeans IDE 6*, Packt Publishing.

I would like to thank my family for supporting me. Special thanks and love to my wife.

Manjeet Singh Sawhney currently works for a large IT consultancy in London, UK, as a Principal Consultant - Enterprise Data Architect within the Global Enterprise Architecture Consulting practice. Previously, he worked for global organizations in various roles, including development, technical solutions consulting, and data management consulting. Although Manjeet has worked across a range of programming languages, he specializes in Java. During his postgraduate studies, he also worked as a Student Tutor for one of the top 100 universities in the world, where he was teaching Java to undergraduate students and was involved in marking exams and evaluating project assignments. Manjeet acquired his professional experience by working on several mission-critical projects serving clients in the financial services, telecommunications, manufacturing, retail, and public sectors.

I am very thankful to my parents; my wife, Jaspal; my son, Kohinoor; and my daughter, Prabhnoor, for their encouragement and patience, as reviewing this book took some of my evenings and weekends from the family.

www.PacktPub.com

Support files, eBooks, discount offers, and more

For support files and downloads related to your book, please visit www.PacktPub.com.

Did you know that Packt offers eBook versions of every book published, with PDF and ePub files available? You can upgrade to the eBook version at www.PacktPub.com and as a print book customer, you are entitled to a discount on the eBook copy. Get in touch with us at service@packtpub.com for more details.

At www.PacktPub.com, you can also read a collection of free technical articles, sign up for a range of free newsletters and receive exclusive discounts and offers on Packt books and eBooks.

https://www2.packtpub.com/books/subscription/packtlib

Do you need instant solutions to your IT questions? PacktLib is Packt's online digital book library. Here, you can search, access, and read Packt's entire library of books.

Why subscribe?

- Fully searchable across every book published by Packt
- Copy and paste, print, and bookmark content
- On demand and accessible via a web browser

Free access for Packt account holders

If you have an account with Packt at www.PacktPub.com, you can use this to access PacktLib today and view 9 entirely free books. Simply use your login credentials for immediate access.

Table of Contents

Preface

Java EE 7, the latest version of the Java EE specification, adds several new features to simplify enterprise application development. New versions of existing Java EE APIs have been included in this latest version of Java EE. JSF 2.2 has been updated to better support wizard-like interfaces via FacesFlows and has been enhanced to better support HTML5. NetBeans supports JPA 2.1 features such as Bean Validation and many others. EJB session beans can be automatically generated by NetBeans, allowing us to easily leverage EJB features such as transactions and concurrency. CDI advanced features such as qualifiers, stereotypes, and others can be easily implemented via NetBeans' wizards. JMS 2.0 has been greatly simplified, allowing us to quickly and easily develop messaging applications. Java EE includes a new Java API for JSON Processing (JSON-P), allowing us to quickly and easily process JSON data. NetBeans includes several features to allow us to quickly and easily develop both RESTful and SOAP-based web services.

This book will guide you through all the NetBeans features that make the development of enterprise Java EE 7 applications a breeze.

What this book covers

Chapter 1, *Getting Started with NetBeans*, provides an introduction to NetBeans, giving time-saving tips and tricks that will result in more efficient development of Java applications.

Chapter 2, *Developing Web Applications Using JavaServer Faces 2.2*, explains how NetBeans can help us easily develop web applications that take advantage of the JavaServer Faces 2.2 framework.

Chapter 3, JSF Component Libraries, covers how NetBeans can help us easily develop JSF applications using popular component libraries such as PrimeFaces, RichFaces, and ICEfaces.

Chapter 4, Interacting with Databases through the Java Persistence API, explains how NetBeans allows us to easily develop applications taking advantage of the Java Persistence API (JPA), including how to automatically generate JPA entities from existing schemas. This chapter also covers how complete web-based applications can be generated with a few clicks from an existing database schema.

Chapter 5, Implementing the Business Tier with Session Beans, discusses how NetBeans simplifies EJB 3.1 session bean development.

Chapter 6, Contexts and Dependency Injection, discusses how the CDI API introduced in Java EE 6 can help us integrate the different layers of our application.

Chapter 7, Messaging with JMS and Message-driven Beans, explains Java EE messaging technologies such as the Java Message Service (JMS) and Message-driven Beans (MDB), covering NetBeans' features that simplify application development taking advantage of these APIs.

Chapter 8, Java API for JSON Processing, explains how to process JSON data using the new JSON-P Java EE API.

Chapter 9, Java API for WebSocket, explains how to use the new Java API for WebSocket to develop web-based applications featuring full duplex communication between the browser and the server.

Chapter 10, RESTful Web Services with JAX-RS, covers RESTful web services with the Java API for RESTful Web Services, including coverage of how NetBeans can automatically generate RESTful web services and both Java and JavaScript RESTful web service clients.

Chapter 11, SOAP Web Services with JAX-WS, explains how NetBeans can help us easily develop SOAP web services based on the Java API for the XML Web Services (JAX-WS) API.

What you need for this book

You need Java Development Kit (JDK) version 7.0 or newer and NetBeans 8.0 or newer Java EE edition.

Who this book is for

If you are a Java developer who wishes to develop Java EE applications while taking advantage of NetBeans' functionality to automate repetitive tasks and ease your software development efforts, this is the book for you. Familiarity with NetBeans or Java EE is not assumed.

Conventions

In this book, you will find a number of text styles that distinguish between different kinds of information. Here are some examples of these styles and an explanation of their meaning.

Code words in text, database table names, folder names, filenames, file extensions, pathnames, dummy URLs, user input, and Twitter handles are shown as follows: "NetBeans uses the JAVA_HOME environment variable to populate the JDK's directory location."

A block of code is set as follows:

```
<package com.ensode.flowscope.namedbeans;

import javax.annotation.PostConstruct;
import javax.annotation.PreDestroy;
import javax.faces.flow.FlowScoped;
import javax.inject.Named;

@Named
@FlowScoped("registration")
public class RegistrationBean {
...
```

When we wish to draw your attention to a particular part of a code block, the relevant lines or items are set in bold:

```
package com.ensode.flowscope.namedbeans;

import javax.annotation.PostConstruct;
import javax.annotation.PreDestroy;
import javax.faces.flow.FlowScoped;
import javax.inject.Named;

@Named
@FlowScoped("registration")
public class RegistrationBean {
...
```

Any command-line input or output is written as follows:

```
chmod +x filename.sh
```

New terms and **important words** are shown in bold. Words that you see on the screen, for example, in menus or dialog boxes, appear in the text like this: " To download NetBeans, we need to click on the **Download** button."

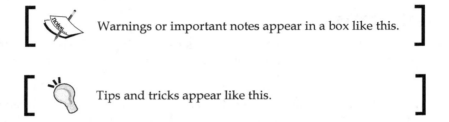

Warnings or important notes appear in a box like this.

Tips and tricks appear like this.

Reader feedback

Feedback from our readers is always welcome. Let us know what you think about this book—what you liked or disliked. Reader feedback is important for us as it helps us develop titles that you will really get the most out of.

To send us general feedback, simply e-mail feedback@packtpub.com, and mention the book's title in the subject of your message.

If there is a topic that you have expertise in and you are interested in either writing or contributing to a book, see our author guide at www.packtpub.com/authors.

Customer support

Now that you are the proud owner of a Packt book, we have a number of things to help you to get the most from your purchase.

Downloading the example code

You can download the example code files from your account at http://www.packtpub.com for all the Packt Publishing books you have purchased. If you purchased this book elsewhere, you can visit http://www.packtpub.com/support and register to have the files e-mailed directly to you.

Errata

Although we have taken every care to ensure the accuracy of our content, mistakes do happen. If you find a mistake in one of our books—maybe a mistake in the text or the code—we would be grateful if you could report this to us. By doing so, you can save other readers from frustration and help us improve subsequent versions of this book. If you find any errata, please report them by visiting http://www.packtpub.com/submit-errata, selecting your book, clicking on the **Errata Submission Form** link, and entering the details of your errata. Once your errata are verified, your submission will be accepted and the errata will be uploaded to our website or added to any list of existing errata under the Errata section of that title.

To view the previously submitted errata, go to https://www.packtpub.com/books/content/support and enter the name of the book in the search field. The required information will appear under the **Errata** section.

Piracy

Piracy of copyrighted material on the Internet is an ongoing problem across all media. At Packt, we take the protection of our copyright and licenses very seriously. If you come across any illegal copies of our works in any form on the Internet, please provide us with the location address or website name immediately so that we can pursue a remedy.

Please contact us at copyright@packtpub.com with a link to the suspected pirated material.

We appreciate your help in protecting our authors and our ability to bring you valuable content.

Questions

If you have a problem with any aspect of this book, you can contact us at questions@packtpub.com, and we will do our best to address the problem.

1
Getting Started with NetBeans

In this chapter, we will learn how to get started with NetBeans. The following topics are covered in this chapter:

- Introduction
- Obtaining NetBeans
- Installing NetBeans
- Starting NetBeans for the first time
- Configuring NetBeans for Java EE development
- Deploying our first application
- NetBeans tips for effective development

Introduction

NetBeans is an **Integrated Development Environment (IDE)** and platform. Although initially, the NetBeans IDE could only be used to develop Java applications, as of version 6, NetBeans supports several programming languages, either through built-in support, or by installing additional plugins. Programming languages natively supported by NetBeans include Java, C, C++, PHP, HTML, and JavaScript. Groovy, Scala, and others are supported via additional plugins.

In addition to being an IDE, NetBeans is also a platform. Developers can use NetBeans' APIs to create both NetBeans plugins and standalone applications.

For a brief history of NetBeans, see http://netbeans.org/ about/history.html.

Although the NetBeans IDE supports several programming languages, because of its roots as a Java only IDE it is more widely used and known within the Java community. As a Java IDE, NetBeans has built-in support for Java SE (Standard Edition) applications, which typically run on a user's desktop or notebook computer; Java ME (Micro Edition) applications, which typically run on small devices such as cell phones or PDAs; and for Java EE (Enterprise Edition) applications, which typically run on "big iron" servers and can support thousands of concurrent users.

In this book, we will be focusing on the Java EE development capabilities of NetBeans, and how to take advantage of NetBeans' features to help us develop Java EE applications more efficiently.

Some of the features we will cover include how NetBeans can help us speed up web application development using **JavaServer Faces** (**JSF**), the standard Java EE component based web framework by providing a starting point for these kinds of artifacts. We will also see how NetBeans can help us generate **Java Persistence API** (**JPA**) entities from an existing database schema (JPA is the standard object-relational mapping tool included with Java EE).

In addition to web development, we will see how NetBeans allows us to easily develop **Enterprise JavaBeans** (**EJBs**); and how to easily develop web services. We will also cover how to easily write both EJB and web service clients by taking advantage of some very nice NetBeans features.

Before taking advantage of all of the aforementioned NetBeans features, we of course need to have NetBeans installed, as covered in the next section.

Obtaining NetBeans

NetBeans can be obtained by downloading it from `http://www.netbeans.org`.

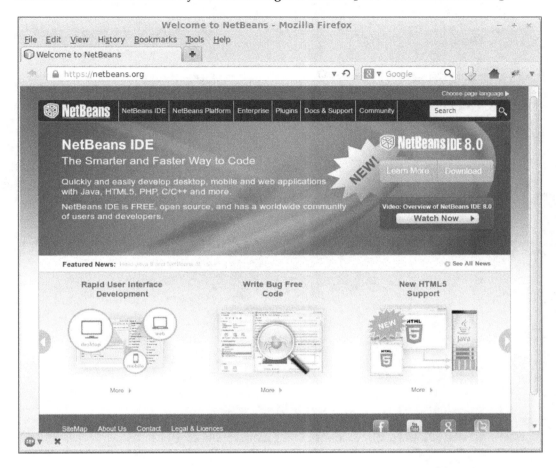

To download NetBeans, we need to click on the **Download** button. Clicking on this button will take us to a page displaying all NetBeans' download bundles.

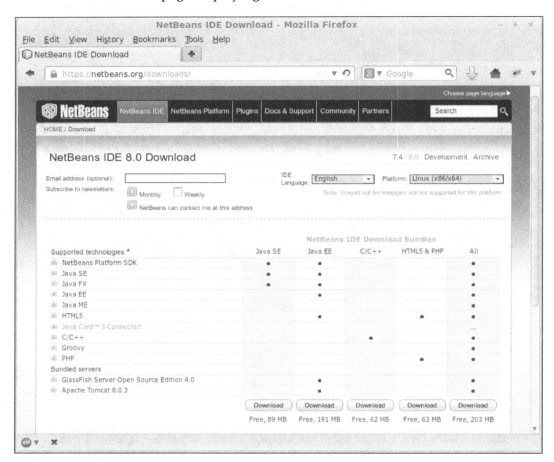

NetBeans' downloads include different NetBeans bundles that provide different levels of functionality. The following table summarizes the different NetBeans bundles available and describes the functionalities they provide.

NetBeans Bundle	Description
Java SE	Allows development of Java desktop applications.
Java EE	Allows development of Java Standard Edition (typically desktop) applications, and Java Enterprise Edition applications (enterprise applications running on "big iron" servers).
C/C++	Allows development of applications written in the C or C++ languages.

NetBeans Bundle	Description
HTML5 and PHP	Allows development of web applications using HTML5 and/or the popular open source PHP programming language.
All	Includes functionalities of all NetBeans bundles.

To follow the examples in this book, either the **Java EE** or the **All** bundle is needed.

> The screenshots in this book were taken with the **Java EE** bundle. NetBeans may look slightly different if the **All** bundle is used, particularly, some additional menu items might be seen.

The following platforms are officially supported by NetBeans:

- Windows
- Linux (x86/x64)
- Mac OS X

Additionally, NetBeans can be executed on any platform containing Java 7 or newer version. To download a version of NetBeans to be executed in one of these platforms, an OS independent of NetBeans is available.

> Although the OS independent version of NetBeans can be executed in all the supported platforms, it is recommended to obtain the platform specific version of NetBeans for your platform.

The NetBeans download page should detect the operating system being used to access it, and the appropriate platform should be selected by default. If this is not the case, or if you are downloading NetBeans with the intention of installing it in another workstation on another platform, the correct platform can be selected from the drop down labeled appropriately enough as **Platform**.

Once the correct platform has been selected, we need to click on the appropriate **Download** button for the NetBeans bundle we wish to install; for Java EE development, we need either the **Java EE,** or the **All** bundle. NetBeans will then be downloaded to a directory of our choice.

Java EE applications need to be deployed on an application server. Several application servers exist in the market; both the **Java EE** and the **All** NetBeans bundles come with GlassFish and Tomcat bundled. Tomcat is a popular open source servlet container, which can be used to deploy applications using JSF. However, it does not support other Java EE technologies such as EJBs or JPA. GlassFish is a 100 percent Java EE compliant application server. We will be using the bundled GlassFish application server to deploy and execute our examples.

Installing NetBeans

NetBeans requires a **Java Development Kit (JDK)** Version 1.7 or newer to be available before it can be installed.

 Since this book is aimed at experienced Java developers, we will not spend much time explaining how to install and configure the JDK. We can safely assume that the target market for the book is more than likely to have a JDK installed. Installation instructions for the Java Development Kit can be found at `http://docs.oracle.com/javase/7/docs/webnotes/install/index.html`.

NetBeans installation varies slightly between the supported platforms. In the following few sections we explain how to install NetBeans on each supported platform.

Microsoft Windows

For Microsoft Windows platforms, NetBeans is downloaded as an executable file named something like `netbeans-8.0-javaee-windows.exe` (exact name depends on the version of NetBeans and the NetBeans bundle that was selected for download). To install NetBeans on Windows platforms, simply navigate to the folder where NetBeans was downloaded and double-click on the executable file.

Mac OS X

For Mac OS X, the downloaded file is called something like `netbeans-8.0-javaee-macosx.dmg` (exact name depends on the NetBeans version and the NetBeans bundle that was selected for download). In order to install NetBeans, navigate to the location where the file was downloaded and double-click on it.

Linux

For Linux, NetBeans is downloaded in the form of a shell script. The name of the file will be similar to `netbeans-8.0-javaee-linux.sh` (exact name will depend on the version of NetBeans and the selected NetBeans bundle).

Before NetBeans can be installed on Linux, the downloaded file needs to be made executable, which can be done using a command line—by navigating to the directory where the NetBeans installer was downloaded and executing the following command:

```
chmod +x filename.sh
```

Substitute `filename.sh` in the preceding command with the appropriate filename for the platform and NetBeans bundle. Once the file is executable it can be installed from the command line as follows:

```
./filename.sh
```

Other platforms

For other platforms, NetBeans can be downloaded as a platform independent ZIP file. The name of the ZIP file will be something like `netbeans-8.0-201403101706-javaee.zip` (exact filename may vary, depending on the exact version of NetBeans downloaded and the NetBeans bundle that was selected).

To install NetBeans on one of these platforms, simply extract the ZIP file to any suitable directory.

Installation procedure

Even though the way to execute the installer varies slightly between platforms, the installer behaves in a similar way between most of them.

 One exception is the platform independent ZIP file, in which there is essentially no installer. Installing this version of NetBeans consists of extracting the ZIP file to any suitable directory.

After executing the NetBeans installation file for our platform, we should see a window similar to the one illustrated in the following screenshot.

The pack shown may vary depending on the NetBeans bundle that was downloaded. The preceding screenshot is for the Java EE bundle.

At this point, we should click on the button labeled **Next>** to continue the installation.

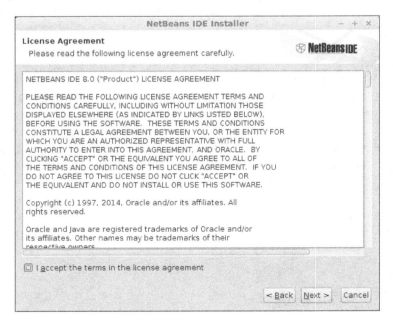

NetBeans is dual licensed, licenses for NetBeans include the **GNU Public License (GPL)** Version 2 with the classpath exception, and the **Common Development and Distribution License (CDDL)**. Both of these licenses are approved by the **Open Source Initiative (OSI)**.

To continue installing NetBeans, click on the checkbox labeled **I accept the terms in the license agreement** and click on the button labeled **Next>**.

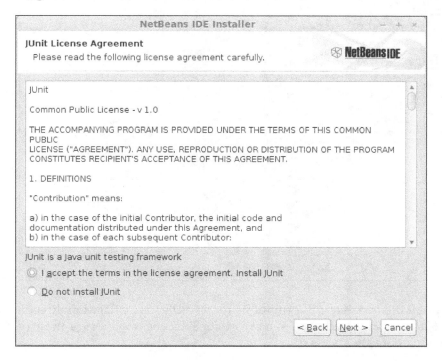

NetBeans comes bundled with JUnit, a popular Java unit testing framework. JUnit's license differs from the NetBeans license, so it needs to be accepted separately. Clicking the **Next>** button takes us to the next step in the installation wizard:

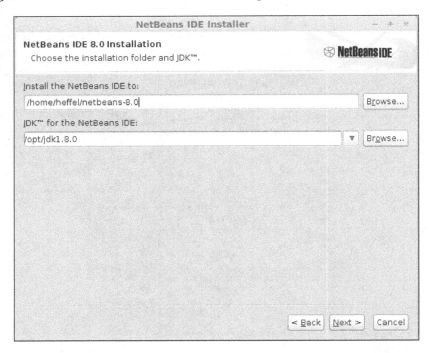

At this point the installer will prompt us for a NetBeans installation directory, and for a JDK to use with NetBeans. We can either select new values for these or retain the provided defaults.

Once we have selected the appropriate installation directory and JDK, we need to click on the button labeled **Next>** to continue the installation.

 NetBeans uses the JAVA_HOME environment variable to populate the JDK's directory location.

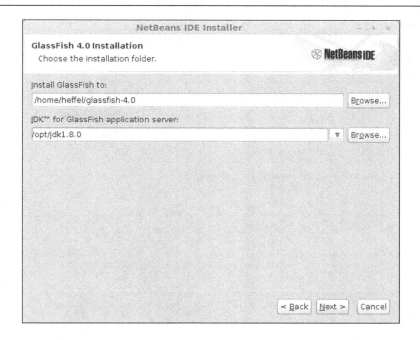

The installer will now prompt us for an installation directory for the GlassFish application server, as well as for the JDK to use for GlassFish; we can either enter a custom directory or accept the default values and then click on **Next>**.

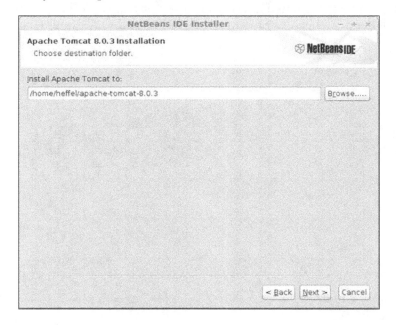

If we chose to install Tomcat, the installer will prompt us for a Tomcat installation directory. Again, we can either enter a custom directory or accept the default values and then click on **Next>**.

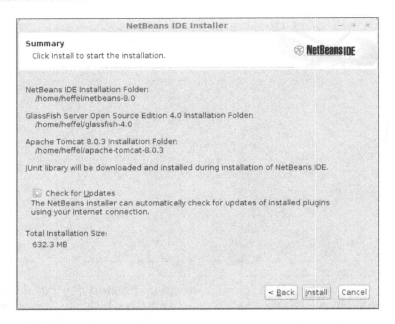

At this point, the installer will display a summary of our choices. After reviewing the summary, we need to click on the button labeled **Install** to begin the installation.

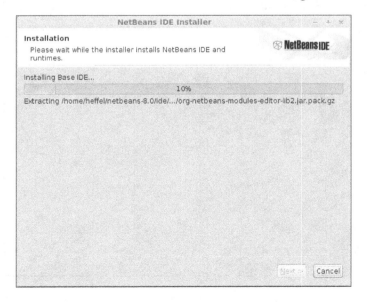

As the installation begins, the installer starts displaying a progress bar indicating the progress of installation.

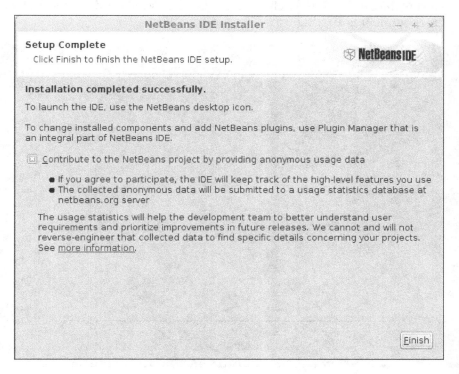

After NetBeans and all related components have been installed, the installer indicates a successful installation, giving us the option to contribute anonymous usage data as shown in the preceding screenshot. After making our selection we can simply click on the **Finish** button to exit the installer.

On most platforms, the installer places a NetBeans icon on the desktop; the icon should look like the following:

We can start NetBeans by double-clicking on the icon.

Starting NetBeans for the first time

We can start NetBeans by double-clicking on its icon. We should see the NetBeans splash screen while it is starting up.

Once NetBeans starts, we should see a page with links to demos, tutorials, and sample projects, among others.

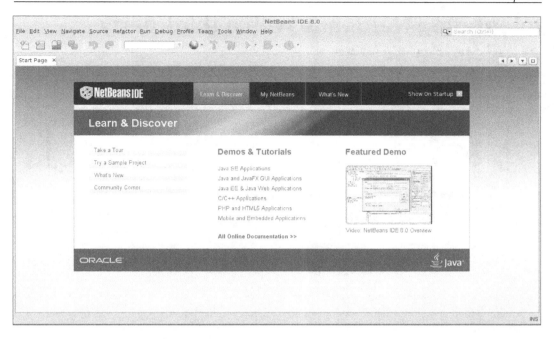

Every time NetBeans is launched, it shows the default start page as illustrated in the preceding screenshot. If we don't want this page to be displayed automatically every time NetBeans is started, we can disable this behavior by un-checking the checkbox labeled as **Show on Startup** at the top of the page. We can always get the start page back by going to **Help | Start Page**.

Configuring NetBeans for Java EE development

NetBeans comes preconfigured with the GlassFish application server, and with the JavaDB RDBMS. If we wish to use the included GlassFish application server and JavaDB RDBMS, then there is nothing we need to do to configure NetBeans. We can, however, integrate NetBeans with other Java EE application servers such as JBoss/WildFly, WebLogic, or WebSphere and with other relational database systems such as MySQL, PostgreSQL, Oracle, or any RDBMS supported by JDBC, which pretty much means any RDBMS.

Integrating NetBeans with a third-party application server

Integrating NetBeans with an application server is very simple. To do so, we need to perform the following steps:

 In this section, we will illustrate how to integrate NetBeans with JBoss, the procedure is very similar for other application servers or servlet containers.

1. First, we need to click on **Window | Services**.

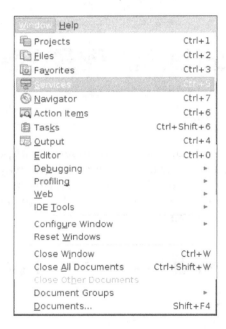

2. Next, we need to right-click on the node labeled **Servers** in the tree inside the **Services** window, and then select **Add Server...** from the resulting pop-up menu.

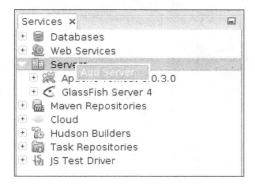

3. Then we need to select the server to install from the list in the resulting window, and click on the button labeled **Next>**.

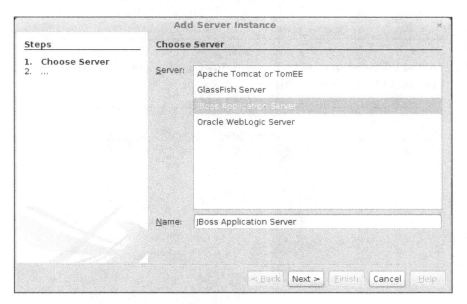

4. We then need to enter a location in the filesystem where the application server is installed and click **Next>**.

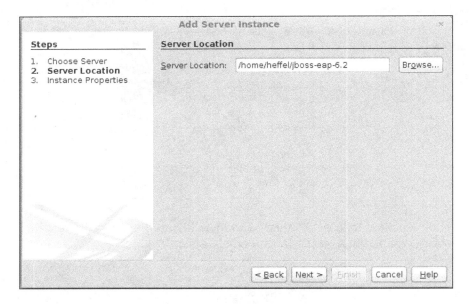

5. Finally, we need to select a domain, host, and port for our application server, then click on the **Finish** button.

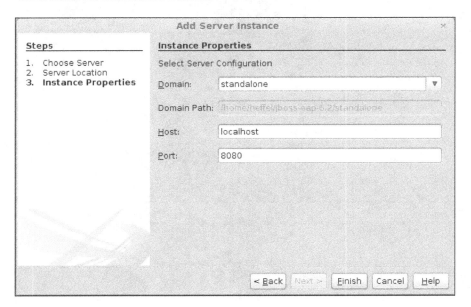

The **Services** window should now display our newly added application server:

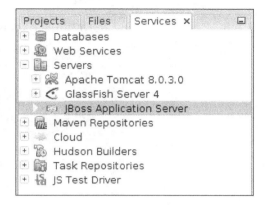

That's it! We have successfully integrated NetBeans with a third-party application server.

Integrating NetBeans with a third-party RDBMS

NetBeans comes with built-in integration with the JavaDB RDBMS system. Additionally, it comes with JDBC drivers for other RDBMS systems such as Oracle, MySQL, and PostgreSQL.

To integrate NetBeans with a third-party RDBMS, we need to tell NetBeans the location of its JDBC driver.

In this section, we will create a connection to HSQLDB, an open source RDBMS written in Java, to illustrate how to integrate NetBeans with a third-party RDBMS; the procedure is very similar for other RDBMS systems such as Oracle, Sybase, SQL Server, among others.

Adding a JDBC driver to NetBeans

Before we can connect to a third-party RDBMS, we need to add its JDBC driver to NetBeans. To add the JDBC driver, we need to right-click on the **Drivers** node under the **Databases** node in the **Services** tab.

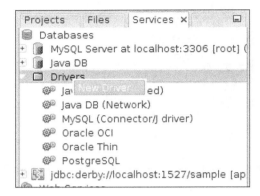

We then need to select a JAR file containing the JDBC driver for our RDBMS, NetBeans guesses the name of the driver class containing the JDBC driver. If more than one driver class is found in the JAR file, the correct one can be selected from the drop-down menu labeled **Driver Class**. We need to click on the **OK** button to add the driver to NetBeans as shown in the following screenshot:

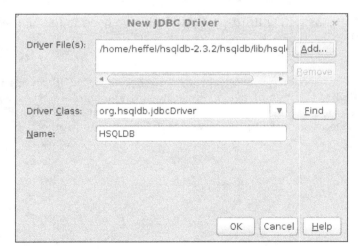

Once we have followed the preceding procedure, our new JDBC driver is displayed in the list of registered drivers.

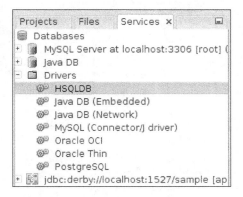

Connecting to a third-party RDBMS

Once we have added the JDBC driver for our RDBMS into NetBeans, we are ready to connect to the third-party RDBMS.

To connect to our third-party RDBMS, we need to right-click on its driver under the **Services** tab, then click on **Connect Using...** on the resulting pop-up menu as shown in the following screenshot:

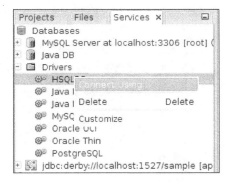

Then we need to enter the JDBC URL, username, and password for our database.

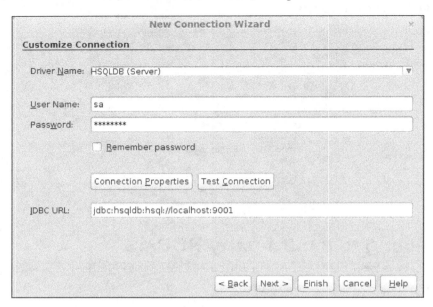

After clicking on the **Next>** button, NetBeans will ask us to select a database schema. In this case, we select **PUBLIC** from the drop-down menu.

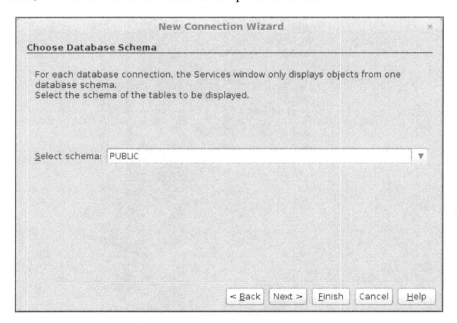

In the next step in the wizard, we are allowed to enter a user-friendly name for our database connection, or we can simply accept the default value.

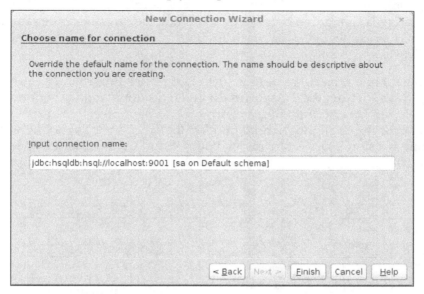

After clicking on the **Finish** button, our database is shown in the list of databases in the **Services** window. We can connect to it by right-clicking on it, selecting **Connect** from the resulting pop-up menu, then entering our username and password for the database (if we chose not to allow NetBeans to remember the password when we added the database).

We have now successfully connected NetBeans to a third party RDBMS.

Deploying our first application

NetBeans comes pre-configured with a number of sample applications. To make sure everything is configured correctly, we will now deploy one of the sample applications to the integrated GlassFish application server that comes bundled with NetBeans.

To open the sample project, we need to go to **File | New Project**, then select **Samples | Java EE** from the **Categories** list in the resulting pop-up window. Once we have selected **Java EE** from the categories list, a list of projects is displayed in the **Projects** list; for this example we need to select the **JavaServer Faces CDI** project. This sample is a simple project involving both JSF and **Contexts and Dependency Injection (CDI)**.

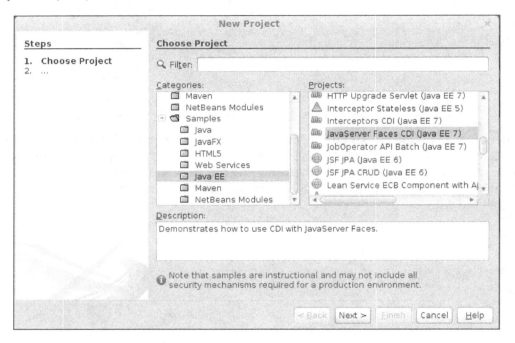

After clicking on the **Next>** button, we are prompted to enter a project location in the next pop-up window. In this case, the default value is sensible.

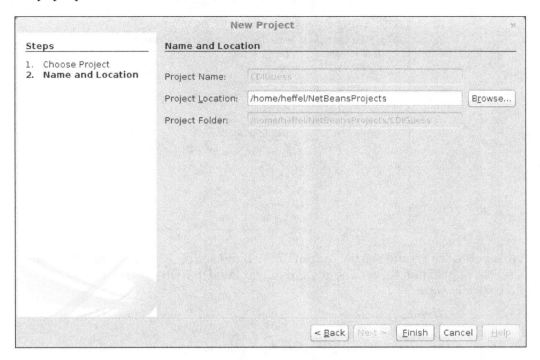

Once we click on the **Finish** button, our new project is displayed in the **Projects** window:

We can compile, package, and deploy our project at one go by right-clicking on it and selecting **Run** from the resulting pop-up menu.

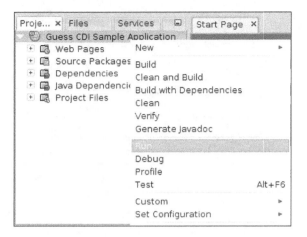

At this point, we should see the output of the build script. Also, both the integrated GlassFish application server and the integrated JavaDB RDBMS system should automatically start.

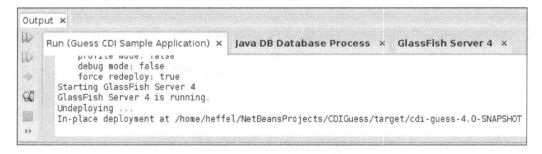

As soon as our application is deployed, a new browser window or tab automatically starts, displaying the default page for our sample application.

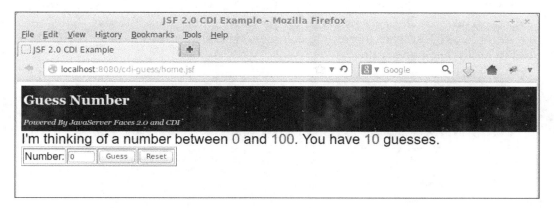

If our browser is displaying a page similar to the preceding one shown, then we can be certain that NetBeans and GlassFish are working properly and we are ready to start developing our own Java EE applications.

NetBeans tips for effective development

NetBeans offers a wide array of features that make Java and Java EE development easier and faster. In the following few sections, we cover some of the most useful features.

Code completion

The NetBeans code editor includes a very good code completion feature, for example, if we wish to create a private variable, we don't need to type the whole `private` word, we can simply write the first three letters (`pri`), then hit *Ctrl* + Space and NetBeans will complete the word `private` for us.

Code completion also works for variable types and method return values, for example, if we want to declare a variable of type `java.util.List`, we simply need to type the first few characters of the type, then hit *Ctrl* + Space NetBeans will try to complete with variable types in any of the packages we have imported in our class. In order to make NetBeans attempt to complete with any type in the classpath, we need to hit *Ctrl* + Space again.

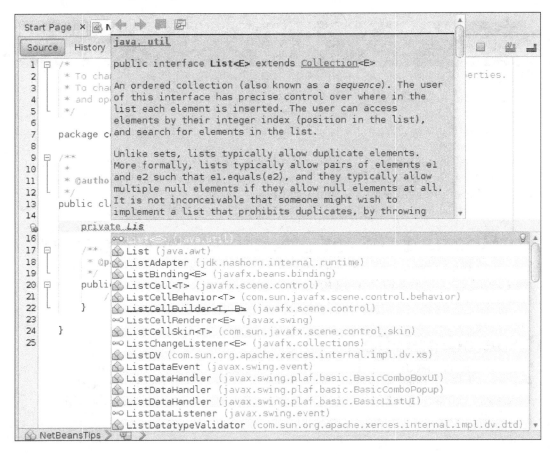

As we can see in the preceding screenshot, NetBeans displays JavaDoc for the class we selected from the code completion options. Another time-saving feature is that the class we selected from the options is automatically imported into our code.

Once we have the type of our variable, we can hit *Ctrl* + Space right after the variable and NetBeans will suggest variable names.

```
 7    package com.ensode.nbbook;
 8
 9 ⊟ import java.util.List;
10
11 ⊟ /**
12    *
13    * @author heffel
14    */
15    public class NetBeansTips {
16
 ⏺        private List
18            ┌─────────────┐
19 ⊟   /**   │ □ l         │
20    * @param│ □ list      │ command line arguments
21    */      └─────────────┘
22 ⊟   public static void main(String[] args) {
23        // TODO code application logic here
24    }
25
26  }
27
```

When we want to initialize our variable to a new value, we can simply hit *Ctrl +
Space* again and a list of valid types is shown as options for code completions
as demonstrated in the following screenshot:

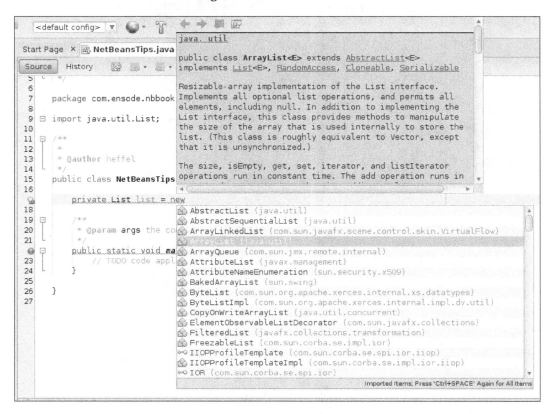

In our example, our type (java.util.List) is an interface, therefore, all classes implementing this interface are shown as possible candidates for code completion. Had our type been a class, both our class and all of its subclasses would have been shown as code completion candidates.

When we are ready to use our variable, we can simply type the first few characters of the variable name, then hit *Ctrl* + Space.

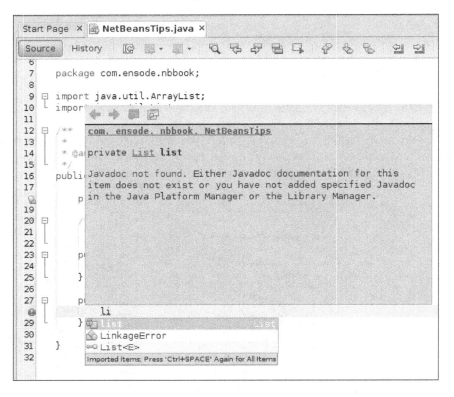

When we wish to invoke a method in our object, we simply type a period at the end of the variable name, and all available methods are displayed as code completion options.

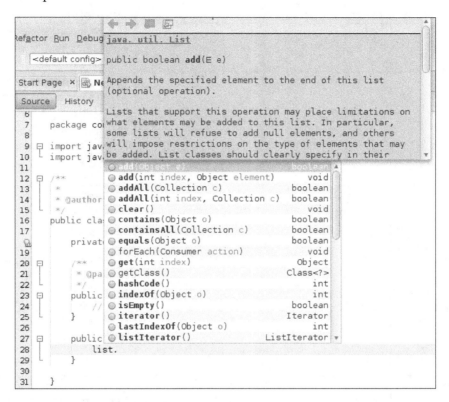

Notice how the JavaDoc for the selected method is automatically displayed.

Code templates

Code templates are abbreviations for frequently used code snippets. To use a code template, we simply type it into the editor and hit the *Tab* key to expand the abbreviations into the full code snippet it represents.

For example, typing `sout` and pressing the *Tab* key will expand into `System.out.println("");`, with the caret placed between the two double quotes.

Some of the most useful code templates are listed in the following table, please note that code templates are case sensitive.

Abbreviation	Example expanded text	Description
Psf	`public static final`	Useful when declaring `public`, `static`, and `final` variables.

fore	```for (Object object : list) {```
	
	 `}`
		Use the enhanced `for` loop to iterate through a collection.

ifelse	```if (boolVar) {```
	
	 ```} else {```
	 `}`
		Generate an `if-else` conditional statement.

psvm	```public static void main(String[] args) {```
	
	 `}`
		Generate a `main` method for our class.

soutv	```System.out.println("boolVar = " +``` `       boolVar);`	Generate a `System.out.println()` statement displaying the value of a variable.

trycatch	`try {`
	
	 `} catch (Exception exception) {`
	 `}`
		Generate a `try-catch` block.

whileit	```while (iterator.hasNext()) {```
	 `       Object object =`
	 `iterator.next();`
	
	 `      }`
		Generate a `while` loop to iterate through an iterator.

To see the complete list of code templates, click on **Tools | Options**, click on the **Editor** icon, then on the **Code Templates** tab.

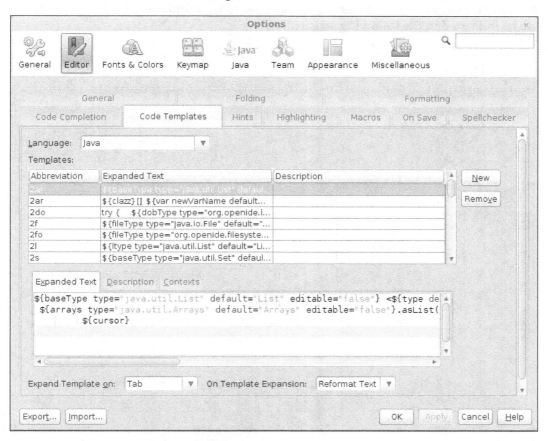

We can add our own templates by clicking on the **New** button. We will be prompted for the template's abbreviation. Once we enter it, our new template will be added to the template list and will automatically be selected. We can then enter the expanded text for our template in the **Expanded Text** tab.

Code templates can be used not only for Java but for HTML, CSS, and all other editors in NetBeans. To view/edit templates for other languages, simply select the desired language from the **Language** drop-down menu under the **Code Templates** tab as indicated in the following screenshot:

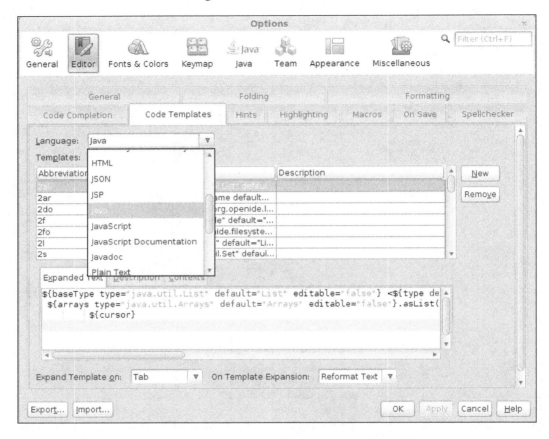

Keyboard shortcuts

NetBeans offers several keyboard shortcuts that allow very fast navigation between source files. Memorizing these keyboard shortcuts allows us to develop code a lot more effectively than relying on the mouse.

> Some of the most useful NetBeans' keyboard shortcuts are listed in this section, but this list is by no means exhaustive. The complete list of NetBeans' keyboard shortcuts can be obtained by clicking on **Help | Keyboard Shortcuts Card**.

One useful keyboard shortcut that allows us to quickly navigate within a large Java file is *Ctrl + F12*. This keyboard shortcut switches focus to the **Navigator** window, which displays an outline of the current Java file and shows all its methods and member variables.

When the **Navigator** window has focus, we can simply start typing to narrow down the list of member variables and methods shown. This keyboard shortcut makes it very fast to navigate through large files.

Hitting *Alt + F12* will open the **Hierarchy** window, which outlines the class hierarchy of the current Java class.

We can use the previous shortcut to quickly navigate to a superclass or a subclass of the current class.

Another useful keyboard shortcut is *Alt + Insert*. This keyboard shortcut can be used to generate frequently used code such as that for constructors, getter and setter methods, among others.

The code will be generated at the current location of the caret.

Additionally, when the caret is right next to an opening or closing brace, hitting *Ctrl + [* results in the caret being placed in the matching brace. This shortcut works for curly braces, parenthesis, and square brackets. Hitting *Ctrl + Shift + [* has a similar effect, but this key combination not only places the caret in the matching brace, it also selects the code between the two carets:

```
31      public void displayListItems(List list){
            for (Object object : list) {
33              System.out.println(object);
34          }
```

Sometimes, we would like to know all the places in our project where a specific method is invoked. Hitting *Alt + F7* while the method is highlighted allows us to easily find out this information.

Usages ×
Usages of **NetBeansTips.displayListItems** [1 occurrence]
NetBeansTips
NetBeansTips.java
26: new NetBeansTips().**displayListItems**(someList);

The keyboard shortcuts works with variables as well.

NetBeans will indicate compilation errors in our code by underlining the erroneous line with a squiggly red line as shown in the following screenshot. Placing the caret over the offending code and hitting *Alt + Enter* will allow us to select from a series of suggestions to fix our code:

Sometimes navigating through all the files in a project can be a bit cumbersome, especially if we know the name of the file we want to open but we are not sure of its location. Luckily, NetBeans provides the *Shift + Alt + O* keyboard shortcut that allows us to quickly open any file in our project:

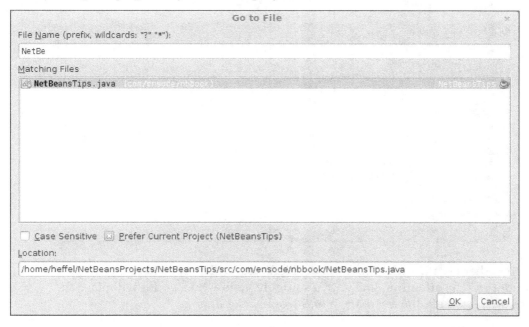

Additional useful keyboard shortcuts include *Shift + Alt + F* to quickly format our code, *Ctrl + E* (*Cmd + E* on Mac OS) to erase the current line, much faster than highlighting the line and hitting backspace. Sometimes we import a class into our code and later decide not to use it. Frequently, the lines where the class is used are deleted but we forget to delete the import line at the top of the source file. NetBeans will generate a warning about the unused import; hitting *Ctrl + Shift + I* will delete all unused imports in one fell swoop, plus it will attempt to add any missing imports.

One last thing worth mentioning, even though it is not strictly a keyboard shortcut, a very useful feature of the NetBeans editor is that left-clicking on a method or variable while pressing *Ctrl* will turn the method or variable into a hyperlink. Clicking on this hyperlink will result in NetBeans taking us to the method or variable declaration.

Understanding NetBeans visual cues

In addition to offering keyboard shortcuts, code templates, and code completion, NetBeans offers a number of visual cues that allow us to better understand our code at a glance. Some of the most useful cues are illustrated in the following screenshot:

```java
package com.ensode.nbbook;

import java.util.Collection;

public class AwesomeNetBeansTips extends NetBeansTips implements Tip{

    @Override
    public void populateList() {
        System.out.println("populateList() in child class");
        super.populateList();
    }

    @Override
    public void someMethod() {
        System.out.println("someMethod() invoked");
        doSomething();
    }
}
```

When there is a warning in our code, NetBeans will alert us in two ways, it will underline the offending line with a squiggly yellow line, and it will place the following icon in the left margin of the offending line:

The light bulb in the icon indicates that NetBeans has a suggestion on how to fix the problem. Moving the caret to the offending line and hitting *Alt + Enter*, as discussed in the previous section, will result in NetBeans offering one or more ways of fixing the problem.

Similarly, when there is a compilation error, NetBeans will underline the offending line with a red squiggly line, and place the following icon on the left margin of said line.

Again, the light bulb indicates that NetBeans has suggestions on how to fix the problem. Hitting *Alt + Enter* in the offending line will allow us to see the suggestions that NetBeans has.

NetBeans not only provides visual cues for errors in our code, it also provides other cues, for example, placing the caret next to an opening or closing brace will highlight both the opening and closing brace, as shown in the populateList() method. This is demonstrated in the previous screenshot.

If one of our methods overrides a method from a parent class, the following icon will be placed in the left margin next to the method declaration:

The icon is an upper case "O" inside a circle, the O stands for "override".

Similarly, when one of our methods is an implementation of a method declared on an interface, the following icon will be placed in the left margin of the method declaration.

The icon is an uppercase "I" inside a green circle, which stands for "implements".

NetBeans also provides visual cues in the form of fonts and font colors, for example, static methods and variables are shown in *italics*, member variables are shown in green, and Java reserved keywords are shown in blue.

Another nice feature of the NetBeans editor is that highlighting a method or variable highlights it everywhere it is used in the currently open file.

Accelerated HTML5 development support

NetBeans has the capability to update deployed web pages in real time as we edit the markup for the page. This feature works both for HTML files and for JSF facelets pages (discussed in the next chapter).

In order for this feature to work, we need to use either the embedded WebKit browser included with NetBeans, or Google's Chrome browser with the NetBeans Connector plugin. To select the browser to run our web application, we need to click on the browser icon on the NetBeans toolbar, then select one of the options under **With NetBeans Connector**, as shown in the following screenshot:

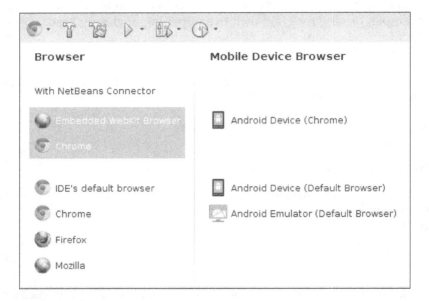

The accelerated HTML5 development support feature works "out of the box" with the embedded WebKit browser. To test it, select the embedded WebKit browser, then run the application we deployed earlier in this chapter in the *Deploying our first application* section. It will run inside NetBeans when using the embedded WebKit browser.

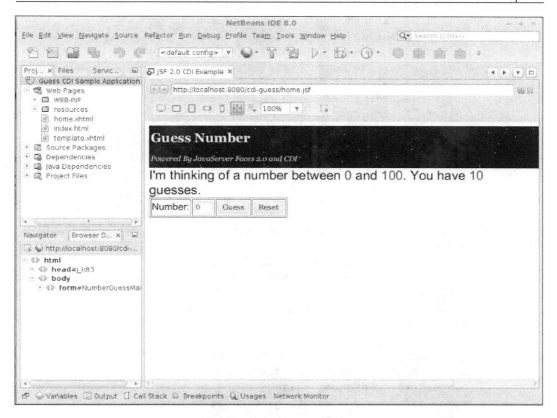

To test the accelerated HTML5 development functionality, let's make a simple change to one of the pages on the application. Open the file called `home.xhtml` and look for a line containing the text **Number**.

```
<h:panelGrid border="1" columns="5" style="font-size: 18px;">
  Number:
    <h:inputText id="inputGuess" value="#{game.guess}"
      required="true" size="3"
      disabled="#{game.number eq game.guess}"
      validator="#{game.validateNumberRange}">
    </h:inputText>
    <h:commandButton id="GuessButton" value="Guess"
      action="#{game.check}"
      disabled="#{game.number eq game.guess}"/>
    <h:commandButton id="RestartButton" value="Reset"
      action="#{game.reset}" immediate="true" />
      <h:outputText id="Higher" value="Higher!"
```

```
      rendered="#{game.number gt game.guess and
        game.guess ne 0}"
      style="color: red"/>
    <h:outputText id="Lower" value="Lower!"
      rendered="#{game.number lt game.guess and
        game.guess ne 0}"
      style="color: red"/>
    </h:panelGrid>
```

Replace the string `Number` with the string `Your Guess`, so that the markup now looks like this:

```
<h:panelGrid border="1" columns="5" style="font-size: 18px;">
    Your Guess:
      <h:inputText id="inputGuess" value="#{game.guess}"
        required="true" size="3"
        disabled="#{game.number eq game.guess}"
        validator="#{game.validateNumberRange}">
      </h:inputText>
      <h:commandButton id="GuessButton" value="Guess"
        action="#{game.check}"
        disabled="#{game.number eq game.guess}"/>
      <h:commandButton id="RestartButton" value="Reset"
        action="#{game.reset}" immediate="true" />
      <h:outputText id="Higher" value="Higher!"
        rendered="#{game.number gt game.guess and
          game.guess ne 0}" style="color: red"/>
      <h:outputText id="Lower" value="Lower!"
        rendered="#{game.number lt game.guess and
          game.guess ne 0}" style="color: red"/>
    </h:panelGrid>
```

Save the file, and without redeploying the application or reloading the page, go back to the embedded browser window. Our change will be reflected on the rendered page.

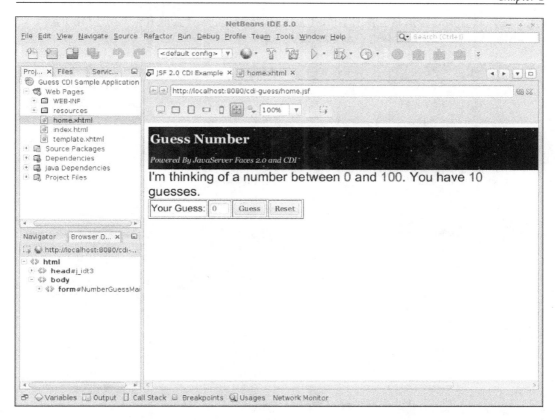

In order for the accelerated HTML5 development feature to work in Chrome, we need to install the NetBeans Connector plugin from the Chrome Web Store. If we select Chrome as our web browser (under the **With NetBeans Connector** section on the menu) and attempt to run our application, NetBeans will prompt us to install the plugin.

Clicking on the button labeled **Go to Chrome Web Store** takes us directly to the download page for the NetBeans Connector plugin:

Clicking on the button labeled **Free** at the upper-right corner results in a pop-up window displaying the permissions for the NetBeans connector plugin:

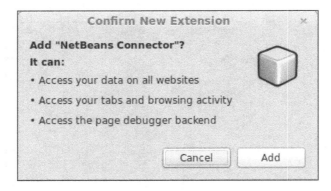

Clicking on the **Add** button automatically installs the plugin. We can then run our project on the Chrome browser and any changes we make to the markup will be instantly reflected on the browser.

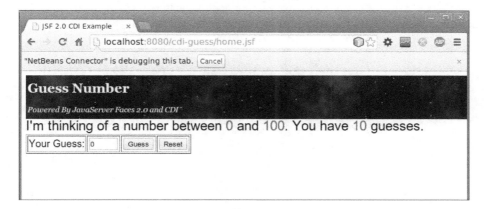

As we can see in this screenshot, when running our application through the NetBeans connector, Chrome displays a message alerting us of the fact.

Summary

In this chapter, we learned how to download and install NetBeans.

We also learned how to set up NetBeans with third-party Java EE application servers and with third-party relational database systems, including how to register a JDBC driver for the RDBMS in question.

We built and deployed our first Java EE application by using one of the sample projects included by NetBeans.

Finally, we covered some of the NetBeans' features such as code completion, code templates, keyboard shortcuts, and visual cues that allow us to do our job more effectively as software developers.

2

Developing Web Applications Using JavaServer Faces 2.2

JavaServer Faces is the standard Java EE framework for building web applications. In this chapter, we will see how using JSF can simplify web application development.

The following topics will be covered in this chapter:

- Creating a JSF project with NetBeans
- Laying out JSF tags by taking advantage of the JSF `<h:panelGrid>` tag
- Using static and dynamic navigation to define navigation between pages
- Developing CDI named beans to encapsulate data and application logic
- Implementing custom JSF validators
- How to easily generate JSF 2.2 templates via NetBeans wizards
- How to easily create JSF 2.2 composite components with NetBeans

Introduction to JavaServer Faces

Before JSF existed, most Java web applications were typically developed using nonstandard (as in, not part of the Java EE specification) web application frameworks such as Apache Struts, Tapestry, and Spring Web MVC, among others. These frameworks are built on top of the Servlet and JSP standards and automate a lot of functionality that needs to be manually coded when using these APIs directly.

Having a wide variety of web application frameworks available often resulted in *analysis paralysis*, that is, developers often spent an inordinate amount of time evaluating frameworks for their applications.

The introduction of JSF to the Java EE specification resulted in a standard, very capable web application framework available in any Java EE-compliant application server. With JSF being the standard Java EE framework, nowadays many Java enterprise application developers choose to use JSF to develop their user interface.

Developing our first JSF application

From an application developer's point of view, a JSF application consists of a series of XHTML pages that contain custom JSF tags, one or more CDI named beans, and an optional configuration file named `faces-config.xml`.

> The `faces-config.xml` file was required in JSF 1.x; however, in JSF 2.0, some conventions were introduced to reduce the need for configuration. Additionally, a number of JSF configurations can be specified using annotations, reducing and, in some cases, eliminating the need for this XML configuration file.

Previous versions of JSF required JSF managed beans to implement server-side functionalities. For backward compatibility, JSF managed beans are still supported; however, CDI named beans are preferred in modern JSF applications.

Creating a new JSF project

To create a new JSF project, we need to go to **File** | **New Project**, select the **Java Web** project category, and select **Web Application** as the project type.

After clicking on **Next**, we need to enter a project name and, optionally, change other information for our project. However, NetBeans provides sensible defaults.

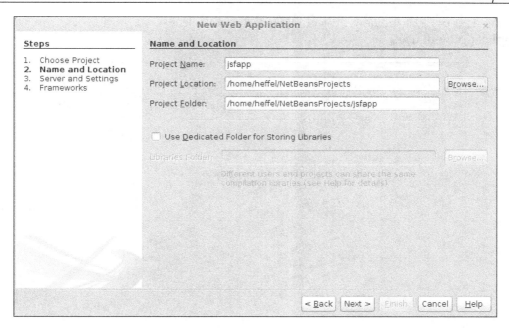

In the next page in the wizard, we can select the server, Java EE version, and the context path of our application. In our example, we will simply pick the default values.

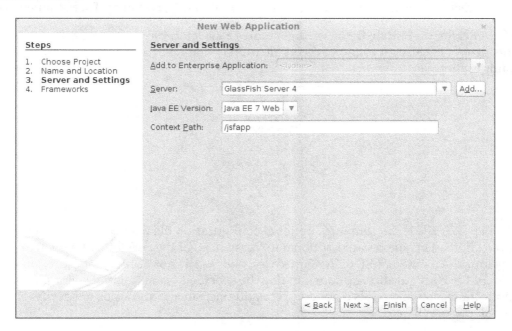

In the next page of the new project wizard, we can select what frameworks our web application will use.

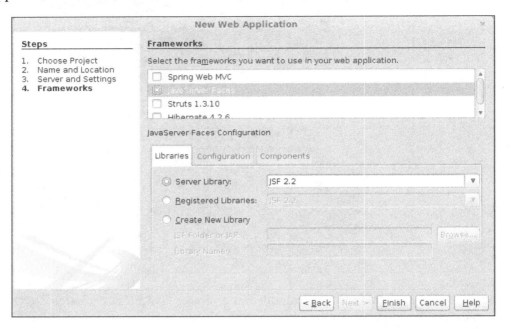

Unsurprisingly, for JSF applications, we need to select the **JavaServer Faces** framework.

After clicking on **Finish**, the wizard generates a skeleton JSF project for us. This project consists of a single facelet file called index.xhtml and a web.xml configuration file.

The web.xml file is the standard, optional configuration file needed for Java web applications. This file became optional in Version 3.0 of the Servlet API, which was introduced in Java EE 6. In many cases, web.xml is not needed anymore, since most of the configuration options can now be specified via annotations. For JSF applications, however, it is a good idea to add one, since it allows us to specify the JSF project stage.

This is shown in the following code:

```xml
<?xml version="1.0" encoding="UTF-8"?>
<web-app version="3.1" xmlns="http://xmlns.jcp.org/xml/ns/javaee"
         xmlns:xsi="http://www.w3.org/2001/XMLSchema-instance"
         xsi:schemaLocation="http://xmlns.jcp.org/xml/ns/javaee
         http://xmlns.jcp.org/xml/ns/javaee/web-app_3_1.xsd">
    <context-param>
        <param-name>javax.faces.PROJECT_STAGE</param-name>
        <param-value>Development</param-value>
    </context-param>
    <servlet>
        <servlet-name>Faces Servlet</servlet-name>
        <servlet-class>javax.faces.webapp.FacesServlet</servlet-class>
        <load-on-startup>1</load-on-startup>
    </servlet>
    <servlet-mapping>
        <servlet-name>Faces Servlet</servlet-name>
        <url-pattern>/faces/*</url-pattern>
    </servlet-mapping>
    <session-config>
        <session-timeout>
            30
        </session-timeout>
    </session-config>
    <welcome-file-list>
        <welcome-file>faces/index.xhtml</welcome-file>
    </welcome-file-list>
</web-app>
```

As we can see, NetBeans automatically sets the JSF project stage to `Development`. Setting the project stage to `Development` configures JSF to provide additional debugging help that is not present in other stages. For example, one common problem when developing a JSF page is that while a page is being developed, validation for one or more fields on the page fails but the developer has not added an `<h:message>` or `<h:messages>` tag to the page (more on this later). When this happens and the form is submitted, the page seems to do nothing, or page navigation doesn't work properly. When setting the project stage to `Development`, these validation errors will automatically be added to the page, without the developer having to explicitly add one of these tags to the page (we should, of course, add the tags before releasing our code to production, since our users will not see the automatically generated validation errors).

The valid values for the `javax.faces.PROJECT_STAGE` context parameter for the `faces` servlet are as follows:

- `Development`
- `Production`
- `SystemTest`
- `UnitTest`

As we previously mentioned, the `Development` project stage adds additional debugging information to ease development. The `Production` project stage focuses on performance. The other two valid values for the project stage (`SystemTest` and `UnitTest`) allow us to implement our own custom behavior for these two phases.

The `javax.faces.application.Application` class has a `getProjectStage()` method that allows us to obtain the current project stage. Based on the value of this method, we can implement code that will only be executed in the appropriate stage. The following code snippet illustrates this:

```
public void someMethod() {
        FacesContext facesContext = FacesContext.getCurrentInstance();
        Application application = facesContext.getApplication();
        ProjectStage projectStage = application.getProjectStage();

        if (projectStage.equals(ProjectStage.Development)) {
            //do development stuff
        } else if (projectStage.equals(ProjectStage.Production)) {
            //do production stuff
        } else if (projectStage.equals(ProjectStage.SystemTest)) {
            // do system test stuff
        } else if (projectStage.equals(ProjectStage.UnitTest)) {
            //do unit test stuff
        }
    }
```

As illustrated in the preceding snippet, we can implement code to be executed in any valid project stage, based on the value returned by the `getProjectStage()` method of the `Application` class.

When creating a Java web project using JSF, a facelet is automatically generated.

The generated facelet file looks like this:

```
<?xml version='1.0' encoding='UTF-8' ?>
<!DOCTYPE html PUBLIC "-//W3C//DTD XHTML 1.0 Transitional//EN"
```

```
       "http://www.w3.org/TR/xhtml1/DTD/xhtml1-transitional.dtd">
<html xmlns="http://www.w3.org/1999/xhtml"
     xmlns:h="http://xmlns.jcp.org/jsf/html">
     <h:head>
         <title>Facelet Title</title>
     </h:head>
     <h:body>
         Hello from Facelets
     </h:body>
</html>
```

As we can see, a facelet is nothing but an XHTML file using some JSF specific XML namespaces. In the automatically generated preceding code the following namespace definition allows us to use the h (for HTML) JSF component library:

```
xmlns:h="http://xmlns.jcp.org/jsf/html"
```

The preceding namespace declaration allows us to use JSF specific tags such as <h:head> and <h:body>, which are a drop-in replacement for the standard HTML/XHTML <head> and <body> tags, respectively.

Another very commonly used namespace in JSF is the f namespace, which is typically defined as follows:

```
xmlns:f= "http://xmlns.jcp.org/jsf/core"
```

The f namespace contains tags that do not render directly in the page, rather it allows us to specify the items in a drop-down list or, for instance, bind actions to our JSF components.

The application generated by the new project wizard is a simple but complete JSF web application. We can see it in action by right-clicking on our project in the project window and selecting **Run**. Now, the application server starts (if it wasn't already running). Then, the application is deployed and the default system browser opens to display our application's default page.

Modifying our page to capture user data

The generated application, of course, is nothing but a starting point for us to create a new application. We will now modify the generated `index.xhtml` file to collect some data from the user.

The first thing we need to do is to add an `<h:form>` tag to our page. The `<h:form>` tag is equivalent to the `<form>` tag in standard HTML pages. After typing the first few characters of the `<h:form>` tag into the page, NetBeans automatically suggests some tags for us to use.

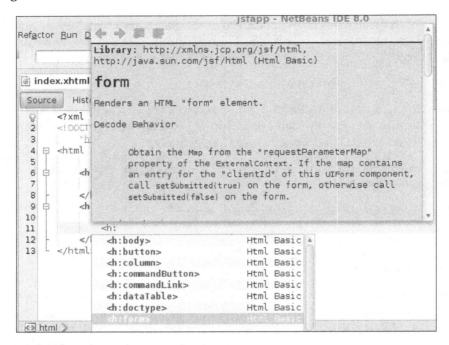

As soon as we highlight the tag we want (`<h:form>` in this case), NetBeans displays that tag's documentation.

After adding the `<h:form>` tag and a number of additional JSF tags, our page markup now looks like this:

```
<?xml version='1.0' encoding='UTF-8' ?>
<!DOCTYPE html PUBLIC "-//W3C//DTD XHTML 1.0 Transitional//EN"
    "http://www.w3.org/TR/xhtml1/DTD/xhtml1-transitional.dtd">
<html xmlns="http://www.w3.org/1999/xhtml"
    xmlns:h="http://xmlns.jcp.org/jsf/html"
    xmlns:f="http://xmlns.jcp.org/jsf/core">
  <h:head>
```

```
        <title>Registration</title>
        <h:outputStylesheet library="css" name="styles.css"/>
    </h:head>
    <h:body>
        <h3>Registration Page</h3>
        <h:form>
            <h:panelGrid columns="3"
                    columnClasses="rightalign,leftalign,leftali
gn">
                <h:outputLabel value="Salutation: " for="salutation"/>
                <h:selectOneMenu id="salutation" label="Salutation"
                        value="#{registrationBean.
salutation}" >
                    <f:selectItem itemLabel="" itemValue=""/>
                    <f:selectItem itemLabel="Mr." itemValue="MR"/>
                    <f:selectItem itemLabel="Mrs." itemValue="MRS"/>
                    <f:selectItem itemLabel="Miss" itemValue="MISS"/>
                    <f:selectItem itemLabel="Ms" itemValue="MS"/>
                    <f:selectItem itemLabel="Dr." itemValue="DR"/>
                </h:selectOneMenu>
                <h:message for="salutation"/>

                <h:outputLabel value="First Name:" for="firstName"/>
                <h:inputText id="firstName" label="First Name"
                        required="true"
                        value="#{registrationBean.firstName}" />
                <h:message for="firstName" />
                <h:outputLabel value="Last Name:" for="lastName"/>
                <h:inputText id="lastName" label="Last Name"
                        required="true"
                        value="#{registrationBean.lastName}" />
                <h:message for="lastName" />

                <h:outputLabel for="age" value="Age:"/>
                <h:inputText id="age" label="Age" size="2"
                        value="#{registrationBean.age}"/>
                <h:message for="age"/>

                <h:outputLabel value="Email Address:" for="email"/>
                <h:inputText id="email" label="Email Address"
                        required="true"
                        value="#{registrationBean.email}">
```

```
                    </h:inputText>
                    <h:message for="email" />

                    <h:panelGroup/>
                    <h:commandButton id="register" value="Register"
                                     action="confirmation" />
                </h:panelGrid>
            </h:form>
        </h:body>
    </html>
```

The following screenshot illustrates how our page will be rendered at runtime:

All JSF input fields must be inside an `<h:form>` tag. The `<h:panelGrid>` tag helps us to easily lay out JSF tags in our page. It can be thought of as a grid where other JSF tags will be placed. The `columns` attribute of the `<h:panelGrid>` tag indicates how many columns the grid will have; each JSF component inside the `<h:panelGrid>` component will be placed in an individual cell of the grid. When the number of components matching the value of the `columns` attribute (3 in our example) has been placed inside `<h:panelGrid>`, a new row is automatically started.

The following table illustrates how tags are laid out inside an `<h:panelGrid>` tag:

First tag	Second tag	Third tag
Fourth tag	Fifth tag	Sixth tag
Seventh tag	Eighth tag	Ninth tag

Each row in our panel grid consists of an `<h:outputLabel>` tag, an input field, and an `<h:message>` tag.

The `columnClasses` attribute of `<h:panelGrid>` allows us to assign CSS styles to each column inside the panel grid. Its `value` attribute must consist of a comma-separated list of CSS styles (defined in a CSS style sheet). The first style will be applied to the first column, the second style will be applied to the second column, the third style will be applied to the third column, and so on. Had our panel grid had more than three columns, then the fourth column would have been styled using the first style in the `columnClasses` attribute, the fifth column would have been styled using the second style in the `columnClasses` attribute, and so on.

If we wish to style rows in a panel grid, we can do so with its `rowClasses` attribute, which works the same way that the `columnClasses` works for columns.

Notice the `<h:outputStylesheet>` tag inside `<h:head>` near the top of the page. This tag was introduced in JSF 2.0. One feature JSF 2.0 brought to the table is standard resource directories. Resources (such as CSS, JavaScript files, and images) can be placed under a top-level directory named `resources`, and JSF tags will have access to those resources automatically. In our NetBeans project, we need to place the `resources` directory under the **Web Pages** folder.

Then, we need to create a subdirectory to hold our CSS style sheet (by convention, this directory should be named `css`). We place our CSS style sheet(s) in this subdirectory.

 The CSS style sheet for our example is very simple; therefore, it is not shown. However, it is part of the code bundle for this chapter.

The value of the library attribute in `<h:outputStylesheet>` must match the directory where our CSS file is located, and the value of its `name` attribute must match the CSS filename.

In addition to CSS files, we should place any JavaScript files in a subdirectory called javascript under the resources directory. The file can then be accessed by the <h:outputScript> tag using javascript as the value of its library attribute and the filename as the value of its name attribute.

Similarly, images should be placed in a directory called images under the resources directory. These images can then be accessed by the JSF <h:graphicImage> tag, where the value of its library attribute will be images and the value of its name attribute will be the corresponding filename.

Now that we have discussed how to lay out elements on the page and how to access resources, let's focus our attention into the input and output elements on the page.

The <h:outputLabel> tag generates a label for an input field in the form; the value of its for attribute must match the value of the id attribute of the corresponding input field.

The <h:message> tag generates an error message for an input field; the value of its for field must match the value of the id attribute for the corresponding input field.

The first row in our grid contains an <h:selectOneMenu> tag. This tag generates an HTML <select> tag on the rendered page.

Every JSF tag has an id attribute. The value for this attribute must be a string containing a unique identifier for the tag. If we don't specify a value for this attribute, one will be generated automatically. It is a good idea to explicitly state the ID of every component; since this ID is used in runtime error messages, affected components are a lot easier to identify if we explicitly set their IDs.

When using the <h:label> tags to generate labels for input fields or when using the <h:message> tags to generate validation errors, we need to explicitly set the value of the id tag, since we need to specify it as the value of the for attribute of the corresponding <h:label> and <h:message> tags.

Every JSF input tag has a label attribute. This attribute is used to generate validation error messages on the rendered page. If we don't specify a value for the label attribute, the field will be identified in the error message by the value of its id attribute.

Each JSF input field has a value attribute; in the case of `<h:selectOneMenu>`, this attribute indicates which of the options in the rendered `<select>` tag will be selected. The value of this attribute must match the value of the `itemValue` attribute of one of the nested `<f:selectItem>` tags. The value of this attribute is usually a value binding expression, which means that the value is read at runtime from a CDI named bean. In our example, the value binding expression `#{registrationBean.salutation}` is used. At runtime, JSF will look for a CDI named bean called `registrationBean` and look for an attribute named `salutation` on this bean. Then, the getter method for this attribute will be invoked, and its return value will be used to determine the selected value of the rendered HTML `<select>` tag.

Nested inside `<h:selectOneMenu>`, there are a number of `<f:selectItem>` tags. These tags generate HTML `<option>` tags inside the HTML `<select>` tag generated by `<h:selectOneMenu>`. The value of the `itemLabel` attribute is the value that the user will see while the value of the `itemValue` attribute will be the value that will be sent to the server when the form is submitted.

All other rows in our grid contain the `<h:inputText>` tag. This tag generates an HTML `input` field of type `text`, which accepts a single line of typed text as input. We explicitly set the `id` attribute of all of our `<h:inputText>` fields, which allows us to refer to them from the corresponding `<h:outputLabel>` and `<h:message>` fields. We also set the `label` attribute for all of our `<h:inputText>` tags, which results in user-friendly error messages.

Some of our `<h:inputText>` fields require a value. These fields have their `required` attributes set to `true`, and each JSF input field has a `required` attribute. If we need the user to enter a value for this attribute, we need to set this attribute to `true`. This attribute is optional; if we don't explicitly set a value for it, then it defaults to `false`.

In the last row of our grid, we added an empty `<h:panelGroup>` tag. The purpose of this tag is to allow you to add several tags into a single cell of a panel grid. Any tag placed inside this tag is placed inside the same cell of the grid where `<h:panelGrid>` is placed. In this particular case, all we want to do is to have an *empty* cell in the grid so that the next tag, `<h:commandButton>`, is aligned with the input fields in the rendered page.

The `<h:commandButton>` tag is used to submit a form to the server. The value of its `value` attribute is used to generate the text of the rendered button. The value of its `action` attribute is used to determine what page to display after the button is clicked.

In our example, we are using static navigation. When using JSF static navigation, the value of the `action` attribute of a command button is hardcoded in the markup. With JSF static navigation, the value of the `action` attribute of `<h:commandButton>` corresponds to the name of the page we want to navigate to, minus its `.xhtml` extension. In our example, when the user clicks on the button, we want to navigate to a file named `confirmation.xhtml`. Therefore, we used the value `confirmation` for its `action` attribute.

An alternative to static navigation is dynamic navigation. When using dynamic navigation, the value of the `action` attribute of the command button is a value binding expression resolving to a method and returning a string in a CDI named bean. The method can return different values based on certain conditions. Navigation would then proceed to a different page depending on the value of the method.

 As long as it returns a string, the CDI named bean method executed when using dynamic navigation can contain any logic inside it, and it is frequently used to save data into a database.

When using dynamic navigation, the return value of the method executed when clicking the button must match the name of the page we want to navigate to (again, minus the file extension).

 In earlier versions of JSF, it was necessary to specify navigation rules in `faces-config.xml`. With the introduction of the conventions discussed in the previous paragraphs, this is no longer necessary.

Creating our CDI named bean

CDI named beans are standard JavaBeans that are used to hold user-entered data in JSF applications.

Since a CDI named bean is a standard Java class, we create one like we create any other Java class: by right-clicking on the **Source Packages** folder in the **Projects** window and going to **New | Java Class...**.

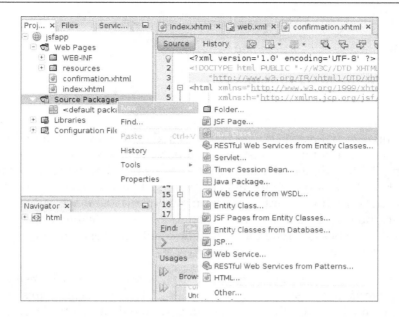

We can then enter a value for the **Class Name** and **Package** fields for our CDI named bean.

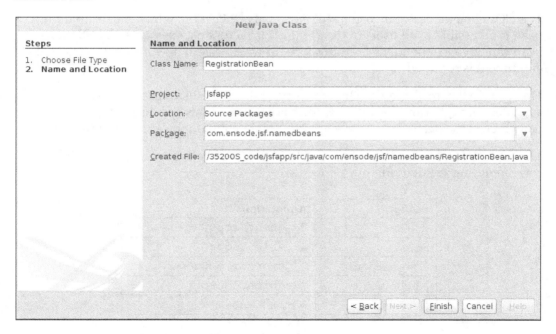

The generated file is an empty Java class:

```
package com.ensode.jsf.namedbeans;

public class RegistrationBean {

}
```

To turn the preceding Java class into a CDI named bean, all we need to do is annotate it with the @Named annotation. The @Named annotation marks the class as a CDI named bean. By default, the CDI named bean name defaults to the class name (in our case, RegistrationBean) with its first character switched to lower case (in our case, registrationBean). If we want to override the default name, we can do it by setting the value attribute of the @Named annotation to the desired value. In general, sticking to the defaults allows more readable and maintainable code; therefore, we shouldn't deviate from them unless we have a good reason.

The CDI named beans can have different scopes. A scope of request means that the bean is only available in a single HTTP request. CDI named beans can also have a session scope, in which case they are available in a single user's HTTP session. CDI named beans can also have a conversation scope, in which the bean is available across several HTTP requests.

The CDI named beans can also have a scope of application, which means that the bean is accessible to all users in the application, across user sessions. A CDI named bean can have a dependent pseudo-scope, in which case a new instance is injected any time it is required.

Finally, a CDI named bean can have a scope of flow, in which case the bean will be available through a specific JSF flow (discussed later in this chapter). To give our CDI named bean the desired scope, we need to decorate it with the appropriate annotation.

The following table summarizes possible CDI named bean scopes along with the corresponding annotation:

Scope	Annotation
Request	@RequestScoped
Session	@SessionScoped
Conversation	@ConversationScoped
Application	@SessionScoped
Dependent	@Dependent
Flow	@FlowScoped

All of the preceding annotations except `@FlowScoped` are defined in the `javax.enterprise.context` package. The `@FlowScoped` annotation is defined in the `javax.faces.flow` package.

We turn our Java class into a request scoped CDI named bean by adding the appropriate annotations:

```
package com.ensode.jsf.namedbeans;

import javax.enterprise.context.RequestScoped;
import javax.inject.Named;

@Named
@RequestScoped
public class RegistrationBean {

}
```

The `@Named` annotation designates our class as a CDI named bean, and the `@RequestScoped` annotation designates that our CDI named bean will have a scope of request.

 NetBeans may not be able to find the `@RequestScoped` annotation, if this the case, we need to add `cdi-api.jar` to our project by right-clicking on **Libraries**, selecting **Add JAR/Folder...**, and selecting `cdi-api.jar` from the `modules` folder of our glassfish installation.

Now, we need to modify our CDI named bean by adding properties that will hold the values entered by the users.

Automatic generation of getter and setter methods

NetBeans can automatically generate getter and setter methods for our properties. We simply need to click the keyboard shortcut to insert code, *Alt + Insert* in Windows and Linux (*Ctrl + I* on Mac OS), and select **Getters and Setters**.

```
package com.ensode.jsf.namedbeans;

import javax.enterprise.context.RequestScoped;
import javax.inject.Named;

@Named
@RequestScoped
public class RegistrationBean {
```

```
private String salutation;
private String firstName;
private String lastName;
private Integer age;
private String email;

//getters and setters omitted for brevity

}
```

We can see that the names of all of the bean's properties (instance variables) match the names we used in the page's value binding expressions. These names must match so that JSF knows how to map the bean's properties to the value binding expressions.

Implementing the confirmation page

Once our user fills out the data on the input page and submits the form, we want to show a confirmation page displaying the values that the user entered. Since we used value binding expressions on every input field on the input page, the corresponding fields on the named bean will be populated with data entered by the user. Therefore, all we need to do in our confirmation page is display the data on the named bean via a series of <h:outputText> JSF tags.

We can create the confirmation page via the **New JSF File** wizard by going to **File | New File**, selecting the **JavaServer Faces** category, and selecting **JSF Page** as the file type.

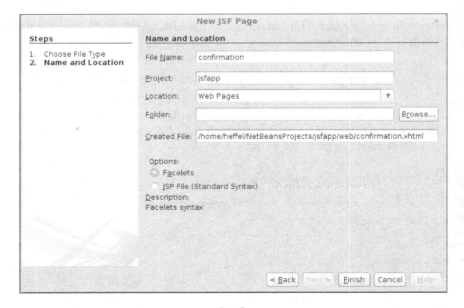

We need to make sure the name the new file matches the value of the action attribute in the command button of the input page (confirmation.xhtml) so that static navigation works properly.

After modifying the generated page to meet our requirements, it should look like this:

```
<?xml version='1.0' encoding='UTF-8' ?>
<!DOCTYPE html PUBLIC "-//W3C//DTD XHTML 1.0 Transitional//EN"
    "http://www.w3.org/TR/xhtml1/DTD/xhtml1-transitional.dtd">
<html xmlns="http://www.w3.org/1999/xhtml"
      xmlns:h="http://xmlns.jcp.org/jsf/html">
    <h:head>
        <title>Confirmation Page</title>
        <h:outputStylesheet library="css" name="styles.css"/>
    </h:head>
    <h:body>
        <h2>Confirmation Page</h2>
        <h:panelGrid columns="2"
                     columnClasses="rightalign-bold,leftalign">
            <h:outputText value="Salutation:"/>
            ${registrationBean.salutation}
            <h:outputText value="First Name:"/>
            ${registrationBean.firstName}
            <h:outputText value="Last Name:"/>
            ${registrationBean.lastName}
            <h:outputText value="Age:"/>
            ${registrationBean.age}
            <h:outputText value="Email Address:"/>
            ${registrationBean.email}
        </h:panelGrid>
    </h:body>
</html>
```

As we can see, our confirmation page is very simple. It consists of a series of <h:outputText> tags that contain labels and value binding expressions bound to our named bean's properties. The JSF <h:outputText> tag simply displays the value of the expression of its value attribute on the rendered page.

Executing our application

We are now ready to execute our JSF application. The easiest way to do so is to right-click on our project and click on **Run** in the resulting pop-up menu.

Now, GlassFish (or whatever application server we are using for our project) will start automatically, if it hadn't been started already. The default browser will open and it will automatically be directed to our page's URL.

After entering some data on the page, it should look something like the following screenshot:

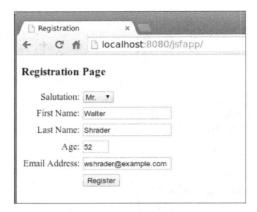

When we click on the **Register** button, our `RegistrationBean` named bean is populated with the values we entered into the page. Each property in the field will be populated according to the value binding expression in each input field.

At this point, JSF navigation kicks in and we are taken to the confirmation page.

The values displayed on the confirmation page are taken from our named bean, confirming that the bean's properties were populated correctly.

JSF validation

Earlier in this chapter, we discussed how the `required` attribute for the JSF input fields allows us to easily make input fields mandatory.

If a user attempts to submit a form with one or more required fields missing, an error message is automatically generated.

The error message is generated by the <h:message> tag corresponding to the invalid field. The string **First Name** in the error message corresponds to the value of the label attribute for the field. Had we omitted the label attribute, the value of the field's id attribute would have been shown instead. As we can see, the required attribute makes it very easy to implement mandatory field functionality in our application.

Recall that the age field is bound to a property of type Integer in our named bean. If a user enters a value that is not a valid integer into this field, a validation error is automatically generated.

Of course, a negative age wouldn't make much sense. However, our application validates that user input is a valid integer with essentially no effort on our part.

The e-mail address input field of our page is bound to a property of type string in our named bean. There is no built-in validation to make sure that the user enters a valid e-mail address. In cases like this, we need to write our own custom JSF validator.

Custom JSF validators must implement the `javax.faces.validator.Validator` interface. This interface contains a single method named `validate()`, and this method takes three parameters, an instance of `javax.faces.context.FacesContext`, an instance of `javax.faces.component.UIComponent` containing the JSF component we are validating, and an instance of `java.lang.Object` containing the value entered by the user for the component. The following example illustrates a typical custom validator:

```java
package com.ensode.jsf.validators;

import java.util.regex.Matcher;
import java.util.regex.Pattern;
import javax.faces.application.FacesMessage;
import javax.faces.component.UIComponent;
import javax.faces.component.html.HtmlInputText;
import javax.faces.context.FacesContext;
import javax.faces.validator.FacesValidator;
import javax.faces.validator.Validator;
import javax.faces.validator.ValidatorException;

@FacesValidator(value ="emailValidator")
public class EmailValidator implements Validator {

    @Override
    public void validate(FacesContext facesContext,
            UIComponent uiComponent, Object value) throws
            ValidatorException {
        Pattern pattern = Pattern.compile("\\w+@\\w+\\.\\w+");
        Matcher matcher = pattern.matcher(
                (CharSequence) value);
        HtmlInputText htmlInputText =
                (HtmlInputText) uiComponent;
        String label;

        if (htmlInputText.getLabel() == null ||
                htmlInputText.getLabel().trim().equals("")) {
            label = htmlInputText.getId();
        } else {
```

```
        label = htmlInputText.getLabel();
    }

    if (!matcher.matches()) {
        FacesMessage facesMessage =
            new FacesMessage(label +
            ": not a valid email address");

        throw new ValidatorException(facesMessage);
    }
  }
}
```

In our example, the `validate()` method does a regular expression match against the value of the JSF component we are validating. If the value matches the expression, validation succeeds; otherwise, validation fails and an instance of `javax.faces.validator.ValidatorException` is thrown.

> The primary purpose of our custom validator is to illustrate how to write custom JSF validations, and not to create a foolproof e-mail address validator. There may be valid e-mail addresses that don't validate using our validator.

The constructor of `ValidatorException` takes an instance of `javax.faces.application.FacesMessage` as a parameter. This object is used to display the error message on the page when validation fails. The message to display is passed as a string to the constructor of `FacesMessage`. In our example, if the `label` attribute of the component is neither `null` nor empty. We use it as part of the error message; otherwise, we use the value of the component's `id` attribute. This behavior follows the pattern established by standard JSF validators.

Our validator needs to be annotated with the `@FacesValidator` annotation. The value of its `value` attribute is the ID that will be used to reference our validator in our JSF pages.

Once we are done implementing our validator, we are ready to use it in our pages.

In our particular case, we need to modify the e-mail field to use our custom validator using the following code:

```
<h:inputText id="email" label="Email Address"
        required="true" value="#{registrationBean.email}">
    <f:validator validatorId="emailValidator"/>
</h:inputText>
```

All we need to do is nest a `<f:validator>` tag inside the input field we wish to have validated using our custom validator. The value of the `validatorId` attribute of `<f:validator>` must match the value of the `value` attribute in the `@FacesValidator` annotation in our validator.

Now, we are ready to test our custom validator.

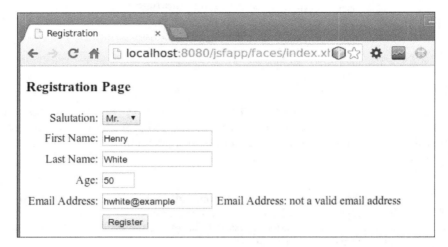

While entering an invalid e-mail address into the e-mail address input field and submitting the form, our custom validator logic was executed and the string we passed as a parameter to `FacesMessage` in our `validator()` method its shown as the error text by the `<h:message>` tag for the field.

Facelets templating

One advantage that Facelets has over JSP is its templating mechanism. Templates allow us to specify page layout in one place. Then, we can have template clients that use the layout defined in the template. Since most web applications have consistent layout across pages, using templates makes our applications much more maintainable because changes to the layout need to be made in a single place. If at one point we need to change the layout for our pages (for example, add a footer or move a column from the left side of the page to the right side of the page), we only need to change the template and the change is reflected in all the template clients.

Adding the Facelets template

We can add a Facelets template to our project simply by going to **File | New File**, selecting the **JavaServer Faces** category, and selecting the **Facelets Template** file type.

NetBeans provides very good support for Facelets templating. It provides several templates "out of the box" using common web page layouts.

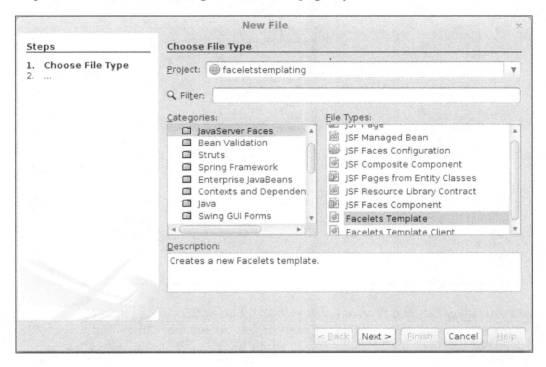

We can then select from one of several predefined templates to use as a base for our template or simply use it "out of the box".

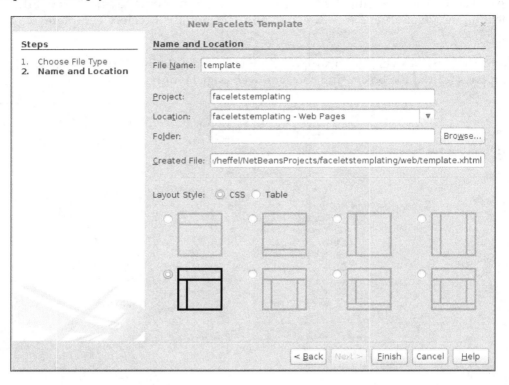

NetBeans gives us the option of using HTML tables or CSS for layout. For most modern web applications, CSS is the preferred approach. For our example, we will pick a layout containing a header area, a single left column, and a main area.

After clicking on **Finish**, NetBeans automatically generates our template, along with the necessary CSS files.

The automatically generated template looks like this:

```
<?xml version='1.0' encoding='UTF-8' ?>
<!DOCTYPE html PUBLIC "-//W3C//DTD XHTML 1.0 Transitional//EN"
"http://www.w3.org/TR/xhtml1/DTD/xhtml1-transitional.dtd">
<html xmlns="http://www.w3.org/1999/xhtml"
      xmlns:ui="http://xmlns.jcp.org/jsf/facelets"
      xmlns:h="http://xmlns.jcp.org/jsf/html">
```

```
    <h:head>
        <meta http-equiv="Content-Type" content="text/html;
charset=UTF-8" />
        <h:outputStylesheet name="./css/default.css"/>
        <h:outputStylesheet name="./css/cssLayout.css"/>
        <title>Facelets Template</title>
    </h:head>

    <h:body>


        <div id="top" class="top">
            <ui:insert name="top">Top</ui:insert>
        </div>
        <div>
            <div id="left">
                <ui:insert name="left">Left</ui:insert>
            </div>
            <div id="content" class="left_content">
                <ui:insert name="content">Content</ui:insert>
            </div>
        </div>
    </h:body>
</html>
```

As we can see, the template doesn't look much different from a regular facelets file.

We can see that the template uses the following namespace: `xmlns:ui="http://xmlns.jcp.org/jsf/facelets"`. This namespace allows us to use the `<ui:insert>` tag. The contents of this tag will be replaced by the content in a corresponding `<ui:define>` tag in template clients.

Using the template

To use our template, we simply need to create a Facelets template client. This can be done by going to **File | New File**, selecting the **JavaServer Faces** category, and selecting the **Facelets Template Client** file type.

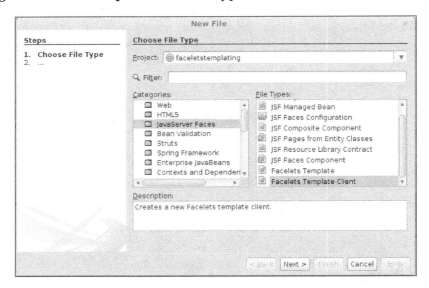

After clicking on **Next**, we need to enter a filename (or accept the default) and select the template that we will use for our template client.

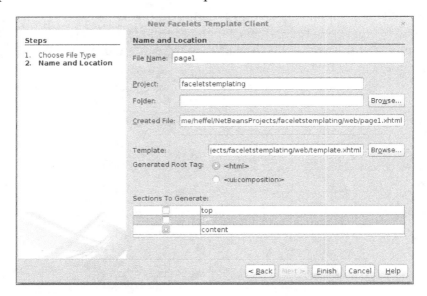

When using Facelets templating, if a template client does not override a section defined on the template, then the template's markup is shown on the rendered page. This allows us to define, for example, a page header that should be the same across all pages in our application in one place (the template), rather than redefining it on every page.

In our example, the `top` and `left` sections should be the same across the application. Therefore, we uncheck these boxes so that those sections are not generated in our template client.

After clicking on **Finish**, our template client is created, with the following content:

```xml
<?xml version='1.0' encoding='UTF-8' ?>
<!DOCTYPE html PUBLIC "-//W3C//DTD XHTML 1.0 Transitional//EN"
"http://www.w3.org/TR/xhtml1/DTD/xhtml1-transitional.dtd">
<html xmlns="http://www.w3.org/1999/xhtml"
    xmlns:ui="http://xmlns.jcp.org/jsf/facelets">

    <body>

        <ui:composition template="./template.xhtml">

            <ui:define name="content">
                content
            </ui:define>

        </ui:composition>
    </body>
</html>
```

As we can see, the template client also uses the `xmlns:ui="http://xmlns.jcp.org/jsf/facelets"` namespace; in a template client, the `<ui:composition>` tag must be the parent tag of any other tag belonging to this namespace. Any markup outside this tag will not be rendered, and the template markup will be rendered instead.

The `<ui:define>` tag is used to insert markup into a corresponding `<ui:insert>` tag in the template. The value of the `name` attribute in `<ui:define>` must match the corresponding `<ui:insert>` tag in the template.

After deploying our application, we can see templating in action by pointing the browser to our template client URL.

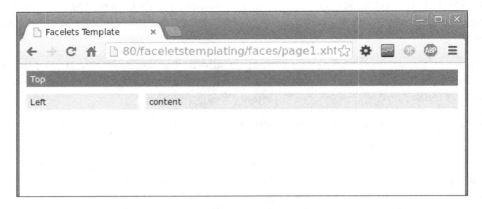

We can see that NetBeans generated a template that allows us to create a fairly elegant page with very little effort on our part. Of course, we should replace the markup in the `<ui:define>` tags to suit our needs.

Here is a modified version of our template, adding markup to be rendered in the corresponding places in the template:

```
<?xml version='1.0' encoding='UTF-8' ?>
<!DOCTYPE html PUBLIC "-//W3C//DTD XHTML 1.0 Transitional//EN"
"http://www.w3.org/TR/xhtml1/DTD/xhtml1-transitional.dtd">
<html xmlns="http://www.w3.org/1999/xhtml"
      xmlns:ui="http://xmlns.jcp.org/jsf/facelets">

    <body>

        <ui:composition template="./template.xhtml">

            <ui:define name="content">
                <p>
                    In this main area we would put our main text,
images, forms, etc. In this example we will simply use the typical
filler text that web designers love to use.
                </p>
                <p>
```

```
                    Lorem ipsum dolor sit amet, consectetur
adipiscing elit. Nunc venenatis, diam nec tempor dapibus, lacus erat
vehicula mauris, id lacinia nisi arcu vitae purus. Nam vestibulum
nisi non lacus luctus vel ornare nibh pharetra. Aenean non lorem
lectus, eu tempus lectus. Cras mattis nibh a mi pharetra ultricies.
In consectetur, tellus sit amet pretium facilisis, enim ipsum
consectetur magna, a mattis ligula massa vel mi. Maecenas id arcu a
erat pellentesque vestibulum at vitae nulla. Nullam eleifend sodales
tincidunt. Donec viverra libero non erat porta sit amet convallis enim
commodo. Cras eu libero elit, ac aliquam ligula. Quisque a elit nec
ligula dapibus porta sit amet a nulla. Nulla vitae molestie ligula.
Aliquam interdum, velit at tincidunt ultrices, sapien mauris sodales
mi, vel rutrum turpis neque id ligula. Donec dictum condimentum arcu
ut convallis. Maecenas blandit, ante eget tempor sollicitudin, ligula
eros venenatis justo, sed ullamcorper dui leo id nunc. Suspendisse
potenti. Ut vel mauris sem. Duis lacinia eros laoreet diam cursus nec
hendrerit tellus pellentesque.
                </p>
            </ui:define>
        </ui:composition>
    </body>
</html>
```

Since the content section is the only one that is specific to our client, we need to define the top and left sections of the template:

```
<?xml version='1.0' encoding='UTF-8' ?>
<!DOCTYPE html PUBLIC "-//W3C//DTD XHTML 1.0 Transitional//EN"
"http://www.w3.org/TR/xhtml1/DTD/xhtml1-transitional.dtd">
<html xmlns="http://www.w3.org/1999/xhtml"
      xmlns:ui="http://xmlns.jcp.org/jsf/facelets"
      xmlns:h="http://xmlns.jcp.org/jsf/html">

    <!-- <h:head> section omitted for brevity -->
    <h:body>

        <div id="top" class="top">
            <ui:insert name="top">
                <h2>Welcome to our Site</h2>
            </ui:insert>
        </div>
        <div>
```

```
            <div id="left">
                <ui:insert name="left">
                    <h3>Links</h3>
                    <ul>
                        <li>
                            <h:outputLink value="http://www.packtpub.
com">
                                <h:outputText value="Packt
Publishing"/>
                            </h:outputLink>
                        </li>
                        <li>
                            <h:outputLink value="http://www.ensode.
net">
                                <h:outputText value="Ensode.net"/>
                            </h:outputLink>
                        </li>
                        <li>
                            <h:outputLink value="http://www.ensode.
com">
                                <h:outputText value="Ensode
Technology, LLC"/>
                            </h:outputLink>
                        </li>

                        <!-- other links omitted for brevity -->
                    </ul>
                </ui:insert>
            </div>
            <div id="content" class="left_content">
                <ui:insert name="content">Content</ui:insert>
            </div>
        </div>
    </h:body>
</html>
```

Since our template client does not override the top and left sections, the markup
from the template will be rendered in the browser.

After making the preceding changes, our template client now renders as follows:

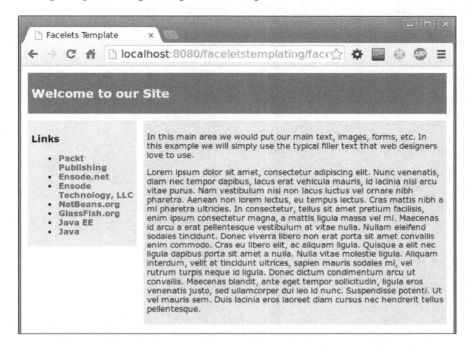

As we can see, creating Facelets templates and template clients with NetBeans is a breeze.

Resource library contracts

Resource library contracts is a new JSF 2.2 feature. It builds on Facelets templates to allow us to build "themable" web applications. For example, we could have an application with multiple customers or we could render the application user interface so that each user sees their own company's logo after logging in. Alternatively, we could have the user select from a predefined set of themes, which is exactly what we are going to do in our next example.

We can create a resource library contract by going to **File** | **New** and selecting **JSF Resource Library Contract** from the **JavaServer Faces** category in the **New File** wizard.

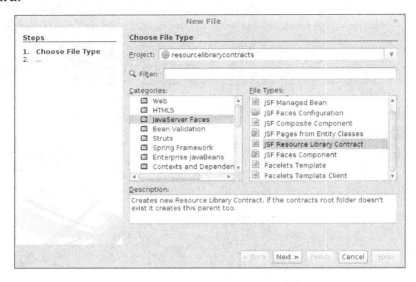

We need to give our resource library contract a name by entering a value into the **Contract Name** input field. We can optionally allow NetBeans to generate the initial templates for our resource library contract.

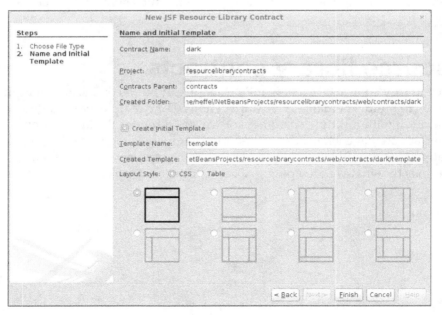

In our example, we are going to have NetBeans generate the initial template and then we'll modify the CSS a bit so that the resulting page will have a dark background with light colored fonts. This will be our "dark" theme.

We'll create a second theme selecting the same layout style as our "dark" theme. We'll leave the CSS as is for the second one (screenshots not shown).

After we create our resource library contracts, NetBeans creates the corresponding files under a `contracts` directory.

Once we have our resource library contracts in place, we need to create a template client as usual (see previous section) to use our contracts in our application's pages. Copy the following code in the `resourcelibrarycontractsdemo.xhtml` file:

```
<?xml version='1.0' encoding='UTF-8' ?>
<!DOCTYPE html PUBLIC "-//W3C//DTD XHTML 1.0 Transitional//EN"
"http://www.w3.org/TR/xhtml1/DTD/xhtml1-transitional.dtd">
<html xmlns="http://www.w3.org/1999/xhtml"
    xmlns:ui="http://xmlns.jcp.org/jsf/facelets"
    xmlns:f="http://xmlns.jcp.org/jsf/core">

  <body>
    <f:view contracts="normal">
        <ui:composition template="/template.xhtml">

            <ui:define name="content">
                <p>
```

```
                              Lorem ipsum dolor sit amet, consectetur
adipiscing elit. Nunc venenatis, diam nec tempor dapibus, lacus erat
vehicula mauris, id lacinia nisi arcu vitae purus. Nam vestibulum
nisi non lacus luctus vel ornare nibh pharetra. Aenean non lorem
lectus, eu tempus lectus. Cras mattis nibh a mi pharetra ultricies.
In consectetur, tellus sit amet pretium facilisis, enim ipsum
consectetur magna, a mattis ligula massa vel mi. Maecenas id arcu a
erat pellentesque vestibulum at vitae nulla. Nullam eleifend sodales
tincidunt. Donec viverra libero non erat porta sit amet convallis enim
commodo. Cras eu libero elit, ac aliquam ligula. Quisque a elit nec
ligula dapibus porta sit amet a nulla. Nulla vitae molestie ligula.
Aliquam interdum, velit at tincidunt ultrices, sapien mauris sodales
mi, vel rutrum turpis neque id ligula. Donec dictum condimentum arcu
ut convallis. Maecenas blandit, ante eget tempor sollicitudin, ligula
eros venenatis justo, sed ullamcorper dui leo id nunc. Suspendisse
potenti. Ut vel mauris sem. Duis lacinia eros laoreet diam cursus nec
hendrerit tellus pellentesque.
                    </p>
                </ui:define>

            </ui:composition>
        </f:view>
    </body>
</html>
```

To use a resource library contract, we need to encapsulate the `<ui:composition>` tag inside an `<f:view>` tag, which has a `contracts` attribute whose value must match the name of the resource library contract we wish to use.

After deploying our application and pointing the browser to the template client URL, we can see the template in action:

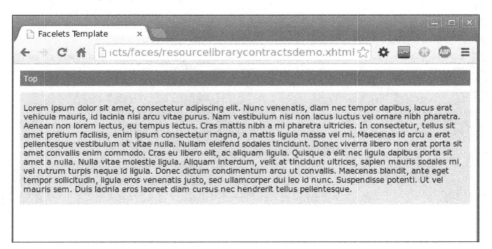

If we change the value of the `contracts` attribute of `<f:view>` to `dark`, we can see the dark theme in action.

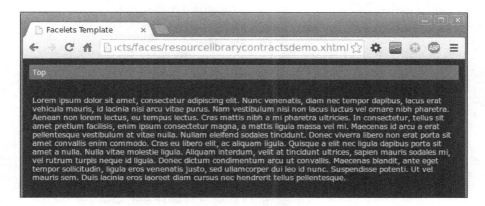

Of course, hardcoding the resource library contract like we did in our example doesn't make a whole lot of sense. To dynamically change the theme, we need to set the value of the `contracts` attribute of `<f:view>` to a value binding expression pointing to a named bean property.

In our project, we will add a `ThemeSelector` named bean to hold the theme selected by the user:

```
package com.ensode.jsf.resourcelibrarycontracts.namedbeans;

import javax.enterprise.context.RequestScoped;
import javax.inject.Named;

@Named
@RequestScoped
public class ThemeSelector {
    private String themeName = "normal";

    public String getThemeName() {
        return themeName;
    }

    public void setThemeName(String themeName) {
        this.themeName = themeName;
    }
}
```

Then, we need to modify our template client to allow the user to change the theme:

```xml
<?xml version='1.0' encoding='UTF-8' ?>
<!DOCTYPE html PUBLIC "-//W3C//DTD XHTML 1.0 Transitional//EN"
"http://www.w3.org/TR/xhtml1/DTD/xhtml1-transitional.dtd">
<html xmlns="http://www.w3.org/1999/xhtml"
      xmlns:ui="http://xmlns.jcp.org/jsf/facelets"
      xmlns:f="http://xmlns.jcp.org/jsf/core"
      xmlns:h="http://xmlns.jcp.org/jsf/html">

  <body>
      <f:view contracts="#{themeSelector.themeName}">
          <ui:composition template="/template.xhtml">
              <ui:define name="top">
                  <h:form>
                      <h:outputLabel for="themeSelector"
                        value="Select a theme"/>
                      <h:selectOneMenu id="themeSelector"
                        value="#{themeSelector.themeName}">
                          <f:selectItem itemLabel="normal"
                            itemValue="normal"/>
                          <f:selectItem itemLabel="dark"
itemValue="dark"/>
                      </h:selectOneMenu>
                      <h:commandButton value="Submit"
                        action="resourcelibrarycontractsdemo"/>
                  </h:form>
              </ui:define>
              <ui:define name="content">
                  <p>
                    <!-- Lorem Ipsum omitted for brevity -->
                  </p>
              </ui:define>
          </ui:composition>
      </f:view>
  </body>
</html>
```

In the preceding markup, we added a `<h:selectOneMenu>` tag and a command button to allow the user to select the desired theme.

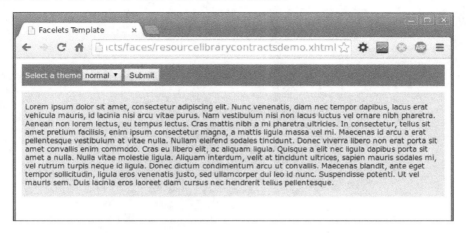

Composite components

A very nice JSF feature is the ability to easily write custom JSF components. With JSF 2, creating a custom component involves little more than creating the markup for it, without any Java code or configuration. Since custom components are typically composed of other JSF components, they are referred to as composite components.

We can generate a composite component by going to **File | New File**, selecting the **JavaServer Faces** category, and selecting the **JSF Composite Component** file type.

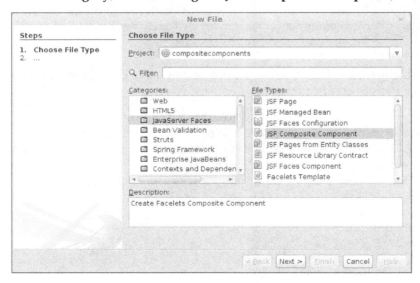

After clicking on **Next,** we can specify the filename, project, and folder for our custom component.

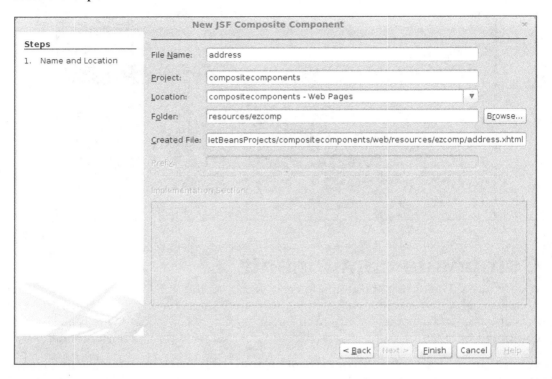

 To take advantage of JSF 2.0's automatic resource handling and conventions, it's not recommended to change the folder where our custom component will be placed.

When we click on **Finish,** NetBeans generates an empty composite component we can use as a base to create our own:

```
<?xml version='1.0' encoding='UTF-8' ?>
<!DOCTYPE html PUBLIC "-//W3C//DTD XHTML 1.0 Transitional//EN"
    "http://www.w3.org/TR/xhtml1/DTD/xhtml1-transitional.dtd">
<html xmlns="http://www.w3.org/1999/xhtml"
    xmlns:cc="http://xmlns.jcp.org/jsf/composite">

    <!-- INTERFACE -->
    <cc:interface>
    </cc:interface>
```

```
    <!-- IMPLEMENTATION -->
    <cc:implementation>
    </cc:implementation>
</html>
```

Every JSF 2 composite component contains two sections: an interface and an implementation.

The interface section must be enclosed inside a `<cc:interface>` tag. In the interface, we define all attributes that our component will have. The implementation section contains the markup that will be rendered when we use our composite component.

In our example, we will develop a simple component we can use to enter addresses. That way, if we have to enter several addresses in an application, we can encapsulate the logic and/or display part in our component. If later we need to change an address entry (for example, to support international addresses), we only need to change our component and all address entry forms in our application will be updated automatically.

After filling in the blanks, our composite component now looks like this:

```
<?xml version='1.0' encoding='UTF-8' ?>
<!DOCTYPE html PUBLIC "-//W3C//DTD XHTML 1.0 Transitional//EN"
    "http://www.w3.org/TR/xhtml1/DTD/xhtml1-transitional.dtd">
<html xmlns="http://www.w3.org/1999/xhtml"
      xmlns:cc="http://xmlns.jcp.org/jsf/composite"
      xmlns:h="http://xmlns.jcp.org/jsf/html"
      xmlns:f="http://xmlns.jcp.org/jsf/core">

    <!-- INTERFACE -->
    <cc:interface>
        <cc:attribute name="addrType"/>
        <cc:attribute name="namedBean" required="true"/>
    </cc:interface>

    <!-- IMPLEMENTATION -->
    <cc:implementation>
        <h:panelGrid columns="2">
            <f:facet name="header">
                <h:outputText value="#{cc.attrs.addrType} Address"/>
            </f:facet>
            <h:outputLabel for="line1" value="Line 1"/>
            <h:inputText id="line1"
              value="#{cc.attrs.namedBean.line1}"/>
            <h:outputLabel for="line2" value="Line 2"/>
```

```
            <h:inputText id="line2"
              value="#{cc.attrs.namedBean.line2}"/>
            <h:outputLabel for="city" value="City"/>
            <h:inputText id="city" value="#{cc.attrs.namedBean.
  city}"/>
            <h:outputLabel for="state" value="state"/>
            <h:inputText id="state" value="#{cc.attrs.namedBean.
  state}"
              size="2" maxlength="2"/>
            <h:outputLabel for="zip" value="Zip"/>
            <h:inputText id="zip" value="#{cc.attrs.namedBean.zip}"
              size="5" maxlength="5"/>
          </h:panelGrid>
      </cc:implementation>
  </html>
```

We specify attributes for our component via the `<cc:attribute>` tag, which has a name attribute used to specify the attribute name, and an optional `required` attribute we can use to specify if the attribute is required.

The body of the `<cc:implementation>` tag looks almost like plain old JSF markup, with one exception. By convention, we can access the tag's attributes by using the `#{cc.attrs.ATTRIBUTE_NAME}` expression that we used to access the attributes we defined in the component's interface section. Note that the `namedBean` attribute of our component must resolve to a named bean. Pages using our component must use a JSF expression resolving to a managed bean as the value of the `namedBean` attribute. We can access the attributes of this named bean by simply using the familiar dot (.) notation we have used before; the only difference here is that instead of using a managed bean name in the expression, we must use the attribute name as defined in the interface section.

Now that we have a simple but complete composite component, using it in our pages is very simple:

```
<?xml version='1.0' encoding='UTF-8' ?>
<!DOCTYPE html PUBLIC "-//W3C//DTD XHTML 1.0 Transitional//EN"
"http://www.w3.org/TR/xhtml1/DTD/xhtml1-transitional.dtd">
<html xmlns="http://www.w3.org/1999/xhtml"
      xmlns:h="http://xmlns.jcp.org/jsf/html"
      xmlns:ezcomp="http://xmlns.jcp.org/jsf/composite/ezcomp">
  <h:head>
      <title>Address Entry</title>
  </h:head>
  <h:body>
      <h:form>
```

```
<h:panelGrid columns="1">
    <ezcomp:address namedBean="#{addressBean}"
                    addrType="Home"/>
    <h:commandButton value="Submit" action="confirmation"
                            style="display: block; margin: 0
auto;"/>
    </h:panelGrid>
  </h:form>
 </h:body>
</html>
```

By convention, the namespace for our custom components will always be
`xmlns:ezcomp="http://xmlns.jcp.org/jsf/composite/ezcomp"` (this is why it
is important not to override the default folder where our component will be placed,
as doing so breaks this convention). NetBeans provides code completion for our
custom composite components, just like it does for standard components.

In our application, we created a simple named bean called `addressBean`. It is a
simple managed bean with a few properties and corresponding getters and setters;
therefore, it is not shown (it is part of this chapter's code download). We use this
bean as the value of the `namedBean` attribute of our component. We also used an
address type of `Home`, and this value will be rendered as a header for our address
input component.

After deploying and running our application, we can see our component in action, as
shown in the following screenshot:

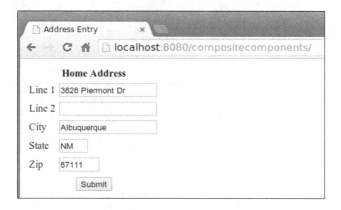

As we can see, creating JSF 2 composite components with NetBeans is a breeze.

Faces flows

Traditional web applications are stateless, that is, a page that just loaded in the browser has no idea of what data the user was working on in previous pages. Java web application frameworks have worked around this inherent limitation of web applications by storing states on the server and attaching Java classes to different application scopes. JSF does this by using the appropriate scope annotation on CDI named beans, as described earlier in this chapter.

If we need to share data between exactly two pages, a scope of request is what we need. If we need to share data across all pages in the application, then a scope of session makes sense. However, what if we need to share data across three or more web pages but not with all pages in the application? There wasn't an appropriate scope we could use until JSF 2.2 added the flow scope.

Since all pages in a flow are related to each other, all pages in the flow must be placed in the same subdirectory. By convention, the name of the subdirectory will be the name of the flow. For example, if we were developing a flow named registration, we would put all pages in the flow in a subdirectory called registration.

In the NetBeans project window, we can create this folder by right-clicking on **Web Pages** node and then going to **New | Other**.

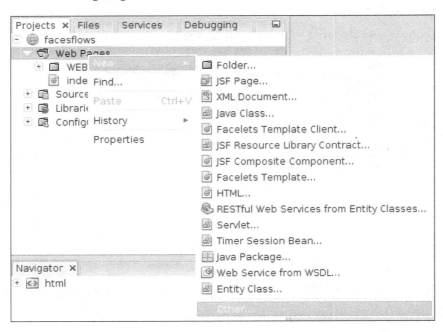

Then, we need to select **Folder** from the **Other** category.

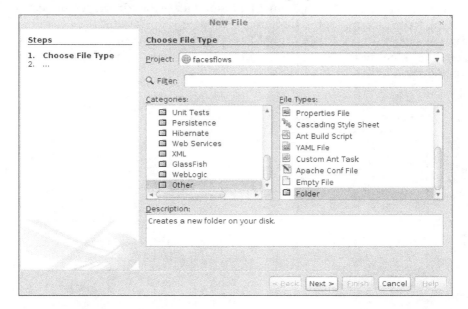

Then, we give our folder the name we want our flow to have; in our case, `registration`.

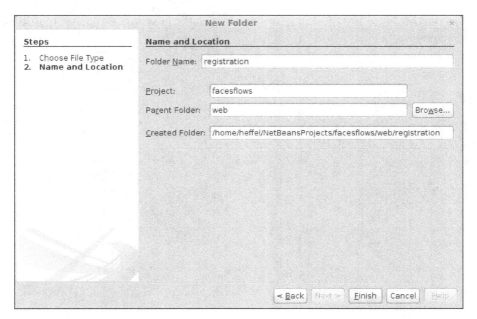

In order for our flow to work properly, we need to add an XML configuration file inside our flow directory. The file must be named after the directory and suffixed with `-flow`. In our example, the filename will be `registration-flow.xml`. In NetBeans, we can add the file by right-clicking on our flow directory (named `registration`), going to **New | Other**, and then selecting **Empty File** from the **Other** category.

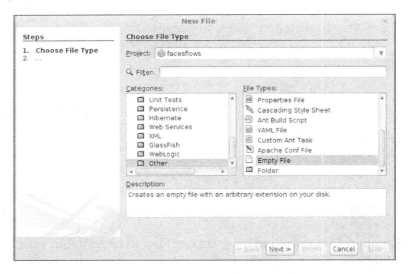

Then, we need to give the file the correct name, making sure we place it inside our flow directory.

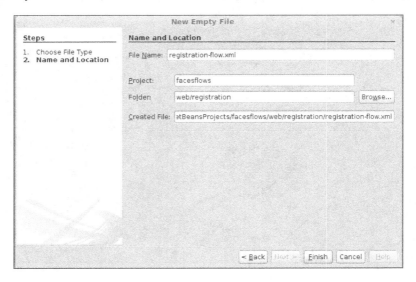

Data for our flow needs to be held in one or more flow-scoped named beans as shown in the following code:

```
package com.ensode.flowscope.namedbeans;

import javax.annotation.PostConstruct;
import javax.annotation.PreDestroy;
import javax.faces.flow.FlowScoped;
import javax.inject.Named;

@Named
@FlowScoped("registration")
public class RegistrationBean {

    private String salutation;
    private String firstName;
    private String lastName;
    private Integer age;
    private String email;

    private String line1;
    private String line2;
    private String city;
    private String state;
    private String zip;

    @PostConstruct
    public void init() {
        System.out.println(this.getClass().getCanonicalName() + "
initialized.");
    }

    @PreDestroy
    public void destroy() {
        System.out.println(this.getClass().getCanonicalName() + "
destroyed.");
    }

    //getters and setters omitted for brevity
}
```

In our example, we use a simple CDI named bean with several properties and corresponding setters and getters. Note the use of the @PostConstruct and @PreDestroy annotations in the example. These are CDI annotations that are invoked just after a CDI named bean is created and just before it is destroyed, respectively. We added these annotations to confirm that our flow-scoped CDI named bean is being created and destroyed as we enter and leave our registration flow.

Now, we need to add the JSF pages in our flow. The first page in the flow needs to be named after the flow itself (in our example, registration.xhtml). There is no restriction about the naming of other pages in the flow. The last page in the flow must be outside the flow directory, and must be named after the flow and suffixed with -return. For our example, the page name will be registration-return.xhtml.

 The markup for the pages doesn't illustrate anything we haven't seen before; therefore, we will not show it. All example code is available as part of this book's code bundle.

After adding all of the necessary files, our project should look like this:

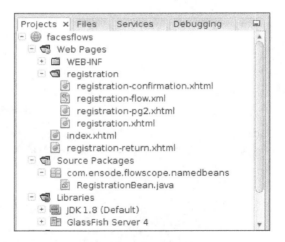

We enter our flow by setting the name of the flow as the value of the action attribute of an <h:commandLink> or <h:commandButton> component.

In our example, we added a simple <h:commandButton> tag to index.xhtml:

```
<h:commandLink action="registration">
        <h:outputText value="Begin Registration"/>
</h:commandLink>
```

When the user clicks on the link, the first page on our flow is displayed.

When the user clicks on the **Continue** button, our flow-scoped named bean is instantiated. In our example, we can verify this by looking at the GlassFish log, where we should see a line like the following:

```
Info:    com.ensode.flowscope.namedbeans.RegistrationBean initialized.
```

The line comes from the `init()` method in `RegistrationBean`, which we annotated with the `@PostConstruct` annotation.

The markup for pages in our flow have `<h:commandButton>` tags to navigate between them, for example, here is the markup for the **Continue** button on the first page of the flow:

```
<h:commandButton id="continue" value="Continue"
                            action="registration-pg2" />
```

The second page on the flow has buttons to navigate forwards and/or backwards:

```
<h:commandButton id="back" value="Go Back"
                            action="registration" />
 <h:commandButton id="continue" value="Continue"
                            action="registration-confirmation" />
```

This takes us to the corresponding page. The last page of the flow has a **Continue** button that takes us out of the flow.

```
<h:commandButton value="Continue" action="registration-return"/>
```

When the user clicks on the **Continue** button, we exit the flow and our flow-scoped named bean is destroyed as expected. Inspecting the GlassFish log confirms this fact:

```
Info:    com.ensode.flowscope.namedbeans.RegistrationBean destroyed.
```

The preceding log entry came from the `destroy()` method on our flow-scoped named bean, which we annotated with the `@PreDestroy` annotation.

HTML5 support

JSF 2.2 added new improvements to support HTML5 features. The two most prominent features for HTML5 support are HTML5-friendly markup and pass-through attributes.

HTML5-friendly markup

HTML5-friendly markup allows us to develop our JSF views using HTML5 tags, as opposed to JSF-specific tags. In order use these tags, we need to include the `http://xmlns.jcp.org/jsf` namespace on our page and specify at least one of the tag attributes with one of the attributes defined in this namespace.

In this section, we will rewrite the application we developed in the *Developing our first JSF application* section earlier in this chapter to utilize HTML5-friendly markup.

To use HTML5-friendly markup with NetBeans, we need to create a web application project from the **Java Web** section and select **JavaServer Faces** as a framework for our application as usual. When adding pages to our application, we need to select the **XHTML** file type from the **Web** category.

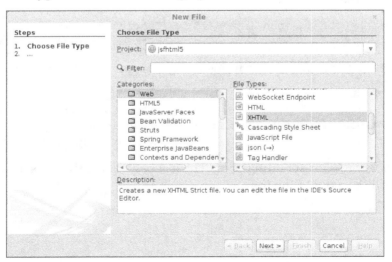

Then, we add HTML markup to our page.

 We can quickly and easily develop HTML pages by dragging-and-dropping components from the NetBeans palette. The palette can be accessed by going to **Window | IDE Tools | Palette**.

After adding the markup for our page, it now looks like this:

```
<?xml version="1.0" encoding="UTF-8"?>
<!DOCTYPE html>
<html xmlns="http://www.w3.org/1999/xhtml"
    xmlns:jsf="http://xmlns.jcp.org/jsf"
    xmlns:f="http://xmlns.jcp.org/jsf/core">
  <head>
      <title>Registration</title>
      <meta name="viewport" content="width=device-width, initial-
scale=1.0"/>
      <link rel="stylesheet" type="text/css" href="css/styles.css"/>
  </head>
  <body>
      <h3>Registration Page</h3>
      <form jsf:id="mainForm" jsf:prependId="false">
          <table border="0" cellspacing="0" cellpadding="0">
              <tbody>
                  <tr>
                      <td class="rightalign">Salutation:</td>

                      <td class="leftalign">
                          <select name="salutation"
jsf:id="salutation"
                                  jsf:value="#{registrationBean.
salutation}" size="1">
                              <f:selectItem itemValue=""
itemLabel=""/>
                              <f:selectItem itemValue="MR"
itemLabel="Mr."/>


                              <!-- other <f:selectItem> tags omitted
for brevity -->
                          </select>
                      </td>
                  </tr>
                  <tr>
```

```
                        <td class="rightalign">
                            First Name:
                        </td>
                        <td class="leftalign">
                            <input type="text" jsf:id="firstName"
                                jsf:value="#{registrationBean.
firstName}"/>
                        </td>
                    </tr>
                    <tr>
                        <td class="rightalign">
                            Last Name:
                        </td>
                        <td class="leftalign">
                            <input type="text" jsf:id="lastName"
                                jsf:value="#{registrationBean.
lastName}"/>
                        </td>
                    </tr>
                    <tr>
                        <td class="rightalign">
                            Age:
                        </td>
                        <td class="leftalign">
                            <input type="number" jsf:id="age"
                                jsf:value="#{registrationBean.age}"/>
                        </td>
                    </tr>
                    <tr>
                        <td class="rightalign">
                            Email Address:
                        </td>
                        <td class="leftalign">
                            <input type="text" jsf:id="email"
                                jsf:value="#{registrationBean.email}"
                                placeholder="username@example.com"/>
                        </td>
                    </tr>
                    <tr>
                        <td></td>
                        <td>
    <input type="submit" value="Submit" jsf:action="confirmation" />
</td>
```

```
        </tr>
      </tbody>
    </table>
  </form>
 </body>
</html>
```

To make JSF interpret HTML tags, we need to add at least one JSF-specific attribute to the tag—any JSF-specific attribute will do. These tags are defined in the `xmlns:jsf= "http://xmlns.jcp.org/jsf"` namespace, which we need to add to the page.

In our example, we transformed an HTML form into a JSF form by adding the `jsf:id` and `jsf:prependId` attributes to the `<form>` tag. To every input field, we added a `jsf:id` and `jsf:value` attribute. These JSF specific attributes let JSF know that these tags should be treated as their JSF equivalents.

We can see in the preceding markup that we used JSF-specific `<f:selectItem>` tags to set the options of our dropdown. One disadvantage of JSF HTML5-friendly markup is that `<option>` tags inside a `<select>` tag are not interpreted correctly, so we still need to use `<f:selectItem>` to set the options of a dropdown.

When we execute our code, we can see our page rendered in the browser.

Pass-through attributes

HTML5 added several new attributes to existing HTML tags. These new attributes were not supported by JSF tags. Instead of updating JSF tags to support these new attributes, the JSF specification team came up with an idea to "future-proof" JSF. This new idea was pass-through attributes.

Pass-through attributes are attributes that are not interpreted by the JSF API, but *passed-through* to the browser to be rendered in the generated HTML. By incorporating this new feature in JSF 2.2, the JSF specification team immediately allowed JSF to support all new HTML5 attributes, along with any new attributes that might be added to HTML in the future.

In the previous section, where we developed a JSF view using HTML5, we used the new `placeholder` HTML5 tag. This tag, as its name implies, places some placeholder text in a text field, giving the user a hint of the format expected for the input. This is a good example of a tag that was added to HTML5 and can be used in JSF pages developed using JSF specific tags:

```
<?xml version='1.0' encoding='UTF-8' ?>
<!DOCTYPE html PUBLIC "-//W3C//DTD XHTML 1.0 Transitional//EN"
    "http://www.w3.org/TR/xhtml1/DTD/xhtml1-transitional.dtd">
<html xmlns="http://www.w3.org/1999/xhtml"
      xmlns:h="http://xmlns.jcp.org/jsf/html"
      xmlns:f="http://xmlns.jcp.org/jsf/core"
      xmlns:p="http://xmlns.jcp.org/jsf/passthrough">
<h:head>
    <title>Registration</title>
    <h:outputStylesheet library="css" name="styles.css"/>
</h:head>
<h:body>
    <h3>Registration Page</h3>
    <h:form>
        <h:panelGrid columns="3"
                     columnClasses="rightalign,leftalign,leftali
gn">

            <!-- Additional markup removed since it is not
                 relevant to the discussion -->

            <h:outputLabel value="Email Address:" for="email"/>
            <h:inputText id="email" label="Email Address"
                    required="true"
```

```
                    p:placeholder="username@example.com"
                      value="#{registrationBean.email}">
               <f:validator validatorId="emailValidator"/>
          </h:inputText>
          <h:message for="email" />

          <h:panelGroup/>
          <h:commandButton id="register" value="Register"
                           action="confirmation" />
       </h:panelGrid>
     </h:form>
   </h:body>
 </html>
```

As we can see in this example, we need to add the `xmlns:jsf= "http://xmlns. jcp.org/jsf/passthrough"` namespace to our JSF page in order to use pass-through attributes. We can then use any arbitrary attributes with our JSF-specific tags by simply prefixing it with the prefix we defined for the namespace (in our case, `p`).

Summary

In this chapter, we saw how NetBeans can help us easily create new JSF projects by automatically adding all the required libraries.

We saw how we can quickly create JSF pages by taking advantage of NetBeans' code completion feature. Additionally, we saw how we can significantly save time and effort by allowing NetBeans to generate JSF 2 templates, including the necessary CSS to easily create fairly elegant pages. We also saw how NetBeans can help us develop JSF 2 custom components.

We also covered some new JSF 2.2 features such as resource library contracts, which allow us to easily develop "themable" applications, as well as the outstanding HTML5 support provided by JSF 2.2—specifically the ability to develop JSF views using HTML5 markup and the ability to use arbitrary HTML5 attributes in JSF markup by employing pass-through attributes.

JSF Component Libraries

3

In the previous chapter, we discussed how to develop web applications using standard JSF components. One nice feature of JSF is its extensibility. It allows application developers to develop their own JSF components. Several ready-made JSF component libraries exist, which makes the job of application developers easier. By far, the three most popular JSF component libraries are PrimeFaces, ICEfaces, and RichFaces. NetBeans includes out-of-the-box support for all three.

In this chapter, we will cover the following topics:

- Using PrimeFaces components in our JSF applications
- Using ICEfaces components in our JSF applications
- Using RichFaces components in our JSF applications

Using PrimeFaces components in our JSF applications

PrimeFaces is a very popular JSF component library, as it allows us to develop elegant and modern-looking web applications with little effort. To use PrimeFaces in our JSF applications, create a new **Web Application** project as usual. When selecting **JavaServer Faces** as a framework, click on the **Components** tab and click on the checkbox labeled **PrimeFaces**.

This step is depicted in the following screenshot:

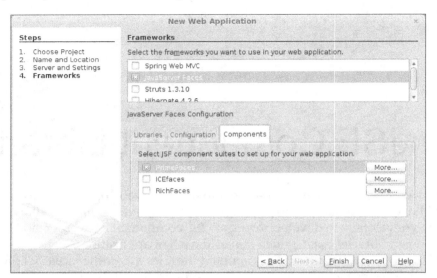

 On selecting PrimeFaces as a JSF component library, you might see an attention message that says **JSF library PrimeFaces not set up properly: Searching valid Primefaces library. Please wait...** near the bottom of the window. Wait a few seconds, and the message should go away.

Right off the bat, NetBeans generates a PrimeFaces application that we can use as a starting point. We can immediately run the generated application to see it in action.

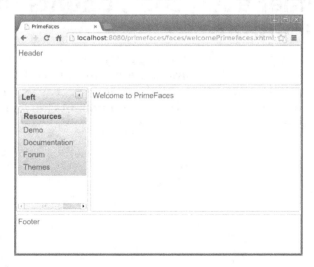

As we can see, the generated application is much more elegant than the JSF applications we developed in the previous chapter. Web applications developed using PrimeFaces render this way without any additional effort (no need to use CSS), since all the CSS and JavaScript is provided by PrimeFaces.

Let's examine the generated `welcomePrimefaces.xhtml` file:

```
<!DOCTYPE HTML PUBLIC "-//W3C//DTD HTML 4.01 Transitional//EN"
"http://www.w3.org/TR/html4/loose.dtd">
<html xmlns="http://www.w3.org/1999/xhtml"
      xmlns:h="http://java.sun.com/jsf/html"
      xmlns:f="http://java.sun.com/jsf/core"
      xmlns:ui="http://java.sun.com/jsf/facelets"
      xmlns:p="http://primefaces.org/ui">

    <f:viewcontentType="text/html">
        <h:head>
            <f:facet name="first">
                <meta content='text/html; charset=UTF-8'
                  http-equiv="Content-Type"/>
                <title>PrimeFaces</title>
            </f:facet>
        </h:head>
        <h:body>

            <p:layoutfullPage="true">

                <p:layoutUnit position="north" size="100"
    resizable="true"
                    closable="true" collapsible="true">
                        Header
                </p:layoutUnit>

                <p:layoutUnit position="south" size="100"
    closable="true"
                    collapsible="true">
                        Footer
                </p:layoutUnit>

                <p:layoutUnit position="west" size="175" header="Left"
    collapsible="true">
                    <p:menu>
                        <p:submenu label="Resources">
                            <p:menuitem value="Demo"
```

```
                                        url=
                            "http://www.primefaces.org/showcase-labs/ui/
home.jsf"
                                />
                                <p:menuitem value="Documentation"
                                url="http://www.primefaces.org/
documentation.html"
                                    />
                                <p:menuitem value="Forum"
                                  url="http://forum.primefaces.org/" />
                                <p:menuitem value="Themes"
                                    url="http://www.primefaces.org/themes.
html" />

                            </p:submenu>

                        </p:menu>
                    </p:layoutUnit>

                    <p:layoutUnit position="center">
                        Welcome to PrimeFaces
                    </p:layoutUnit>

                </p:layout>
            </h:body>
        </f:view>
</html>
```

To use PrimeFaces components in our JSF pages, we need to use the xmlns:p="http://primefaces.org/ui" namespace. NetBeans automatically adds this namespace to the generated page.

Notice that the rendered page is divided into sections (a header, footer, left hand-side menu, and the main content area of the application). Normally, we would have to use HTML <div> tags and CSS to create a layout like this. PrimeFaces, however, includes the <p:layout> component that takes care of all the difficult tasks for us.

Inside <p:layout>, we need to have some nested <p:layoutUnit> components to create specific sections for the page. The <p:layoutUnit> element has a position attribute that we can use to specify what section the layout unit corresponds to:

- A value of north will result in the layout unit being rendered at the top of the page. The width of the section will automatically cover all available horizontal space in the browser window. This value is used to generate the **Header** section in the NetBeans-generated markup.

- A value of west will render to the left of the page. The height of the section will automatically cover all available vertical space. This value is used on the **Left** section on the NetBeans-generated markup.

- A value of south will result in the layout unit being rendered at the bottom of the page. The width of the section will span through all available horizontal space. This value is used to generate the **Footer** section on the NetBeans-generated markup.

- A value of center will result in a layout that renders in the center of the page. Both the width and the height of the section will expand to take all available horizontal and vertical space, respectively.

- We can also use a value of east for the position attribute of <p:layoutUnit> (not used in the NetBeans-generated markup). This value will generate a section rendered on the right side of the page, with its vertical size expanding to take all available vertical space.

The <p:layoutUnit> component has a size attribute that we can use to set the width (for a position attribute value of east or west) or height (for a position attribute value of north or south) of the layout unit. When using center as the value of the position attribute, the value of the size attribute is ignored and the layout unit expands to take all available vertical and horizontal space.

The <p:layoutUnit> component also has resizable, closeable, and collapsible attributes; setting these attributes to true allows us to resize, close, and collapse the rendered section, respectively.

The NetBeans-generated PrimeFaces markup also employs the <p:menu> PrimeFaces component. This component allows us to easily create menus to aid the users navigate though our application.

We can use one or more nested <p:submenu> components inside <p:menu>. This tag allows us to group related menu items together. The <p:submenu> component has a label attribute we can use to label our menu items. In the NetBeans-generated markup, a <p:submenu> component with a label of **Resources** is used. We can add one or more <p:menuitem> tags inside <p:submenu>, one for each menu item. The <p:submenu> component has a value attribute, whose value will render as the text of the menu item, and a url attribute that we can use to set the URL of the page the menu will navigate to.

PrimeFaces has drop-in replacements for most standard JSF components, for example, there is a PrimeFaces-specific <p:inputText> tag that is analogous to the standard <h:inputText> tag. This fact makes porting standard JSF applications to PrimeFaces very easy, mostly by replacing the h: prefix of standard JSF applications with the PrimeFaces-specific p: prefix.

The following screenshot shows a PrimeFaces-specific version of the registration application we developed in the previous chapter:

As we can see, the application renders beautifully and all we had to do was replace standard JSF components with their PrimeFaces-specific counterparts. Notice that an asterisk is automatically added to the label for all the required fields.

The following snippet shows the relevant parts of the markup to generate the registration page:

```
<p:messages/>
<h:form>
    <p:panelGrid columns="2"
                        columnClasses="rightalign,leftalign">
        <p:outputLabel value="Salutation: " for="salutation"/>
        <p:selectOneMenu id="salutation" label="Salutation"
                                        value="#{registrationBean.
salutation}">
            <f:selectItem itemLabel="" itemValue=""/>
            <f:selectItem itemLabel="Mr." itemValue="MR"/>
            <f:selectItem itemLabel="Mrs." itemValue="MRS"/>
            <f:selectItem itemLabel="Miss" itemValue="MISS"/>
            <f:selectItem itemLabel="Ms" itemValue="MS"/>
            <f:selectItem itemLabel="Dr." itemValue="DR"/>
        </p:selectOneMenu>
        <p:outputLabel value="First Name:" for="firstName"/>
        <p:inputText id="firstName" label="First Name"
                        required="true"
                        value="#{registrationBean.firstName}" />
        <p:outputLabel value="Last Name:" for="lastName"/>
        <p:inputText id="lastName" label="Last Name"
                        required="true"
```

```
                              value="#{registrationBean.lastName}" />
        <p:outputLabel for="age" value="Age:"/>
        <p:inputText id="age" label="Age" size="2"
                              value="#{registrationBean.age}"/>
        <p:outputLabel value="Email Address:" for="email"/>
        <p:inputText id="email" label="Email Address"
                              required="true"
                              value="#{registrationBean.email}">
            <f:validatorvalidatorId="emailValidator"/>
        </p:inputText>
        <h:panelGroup/>
        <p:commandButton id="register" value="Register"
                                      action="confirmation"
    ajax="false"/>
        </p:panelGrid>
    </h:form>
```

As we can see, for the most part, all we had to do was to replace JSF-specific tags with their PrimeFaces-specific counterparts. For aesthetic reasons, we also changed the number of columns of `<p:panelGrid>` to two (as opposed to three in the original `<h:panelGrid>` tag) and replaced the `<h:message>` tags in the original page with a top-level `<p:messages>` tag.

By default, PrimeFaces command buttons are Ajax enabled. So, for this particular example, we explicitly disabled Ajax on our command button by setting its `ajax` attribute to `false`.

Another nice feature of PrimeFaces is that validation messages are nicely styled and all fields that fail validation are highlighted in red, as shown in the following screenshot:

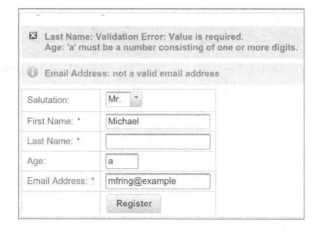

In this section, we provided a brief introduction to PrimeFaces. There are many other PrimeFaces custom components and features we didn't cover. You can visit http://www.primefaces.org for more information.

Using ICEfaces components in our JSF applications

ICEfaces is another popular JSF library that simplifies JSF application development. To use ICEfaces in our JSF applications, create a new web application project. When selecting **JavaServer Faces** as a framework, click on the **Components** tab and click on the checkbox labeled **ICEfaces**.

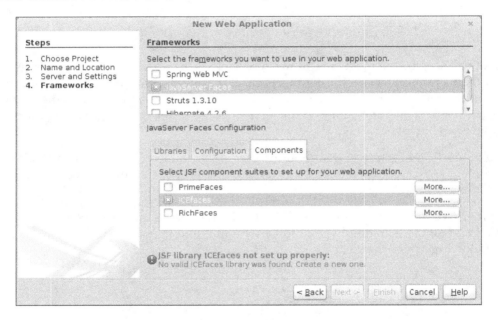

Unlike PrimeFaces, the ICEfaces libraries are not included with NetBeans. Therefore, we need to download them from http://www.icesoft.com and create a new library.

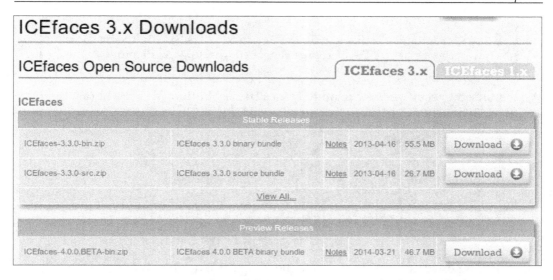

The file we need to download is the latest stable binary distribution of ICEfaces (the filename was `ICEfaces-3.3.0-bin.zip` at the time of writing).

 You need to register on the ICESoft website (`www.icesoft.org`) to download the ICEfaces libraries.

After extracting the downloaded ZIP file, the JAR files we need to add to our library can be found under `icefaces/lib`.

To create a new ICEfaces library in NetBeans, click on the **More...** button next to **ICEfaces**. The following dialog window pops up:

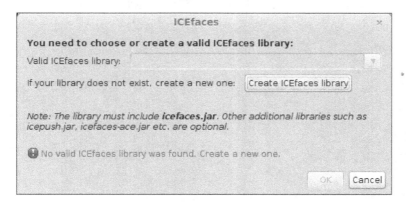

Although the dialog indicates `icefaces-ace.jar` is optional, it is necessary for the NetBeans-generated markup to work properly.

We then need to click on the **Create ICEfaces library** button, give the library an appropriate name (like `ICEfaces`), and click on **OK**.

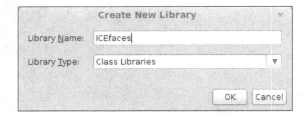

After clicking on **OK**, we need to locate the ICEfaces JAR files on the filesystem by clicking on the **Add JAR/Folder...** button to add them to our library.

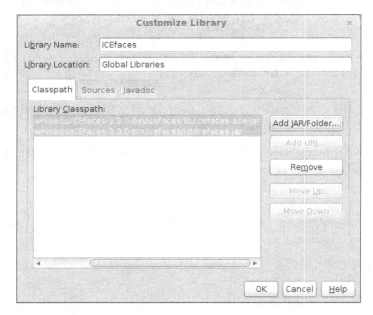

After we click on **OK**, the NetBeans ICEfaces library is created.

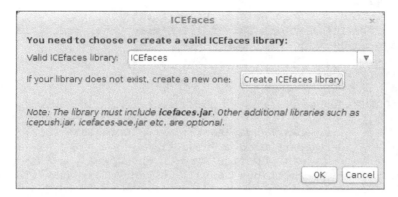

Now, click on **OK** and click on **Finish** on the new JSF project wizard to create our new project.

Like with PrimeFaces, when using ICEfaces, NetBeans generates a sample ICEfaces application that we can use as a starting point.

The generated page provides links to additional ICEfaces resources, as shown in the following code:

```
<?xml version='1.0' encoding='UTF-8' ?>
<!DOCTYPE html PUBLIC "-//W3C//DTD XHTML 1.0 Transitional//EN"
"http://www.w3.org/TR/xhtml1/DTD/xhtml1-transitional.dtd">
<html xmlns="http://www.w3.org/1999/xhtml"
      xmlns:ui="http://java.sun.com/jsf/facelets"
      xmlns:f="http://java.sun.com/jsf/core"
      xmlns:h="http://java.sun.com/jsf/html"
      xmlns:icecore="http://www.icefaces.org/icefaces/core"
```

```
        xmlns:ace="http://www.icefaces.org/icefaces/components">
    <h:head>
        <title>ICEfaces Welcome Page</title>
        <!-- This line is only for ICE component, remove it if no ice
component is used in this page.-->
        <link rel="stylesheet" type="text/css" href="./xmlhttp/css/
rime/rime.css"/>
    </h:head>
    <h:body>
        <h:form>
            <ace:panel header="Welcome to ICEfaces">
                <h:panelGrid columns="1">
                    <!-- NOTICE -To run this page you must have
also ICEfaces ACE components library on your classpath (project
dependencies). -->
                    <ace:linkButton id="linkButton1"
                      value="ICEfaces Overview"  href="http://wiki.
icesoft.org/display/ICE/ICEfaces+Overview">
                    </ace:linkButton>
                    <ace:linkButton id="linkButton2"
                       value="General Documentation" href="http://
wiki.icesoft.org/display/ICE/ICEfaces+Documentation">
                    </ace:linkButton>
                    <ace:linkButton id="linkButton3"
                       value="ICEfaces Demos" href="http://www.icesoft.
org/demos/icefaces-demos.jsf">
                    </ace:linkButton>
                    <ace:linkButton id="linkButton4" value="Tutorials"
href="http://www.icesoft.org/community/tutorials-samples.jsf">
                    </ace:linkButton>
                    <ace:linkButton id="linkButton5"
                       value="ACE components" href="http://wiki.
icesoft.org/display/ICE/ACE+Components"></ace:linkButton>
                    <ace:linkButton id="linkButton6"
                       value="ICE components" href="http://wiki.
icesoft.org/display/ICE/ICE+Components">
                    </ace:linkButton>
                    <!-- You can also use ICE components. Adds ICE
namespace in that case: xmlns:ice="http://www.icesoft.com/icefaces/
component" -->
                    <!-- <ice:outputLink id="aceLink" value="http://
wiki.icesoft.org/display/ICE/ACE+Components" target="_blank">ACE
components</ice:outputLink> -->
                    <!-- <ice:outputLink id="iceLink" value="http://
wiki.icesoft.org/display/ICE/ICE+Components" target="_blank">ICE
components</ice:outputLink> -->
                </h:panelGrid>
            </ace:panel>
```

```
        </h:form>
    </h:body>
</html>
```

ICEfaces includes two sets of components: the ICE components, whose functionality is primarily implemented as server-side code with limited JavaScript, and the newer ACE components that are implemented using a combination of server-side and client-side code. According to ICESoft (the company behind ICEfaces), ICE components should be used when we need to support legacy browsers, when migrating from older ICEfaces versions, or when we need to minimize JavaScript rendering or data processing. ACE components should be used to leverage modern browsers.

The NetBeans-generated ICEfaces application uses only ICEfaces ACE components and standard JSF components. An ICEfaces `<ace:panel>` tag is used to generate the panel enclosing the links on the rendered page. This tag has a `header` attribute we can use, appropriately enough, to render a header for our panel.

Inside the `<ace:panel>` tag, there are some `<ace:linkButton>` tags that are used to render the links on the page. The `<ace:linkButton>` tag provides functionality similar to the standard JSF `<h:outputLink>` and `<h:commandLink>` tags. In the NetBeans-generated markup, the button behaves like a standard `<h:outputLink>` component. The URL that the generated link navigates to is defined in its `href` attribute. To make `<ace:linkButton>` behave as a standard JSF command link, we use its `action` attribute just like we do with.

The following screenshot illustrates an ICEfaces version of our sample registration application:

The following code snippet shows the relevant markup for the ICEfaces-specific registration application:

```
<h:form>
    <ace:panel header="Registration">
        <ace:messages/>
        <h:panelGrid columns="2"
                columnClasses="rightalign,leftalign">
            <h:outputLabel value="Salutation: "
for="salutation"/>
            <ace:selectMenu id="salutation" label="Salutation"
                    value="#{registrationBean.
salutation}" >
                <f:selectItem itemLabel="" itemValue=""/>
                <f:selectItem itemLabel="Mr." itemValue="MR"/>
                <f:selectItem itemLabel="Mrs."
itemValue="MRS"/>
                <f:selectItem itemLabel="Miss"
itemValue="MISS"/>
                <f:selectItem itemLabel="Ms" itemValue="MS"/>
                <f:selectItem itemLabel="Dr." itemValue="DR"/>
            </ace:selectMenu>

            <h:outputLabel value="First Name:"
for="firstName"/>
            <h:inputText id="firstName" label="First Name"
                    required="true"
                    value="#{registrationBean.firstName}"
/>
            <h:outputLabel value="Last Name:" for="lastName"/>
            <h:inputText id="lastName" label="Last Name"
                    required="true"
                    value="#{registrationBean.lastName}"
/>
            <h:outputLabel for="age" value="Age:"/>
            <ace:sliderEntry id="age"
                    value="#{registrationBean.age}"
                    min="0" max="100" showLabels="true"
/>
            <h:outputLabel value="Email Address:"
for="email"/>
            <h:inputText id="email" label="Email Address"
                    required="true"
                    value="#{registrationBean.email}">
                <f:validatorvalidatorId="emailValidator"/>
```

```
                    </h:inputText>
                    <h:panelGroup/>
                    <ace:pushButton id="register" value="Register"
                                    action="confirmation" />
                </h:panelGrid>
            </ace:panel>
        </h:form>
```

In our example, we use the previously explained `<ace:panel>` component to encapsulate our form's input fields. Similar to PrimeFaces, ICEfaces has an `<ace:messages>` component that renders messages nicely styled; therefore, we added this component to our page to avoid styling the JSF messages.

ICEfaces does not have replacements for `<h:outputText>` or `<h:inputText>`, so we simply used these standard components in our ICEfaces application:

- The `<ace:selectMenu>` component is a replacement for the standard `<h:selectOneMenu>` component. It renders as a dropdown and works pretty much the same way as the standard `<h:selectOneMenu>`.

- The `<ace:sliderEntry>` component allows us to enter numeric values by moving a slider with the mouse.

- The `<ace:pushButton>` component is equivalent to the standard JSF `<h:commandButton>` component. When the user clicks on the button, the method specified in its `action` attribute is automatically executed.

In this section, we only scratched the surface of what is available with ICEfaces. For more information, you can visit the ICEfaces documentation wiki page at `http://wiki.icesoft.org/display/ICE/ICEfaces+Documentation`.

Using RichFaces components in our JSF applications

The third JSF component library we can select when starting a new Java web application in NetBeans is RichFaces. NetBeans does not bundle the RichFaces JAR files out of the box; therefore, like with ICEfaces, we need to download the RichFaces libraries and create a NetBeans library from them.

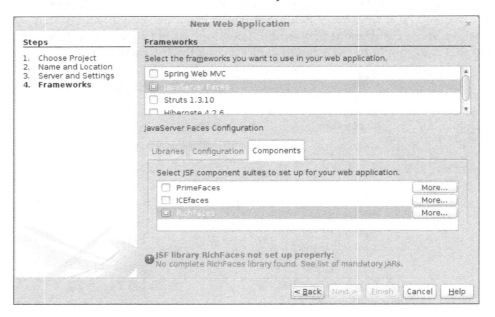

The latest stable version of RichFaces can be downloaded from http://www.jboss. org/richfaces/download/stable.html.

We need to click on the **Download** link on the RichFaces final distribution (ZIP) row to get the latest version of RichFaces. Once we extract the ZIP file, the files we need to add to the NetBeans library will have names similar to the following (exact name will vary depending on the RichFaces version):

- `richfaces-components-a4j-4.5.1.Final.jar`

- `richfaces-components-rich-4.5.1.Final.jar`

- `richfaces-core-4.5.1.Final.jar`

- RichFaces also has some external dependencies that can be found under the lib directory of the extracted ZIP file (exact names may vary depending on the RichFaces version):

  - `guava-18.0.jar`

  - `sac-1.3.jar`

  - `cssparser-0.9.14.jar`

Once we have downloaded RichFaces and its external dependencies, we are ready to create the RichFacesNetBeans library.

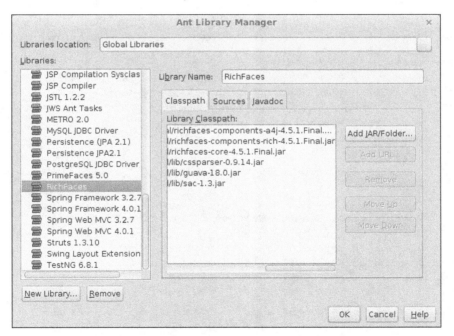

After we create the RichFacesNetBeans library, our project is ready and NetBeans generates a sample RichFaces application that we can use as a starting point.

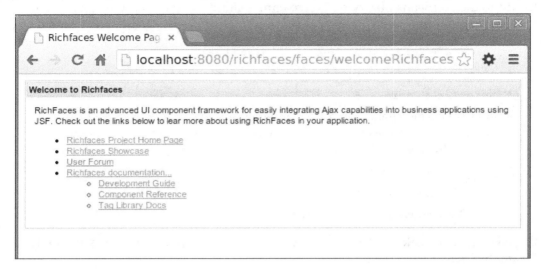

Like with PrimeFaces and ICEfaces, the RichFaces page generated by NetBeans provides links to additional RichFaces resources, as shown in the following code:

```
<?xml version='1.0' encoding='UTF-8' ?>
<!DOCTYPE html PUBLIC "-//W3C//DTD XHTML 1.0 Transitional//EN"
"http://www.w3.org/TR/xhtml1/DTD/xhtml1-transitional.dtd">
<html xmlns="http://www.w3.org/1999/xhtml"
      xmlns:rich="http://richfaces.org/rich"
      xmlns:h="http://java.sun.com/jsf/html">
    <h:head>
        <title>Richfaces Welcome Page</title>
    </h:head>
    <h:body>
        <rich:panel header="Welcome to Richfaces">
            RichFaces is an advanced UI component framework for easily
integrating Ajax capabilities into business applications using JSF.
Check out the links below to learn more about using RichFaces in your
application.
            <ul>
                <li>
                  <h:outputLink value="http://richfaces.org" >
                    Richfaces Project Home Page</h:outputLink>
                </li>
                <li>
```

```
                    <h:outputLink
                        value="http://showcase.richfaces.org" >
                        Richfaces Showcase</h:outputLink>
                </li>
                <li>
                    <h:outputLink value="https://community.jboss.org/en/
richfaces?view=discussions" >
 User Forum
                    </h:outputLink>
                </li>
                <li>
                    <h:outputLink value="http://www.jboss.org/richfaces/
docs" >Richfaces documentation...
                    </h:outputLink>
                    <ul>
                      <li>
                        <h:outputLink value="http://docs.jboss.org/
richfaces/latest_4_X/Developer_Guide/en-US/html_single/" >
                            Development Guide</h:outputLink>
                      </li>
                      <li>
                        <h:outputLink value="http://docs.jboss.org/
richfaces/latest_4_X/Component_Reference/en-US/html/" >
                            Component Reference</h:outputLink>
                      </li>
                      <li>
                        <h:outputLink value="http://docs.jboss.org/
richfaces/latest_4_X/vdldoc/" >
                            Tag Library Docs</h:outputLink>
                      </li>
                    </ul>
                </li>
            </ul>
        </rich:panel>
    </h:body>
</html>
```

The only RichFaces-specific tag used in the NetBeans-generated RichFaces page is the `<rich:panel>` tag, which is used to create the panel containing the text and links on the page.

Porting our registration page to RichFaces results in a page that looks like the following screenshot:

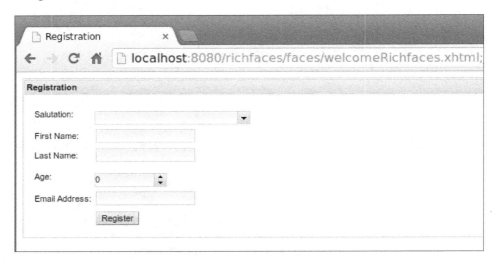

The relevant markup for the RichFaces-specific version of our application looks like this:

```
<rich:panel header="Registration">
        <h:formprependId="false">
            <h:panelGrid columns="3"
                        columnClasses="rightalign,leftalign,left
align">
                <h:outputLabel value="Salutation: " for="salutati
on"/>
                <rich:select id="salutation"
                        value="#{registrationBean.
salutation}">
                    <f:selectItem itemLabel="" itemValue=""/>
                    <f:selectItem itemLabel="Mr." itemValue="MR"/>
                    <f:selectItem itemLabel="Mrs."
itemValue="MRS"/>
                    <f:selectItem itemLabel="Miss"
itemValue="MISS"/>
                    <f:selectItem itemLabel="Ms" itemValue="MS"/>
                    <f:selectItem itemLabel="Dr." itemValue="DR"/>
                </rich:select>
                <rich:message for="salutation"/>

                <h:outputLabel value="First Name:"
for="firstName"/>
```

```
                        <h:inputText id="firstName" label="First Name"
                                required="true"
                                value="#{registrationBean.firstName}"
    />
                        <rich:message for="firstName" />
                        <h:outputLabel value="Last Name:" for="lastName"/>
                        <h:inputText id="lastName" label="Last Name"
                                required="true"
                                value="#{registrationBean.lastName}"
    />
                        <rich:message for="lastName" />

                        <h:outputLabel for="age" value="Age:"/>
                        <rich:inputNumberSpinner id="age" label="age"

value="#{registrationBean.age}"
                                                minValue="0"
maxValue="110"/>
                        <rich:message for="age"/>

                        <h:outputLabel value="Email Address:"
for="email"/>
                        <h:inputText id="email" label="Email Address"
                                required="true"
                                value="#{registrationBean.email}">
                    <f:validatorvalidatorId="emailValidator"/>
                        </h:inputText>
                        <rich:message for="email" />

                        <h:panelGroup/>
                        <h:commandButton id="register" value="Register"
                                action="confirmation" />
                </h:panelGrid>
            </h:form>
        </rich:panel>
```

We encapsulate our form inside a `<rich:panel>` tag so that it is rendered
inside a panel. The `<rich:select>` tag is a RichFaces-specific component that
renders as a drop-down list. One advantage of `<rich:select>` over regular JSF
`<h:selectOneMenu>` is that `<rich:select>` can be configured as a combobox, in
which case it will accept typed input. To configure `<rich:select>` to be used as
a combobox, set its `enableManualInput` attribute to `true`.

The `<rich:inputNumberSpinner>` component allows the user to enter numeric
input either by directly typing it in or by clicking on arrows.

RichFaces provides both a <rich:messages> and a <rich:message> component, which are analogous to standard JSF <h:messages> and <h:message>. The RichFaces-specific versions render messages nicely formatted. The following screenshot illustrates how the RichFaces <rich:message> component renders validation messages:

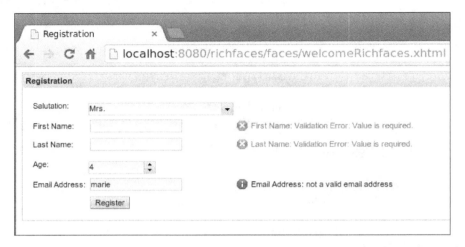

Once again, we only scratched the surface of what RichFaces offers. For more information on RichFaces, refer to the RichFaces documentation at http://www.jboss.org/richfaces/docs.

Summary

In this chapter, we covered NetBeans support for three of the most popular JSF component libraries: PrimeFaces, ICEfaces, and RichFaces.

We covered how to develop an application using the bundled PrimeFaces library included with NetBeans. We also discussed how to configure NetBeans to be able to develop JSF applications using the ICEfaces and RichFaces component libraries. Finally, we discussed how NetBeans generates a skeleton application that we can use as a starting point for our PrimeFaces, ICEfaces, or RichFaces applications.

4
Interacting with Databases through the Java Persistence API

The **Java Persistence API (JPA)** is an **object-relational mapping (ORM)** API. ORM tools help us to automate the mapping of Java objects to relational database tables. Earlier versions of J2EE used Entity Beans as the standard approach for ORM. Entity Beans attempted to always keep the data in memory synchronized with the database data, a good idea in theory, however, in practice this feature resulted in poorly performing applications.

Several ORM APIs were developed to overcome the limitations of Entity Beans, such as Hibernate, iBatis, Cayenne, and TopLink, among others.

Java EE 5 deprecated Entity Beans in favor of JPA. JPA took ideas from several ORM tools and incorporated them in the standard. As we will see in this chapter, NetBeans has several features that make development with JPA a breeze.

The following topics will be covered in this chapter:

- Creating our first JPA entity
- Interacting with JPA entities using EntityManager
- Generating JPA entities from an existing database schema
- JPA named queries and **Java Persistence Query Language (JPQL)**
- Entity relationships
- Generating complete JSF applications from JPA entities

Creating our first JPA entity

JPA entities are Java classes whose fields are persisted to a database by the JPA API. These Java classes are **Plain Old Java Objects** (**POJOs**), and as such, they don't need to extend any specific parent class or implement any specific interface. A Java class is designated as a JPA entity by decorating it with the @Entity annotation.

In order to create and test our first JPA entity, we will create a new web application using the JavaServer Faces framework. In this example, we will name our application jpaweb, and (as with all of our examples) we will use the bundled GlassFish application server.

> Refer to *Chapter 2, Developing Web Applications Using JavaServer Faces 2.2*, for instructions on creating a new JSF project.

To create a new JPA entity, select the **Persistence** category from the new file dialog and select **Entity Class** as the file type.

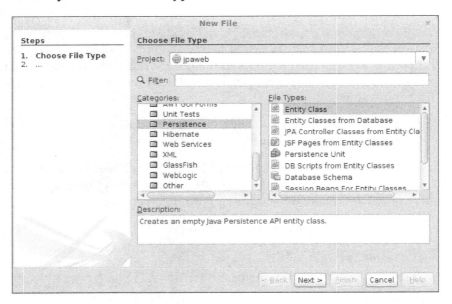

After doing so, NetBeans presents the **New Entity Class** wizard.

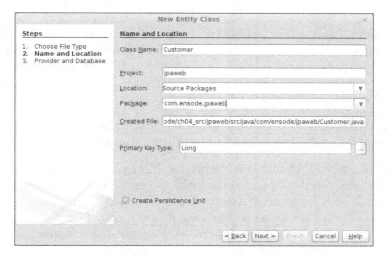

At this point, we should specify the values for the **Class Name** and **Package** fields (Customer and com.ensode.jpaweb in our example).

Projects using JPA require a persistence unit. This persistence unit is defined in a file called persistence.xml. When we create our first JPA entity for the project, NetBeans detects that no persistence.xml exists and automatically checks the checkbox labeled **Create Persistence Unit**. The next step in the wizard allows us to enter the information necessary to create the persistence unit. This is shown in the following screenshot:

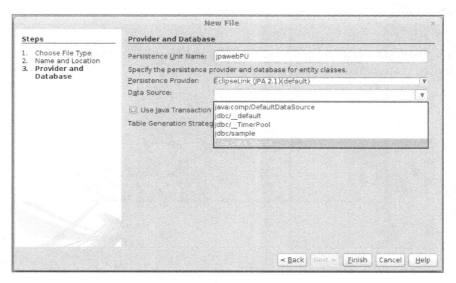

The **Provider and Database** wizard will suggest a name for our persistence unit; in most cases the default can be safely accepted.

JPA is a specification for which several implementations exist. NetBeans supports several JPA implementations, including EclipseLink, TopLink Essentials, Hibernate, KODO, and OpenJPA. Since the bundled GlassFish application server includes EclipseLink as its default JPA implementation, it makes sense to take this default value for the **Persistence Provider** field when deploying our application to GlassFish.

Before we can interact with a database from any Java EE application, a database connection pool and data source need to be created in the application server.

A database connection pool contains connection information that allows us to connect to our database, such as the server name, port, and credentials. The advantage of using a connection pool instead of directly opening a JDBC connection to a database is that database connections in a connection pool are never closed, they are simply allocated to applications as they need them. This improves performance, since the operations of opening and closing database connections are expensive in terms of performance.

Data sources allow us to obtain a connection from a connection pool, and then invoke its `getConnection()` method to obtain a database connection from a connection pool. When dealing with JPA, we don't need to directly obtain a reference to a data source, it is all done automatically by the JPA API. However, we still need to indicate the data source to use in the application's persistence unit.

NetBeans comes with a few data sources and connection pools preconfigured. We can use one of these preconfigured resources for our application. However, NetBeans also allows us to create these resources "on the fly", which is what we will be doing in our example.

To create a new data source, we need to select the **New Data Source...** item from the **Data Source** combobox.

A data source needs to interact with a database connection pool. NetBeans comes preconfigured with a few connection pools out of the box. However, as with data sources, it allows us to create a new connection pool "on demand". In order to do this, we need to select the **New Database Connection...** item from the **Database Connection** combobox.

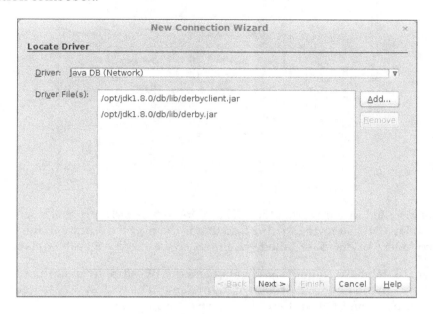

NetBeans includes JDBC drivers for a few **relational database management systems (RDBMS)** such as JavaDB, MySQL, PostgreSQL out of the box. JavaDB is bundled with both GlassFish and NetBeans; therefore, we selected JavaDB for our example to avoid installing an external RDBMS.

For RDBMS systems that are not supported out of the box, we need to obtain a JDBC driver and let NetBeans know of its location by selecting **New Driver** from the **Driver Name** combobox. Then, we need to navigate to the location of the JAR file that contains the JDBC driver. Consult your RDBMS documentation for details.

Click on **Next >** to enter your connection details as shown in the following screenshot:

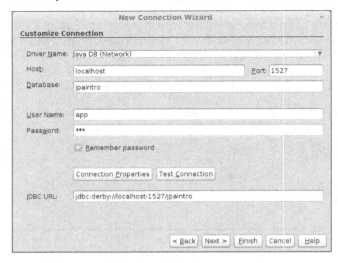

JavaDB is installed in our workstation. Therefore, use `localhost` as the server name. By default, JavaDB listens to port 1527, so that is the port we specify in the URL. We wish to connect to a database called `jpaintro`, so we specify it as the database name.

Every JavaDB database contains a schema named **APP**, since by default each user uses a schema named after his/her own login name. The easiest way to get going is to create a user named `APP` and selecting a password for this user.

Since the `jpaintro` database does not exist yet, we need to create it. We can do this by clicking on **Connection Properties** and entering a property named `create` with a value `true`.

In the next step in the wizard, we need to select a schema to use for our application. The **APP** schema is the one typically used by applications using JavaDB as their RDBMS.

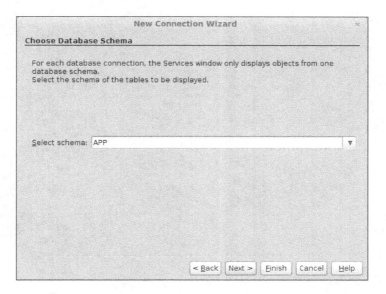

In the next step, NetBeans asks us to enter a descriptive name for our connection.

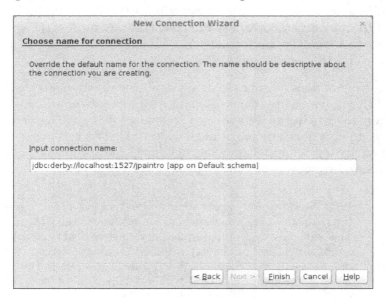

We can choose to do so or simply accept the default connection name. Once we have created our new data source and connection pool, we can continue configuring our persistence unit.

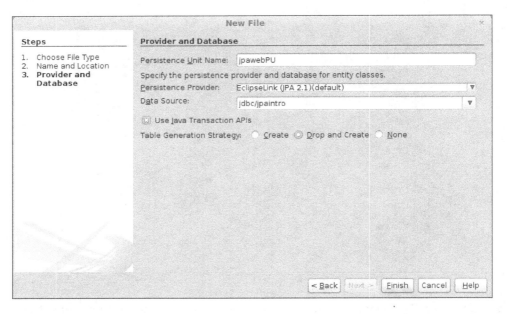

It is a good idea to leave the **Use Java Transaction APIs** checkbox checked. This will instruct our JPA implementation to use the **Java Transaction API (JTA)** to allow the application server to manage transactions. If we uncheck this box, we will need to manually write code to manage transactions.

Most JPA implementations allow us to define a table generation strategy. We can instruct our JPA implementation to create tables for our entities when we deploy our application, to drop the tables and then regenerate them when our application is deployed, or to not create any tables at all. NetBeans allows us to specify the table generation strategy for our application by clicking on the appropriate value in the **Table Generation Strategy** radio button group.

When working with a new application, it is a good idea to select the **Drop and Create** table generation strategy in the wizard. This will allow us to add, remove, and rename fields in our JPA entity at will, without having to make the same changes in the database schema. When selecting this table generation strategy, tables in the database schema will be dropped and recreated every time we deploy our application. Therefore, any data previously persisted will be lost.

Once we have created our new data source, database connection, and persistence unit, we are ready to create our new JPA entity.

We can do so by simply clicking on the **Finish** button. At this point, NetBeans generates the source for our JPA entity.

 JPA allows the primary field of a JPA entity to map to any column type (VARCHAR, NUMBER, and so on). It is a best practice to have a numeric surrogate primary key, that is, a primary key that serves only as an identifier and has no business meaning in the application. Selecting the default **Primary Key Type** of **Long** will allow a wide range of values to be available for the primary keys of our entities.

The Customer class has some important things to consider, as highlighted in the following code:

```
package com.ensode.jpaweb;

import java.io.Serializable;
import javax.persistence.Entity;
import javax.persistence.GeneratedValue;
import javax.persistence.GenerationType;
import javax.persistence.Id;

@Entity
public class Customer implements Serializable {
    private static final long serialVersionUID = 1L;
    @Id
    @GeneratedValue(strategy = GenerationType.AUTO)
    private Long id;

    public Long getId() {
        return id;
    }

    public void setId(Long id) {
        this.id = id;
    }

    //Other generated methods (equals(), hashCode(), toString())
omitted for brevity
    }
```

As we can see, a JPA entity is a standard Java object. There is no need to extend any special class or implement any special interface. What differentiates a JPA entity from other Java objects are a few JPA-specific annotations.

The `@Entity` annotation is used to indicate that our class is a JPA entity. Any object we want to persist to a database via JPA must be annotated with this annotation.

The `@Id` annotation is used to indicate what field in our JPA entity is its primary key. The primary key is a unique identifier for our entity. No two entities may have the same value for their primary key field. This annotation can be used on the field that serves as a primary key; this is the strategy that the NetBeans wizard uses. It is also correct to annotate the getter method for the entity's primary key field.

The `@Entity` and the `@Id` annotations are the bare minimum two annotations that a class needs in order to be considered a JPA entity. JPA allows primary keys to be automatically generated; in order to take advantage of this functionality, the `@GeneratedValue` annotation can be used. As we can see, the NetBeans-generated JPA entity uses this annotation. This annotation is used to indicate the strategy to use to generate primary keys. All possible primary key generation strategies are listed in the following table:

Primary key generation strategy	Description
`GenerationType.AUTO`	This indicates that the persistence provider will automatically select a primary key generation strategy. This is used by default if no primary key generation strategy is specified.
`GenerationType.IDENTITY`	This indicates that an identity column in the database table the JPA entity maps to must be used to generate the primary key value.
`GenerationType.SEQUENCE`	This indicates that a database sequence should be used to generate the entity's primary key value.
`GenerationType.TABLE`	This indicates that a database table should be used to generate the entity's primary key value.

In most cases, the `GenerationType.AUTO` strategy works properly, so it is almost always used. For this reason, the **New Entity Class** wizard uses this strategy.

> When using the sequence or table generation strategies, we might have to indicate the sequence or table used to generate the primary keys. These can be specified by using the `@SequenceGenerator` and `@TableGenerator` annotations, respectively. Refer to the Java EE 7 JavaDoc at `http://download.oracle.com/javaee/7/api/` for details.

Adding persistent fields to our entity

At this point, our JPA entity contains a single field: its primary key. This is admittedly not very useful. We need to add a few fields to be persisted to the database, as shown in the following code:

```java
package com.ensode.jpaweb;

import java.io.Serializable;
import javax.persistence.Entity;
import javax.persistence.GeneratedValue;
import javax.persistence.GenerationType;
import javax.persistence.Id;

@Entity
public class Customer implements Serializable {

    private static final long serialVersionUID = 1L;
    @Id
    @GeneratedValue(strategy = GenerationType.AUTO)
    private Long id;
    private String firstName;
    private String lastName;

    public Long getId() {
        return id;
    }

    public void setId(Long id) {
        this.id = id;
    }

    public String getFirstName() {
        return firstName;
    }

    public void setFirstName(String firstName) {
        this.firstName = firstName;
    }

    public String getLastName() {
        return lastName;
    }
```

```
public void setLastName(String lastName) {
    this.lastName = lastName;
}
}
```

In this modified version of our JPA entity, we added two fields to be persisted to the database: firstName and lastName, which will be used to store the user's first name and last name respectively. JPA entities need to follow standard JavaBean coding conventions. This means that they must have a public constructor that takes no arguments (one is automatically generated by the Java compiler if we don't specify any other constructors), and all fields must be private and accessed via public getter and setter methods.

Automatically generating getters and setters

In NetBeans, getter and setter methods can be generated automatically: simply declare new fields as usual, use the keyboard shortcut *Alt + Insert*, select **Getter and Setter** from the resulting pop-up window, click on the checkbox next to the class name to select all fields, and click on the **Generate** button.

Before we can use JPA to persist our entity's fields into our database, we need to write some additional code.

Creating a data access object

It is a good idea to follow the **data access object (DAO)** design pattern whenever we write code that interacts with a database. The DAO design pattern keeps all database access functionality in DAO classes. This creates a clear separation of concerns, leaving other layers in our application, such as the user interface logic and the business logic, free of any persistence logic.

NetBeans can help us generate JPA controller classes from existing entities. These JPA controller classes follow the DAO design pattern. To generate a JPA controller class, we simply need to go to **File | New**, select the **Persistence** category, and select the **JPA Controller Classes from Entity Classes** file type from the **New File** dialog.

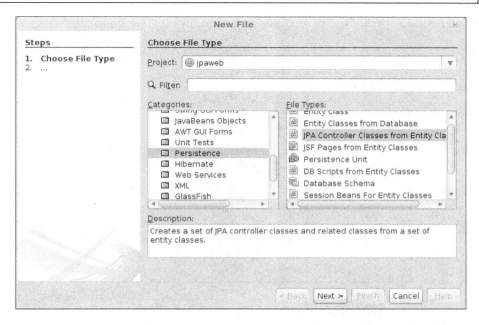

In the next step in the wizard, we need to select the entity classes we wish to generate JPA controller classes for.

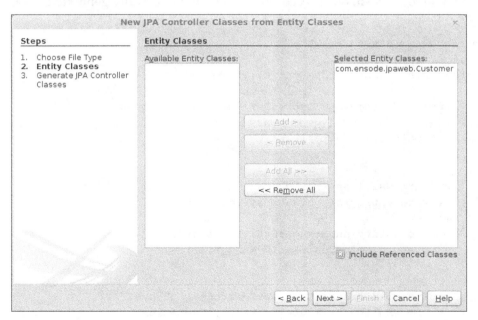

Then, we need to specify the project and package for our JPA controller classes.

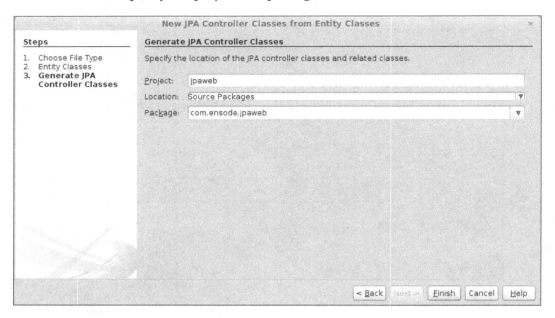

After clicking on **Finish**, our JPA controller class is successfully generated, as shown here:

```java
package com.ensode.jpaweb;
//imports omitted
public class CustomerJpaController implements Serializable {

    public CustomerJpaController(UserTransaction utx,
            EntityManagerFactory emf) {
        this.utx = utx;
        this.emf = emf;
    }
    private UserTransaction utx = null;
    private EntityManagerFactory emf = null;

    public EntityManager getEntityManager() {
        return emf.createEntityManager();
    }

    public void create(Customer customer) throws
            RollbackFailureException, Exception {
        EntityManager em = null;
        try {
```

```
            utx.begin();
            em = getEntityManager();
        em.persist(customer);
            utx.commit();
        } catch (Exception ex) {
            try {
                utx.rollback();
            } catch (Exception re) {
                throw new RollbackFailureException(
                        "An error occurred attempting to roll back the
transaction.",
                        re);
            }
            throw ex;
        } finally {
            if (em != null) {
                em.close();
            }
        }
    }


    public void edit(Customer customer) throws
        NonexistentEntityException, RollbackFailureException, Exception
{
        EntityManager em = null;
        try {
            utx.begin();
            em = getEntityManager();
        customer = em.merge(customer);
            utx.commit();
        } catch (Exception ex) {
            try {
                utx.rollback();
            } catch (Exception re) {
                throw new RollbackFailureException(
                        "An error occurred attempting to roll back the
transaction.",
                        re);
            }
            String msg = ex.getLocalizedMessage();
            if (msg == null || msg.length() == 0) {
                Long id = customer.getId();
                if (findCustomer(id) == null) {
                    throw new NonexistentEntityException(
```

```
                                "The customer with id " + id
                                + " no longer exists.");
                }
            }
            throw ex;
        } finally {
            if (em != null) {
                em.close();
            }
        }
    }

    public void destroy(Long id) throws NonexistentEntityException,
        RollbackFailureException, Exception {
        EntityManager em = null;
        try {
            utx.begin();
            em = getEntityManager();
            Customer customer;
            try {
                customer = em.getReference(Customer.class, id);
                customer.getId();
            } catch (EntityNotFoundException enfe) {
                throw new NonexistentEntityException(
                        "The customer with id " + id
                        + " no longer exists.", enfe);
            }
    em.remove(customer);
            utx.commit();
        } catch (Exception ex) {
            try {
                utx.rollback();
            } catch (Exception re) {
                throw new RollbackFailureException(
                        "An error occurred attempting to roll back the
transaction.",
                        re);
            }
            throw ex;
        } finally {
            if (em != null) {
                em.close();
            }
```

```
        }
    }

    public List<Customer> findCustomerEntities() {
        return findCustomerEntities(true, -1, -1);
    }

    public List<Customer> findCustomerEntities(int maxResults,
            int firstResult) {
        return findCustomerEntities(false, maxResults, firstResult);
    }

    private List<Customer> findCustomerEntities(boolean all, int
maxResults,
        int firstResult) {
        EntityManager em = getEntityManager();
        try {
        CriteriaQuery cq = em.getCriteriaBuilder().createQuery();
        cq.select(cq.from(Customer.class));
        Query q = em.createQuery(cq);
            if (!all) {
                q.setMaxResults(maxResults);
                q.setFirstResult(firstResult);
            }
        return q.getResultList();
        } finally {
            em.close();
        }
    }

    public Customer findCustomer(Long id) {
        EntityManager em = getEntityManager();
        try {
        return em.find(Customer.class, id);
        } finally {
            em.close();
        }
    }

    public int getCustomerCount() {
        EntityManager em = getEntityManager();
        try {
        CriteriaQuery cq = em.getCriteriaBuilder().createQuery();
        Root<Customer> rt = cq.from(Customer.class);
```

```
        cq.select(em.getCriteriaBuilder().count(rt));
        Query q = em.createQuery(cq);
        return ((Long) q.getSingleResult()).intValue();
            } finally {
                em.close();
            }
    }


    }
```

As we can see, NetBeans generates methods to create, read, update, and delete JPA entities.

The method to create a new entity is called `create()`, and it takes an instance of our JPA entity as its sole argument. This method simply invokes the `persist()` method on `EntityManager`, which takes care of persisting the data on the JPA entity to the database.

For read operation, several methods are generated. The `findCustomer()` method takes the primary key of the JPA entity we wish to retrieve as its sole parameter, invokes the `find()` method on `EntityManager` to retrieve the data from the database, and returns an instance of our JPA entity. Several overloaded versions of the `findCustomerEntities()` method are generated, and these methods allow us to retrieve more than one JPA entity from the database. The version of this method that does all the real work is the one that contains the following signature:

```
private List<Customer> findCustomerEntities(boolean all, int
maxResults,
    int  firstResult)
```

The first parameter is a Boolean, which we can use to indicate if we want to retrieve all values in the database; the second parameter allows us to specify the maximum number of results we wish to retrieve; the last parameter allows us to indicate the first result we wish to retrieve. This method uses the Criteria API that was introduced in JPA 2.0 to build a query programmatically. If the value of the `all` parameter is false, then this method sets the maximum number of results and the first result by passing the appropriate parameters to the `setMaxResults()` and `setFirstResult()` methods in the Query object.

The `edit()` method is used to update existing entities. It takes an instance of our JPA entity as its sole parameter. This method invokes the `merge()` method on `EntityManager`, which updates the data in the database with the data in the JPA entity it receives as a parameter.

The `destroy()` method is used to delete an entity. It takes the primary key of the object to be deleted as its sole parameter. It first checks to see if the object exists in the database. If it doesn't exist, this method throws an exception, otherwise it deletes the corresponding row from the database by invoking the `remove()` method on `EntityManager`.

At this point, we have all the code we need to persist our entity's properties in the database, and all we need to do to perform CRUD (short for Create, Read, Update, and Delete) operations involving our JPA entity is invoke these methods on the generated JPA controller from our code.

Automated generation of JPA entities

In many projects, we will be working with an existing database schema created by a database administrator. NetBeans can generate JPA entities from an existing database schema, which saves us a lot of potentially tedious work.

In this section, we will use a custom database schema. In order to create the schema, we need to execute an SQL script that will create the schema and populate some of its tables. In order to do this, we need to go to the **Services** window, expand **Databases**, right-click on **JavaDB**, and select the **Create Database...** option.

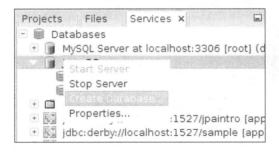

Then, we need to add the database information in the **Create Java DB Database** wizard.

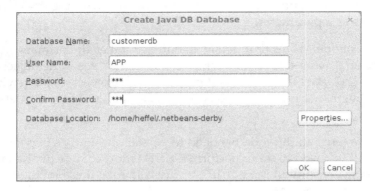

At this point, we can open our SQL script file by going to **File | Open File...** and navigating to its location on our disk and opening it. The filename of our script is create_populate_tables.sql. It is included as part of the source bundle for this chapter. The following screenshot shows the file as soon as we open it in our project:

Once we have opened the SQL script, we need to select our newly-created connection `customerdb` from the **Connection** combobox.

After selecting the connection, we need to click on the  icon to execute the database script.

Our database will now have a number of tables:

To generate JPA entities from an existing schema such as the one we just created, we need to create a new project. Go to **File | New**, and select the **Persistence** category and the **Entity Classes from Database** file type from the **New File** dialog.

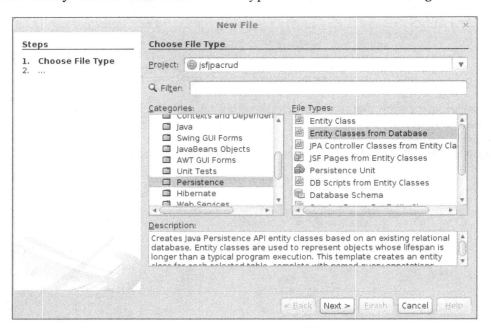

 NetBeans allows us to generate JPA entities from pretty much any kind of Java project. In our example we will be using a **Web Application** project.

At this point, we can either select an existing data source, or, like we did in the previous example, create one "on the fly". In our example, we created a new one and selected the database connection we created earlier in this section.

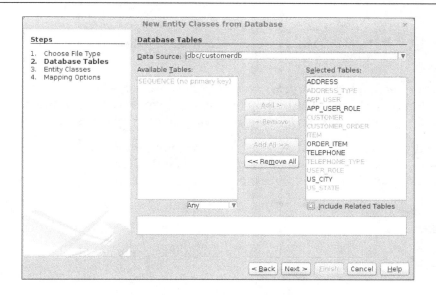

Once we have created or selected our data source, we need to select one or more tables to use to generate our JPA entities. If we wish to create JPA entities for all tables, we can simply click on the **Add All** button.

After clicking on **Next**, NetBeans gives us the opportunity to change the names of the generated classes, although the defaults tend to be sensible. We should also specify a package for our classes, and it is a good idea to check the **Generate Named Query Annotations for Persistent Fields** checkbox. We can optionally generate JAXB (short for Java API for XML Binding) annotations and create a persistence unit.

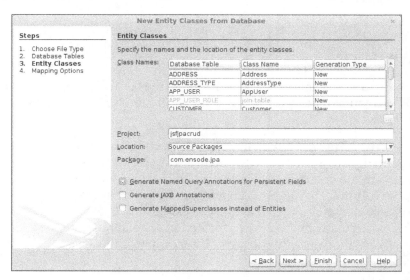

Named queries are explained in detail in the next subsection.

In the next screen in the wizard, we can select how associated entities will be fetched (eagerly or lazily). The default behavior is to fetch *one-to-one* and *many-to-one* relationships eagerly, and *one-to-many* and *many-to-many* relationships lazily.

Additionally, we can select what collection type to use for the many side of a *one-to-many* or *many-to-many* relationship. The default value is `java.util.Collection`, and other valid values are `java.util.List` and `java.util.Set`.

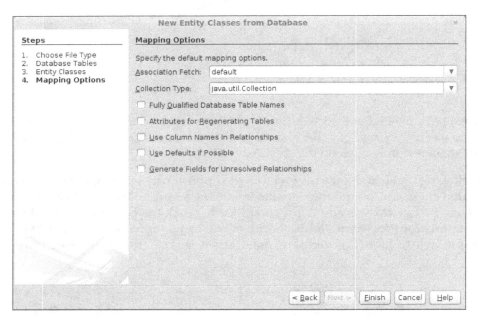

Checking the **Fully Qualified Database Table Names** checkbox results in the catalog and schema elements of the table being mapped to the `@Table` annotation for each generated entity.

Checking the **Attributes for Regenerating Tables** checkbox results in the generated `@Column` annotations having attributes such as `length`, which specifies the maximum length allowed in the column; `nullable`, which specifies whether `null` values are allowed in the column; and `precision` and `scale`, which specify the precision and scale of decimal values, respectively. Checking this checkbox also adds the `uniqueConstraints` attribute to the generated `@Table` annotation to specify any unique constraints that apply to the table, if necessary.

Checking the **Use Column Names in Relationships** checkbox results in fields for one-to-many and one-to-one to be named after the column name in the database table the generated entity maps to. This field is checked by default. However, in our experience, unchecking it results in more readable code.

Checking the **Use Defaults if Possible** checkbox results in NetBeans only generating annotations that override the default behavior.

Checking the **Generate Fields for Unresolved Relationships** checkbox results in NetBeans generating fields whose entities cannot be resolved.

After clicking on **Finish**, NetBeans generates JPA entities for all tables in the database.

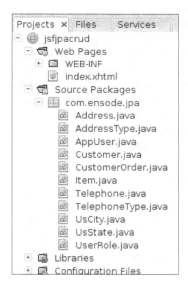

Our database contains a table named CUSTOMER. Let's take a look at the generated Customer JPA entity:

```
package com.ensode.jpa;

import java.io.Serializable;
import java.util.Collection;
import javax.persistence.Basic;
import javax.persistence.Column;
import javax.persistence.Entity;
import javax.persistence.Id;
import javax.persistence.NamedQueries;
```

```
import javax.persistence.NamedQuery;
import javax.persistence.OneToMany;
import javax.persistence.Table;
import javax.validation.constraints.NotNull;
import javax.validation.constraints.Size;

@Entity
@Table(name = "CUSTOMER")
@NamedQueries({
    @NamedQuery(name = "Customer.findAll", query = "SELECT c FROM
Customer c"),
    @NamedQuery(name = "Customer.findByCustomerId", query = "SELECT c
FROM Customer c WHERE c.customerId = :customerId"),
    @NamedQuery(name = "Customer.findByFirstName", query = "SELECT c
FROM Customer c WHERE c.firstName = :firstName"),
    @NamedQuery(name = "Customer.findByMiddleName", query = "SELECT c
FROM Customer c WHERE c.middleName = :middleName"),
    @NamedQuery(name = "Customer.findByLastName", query = "SELECT c
FROM Customer c WHERE c.lastName = :lastName"),
    @NamedQuery(name = "Customer.findByEmail", query = "SELECT c FROM
Customer c WHERE c.email = :email")})
public class Customer implements Serializable {
    private static final long serialVersionUID = 1L;
    @Id
    @Basic(optional = false)
    @NotNull
    @Column(name = "CUSTOMER_ID")
    private Integer customerId;
    @Size(max = 20)
    @Column(name = "FIRST_NAME")
    private String firstName;
    @Size(max = 20)
    @Column(name = "MIDDLE_NAME")
    private String middleName;
    @Size(max = 20)
    @Column(name = "LAST_NAME")
    private String lastName;
    // @Pattern(regexp="[a-z0-9!#$%&'*+/=?^_`{|}~-]+(?:\\.
[a-z0-9!#$%&'*+/=?^_`{|}~-]+)*@(?:[a-z0-9](?:[a-z0-9-]*[a-z0-
9])?\\.)+[a-z0-9](?:[a-z0-9-]*[a-z0-9])?", message="Invalid email")//
if the field contains email address consider using this annotation to
enforce field validation
    @Size(max = 30)
    @Column(name = "EMAIL")
    private String email;
```

```
@OneToMany(mappedBy = "customer")
private Collection<Telephone> telephoneCollection;
@OneToMany(mappedBy = "customer")
private Collection<CustomerOrder> customerOrderCollection;
@OneToMany(mappedBy = "customer")
private Collection<Address> addressCollection;

//generated constructors and methods omitted for brevity.
}
```

As we can see, NetBeans generates a class decorated with the `@Entity` annotation, which marks the class as a JPA entity. Notice that NetBeans automatically decorated one of the fields with the `@Id` annotation based on the primary key constraint in the table used to generate the JPA entity. We can also see that no primary key generation strategy is used; we either need to populate the primary key ourselves, or add the `@GeneratedValue` annotation manually. The `@Basic` annotation is used to mark this field as nonoptional.

Notice the `@Table` annotation. This is an optional annotation that indicates what table our JPA entity maps to. If the `@Table` annotation is not used, then our entity will map to a table having the same name as the entity class (case insensitive). In our particular example, the `@Table` annotation is redundant, but there are cases where it is useful. For example, some database schemas have tables named in plural (CUSTOMERS), but it makes sense to name our entities in the singular (Customer). Additionally, the standard naming convention for database tables that contain more than one word is to use underscores to separate the words (CUSTOMER_ORDER), whereas in Java the standard is to use camel case (CustomerOrder). The `@Table` annotation allows us to follow the established naming standards in both the relational database and the Java world.

Named queries and JPQL

Notice the `@NamedQueries` annotation in the generated code (this annotation is only generated if we click on the **Generate Named Query Annotations for Persistent Fields** checkbox of the **New Entity Classes from Database** wizard), this annotation contains a `value` attribute (the attribute `name` can be omitted from the code since it is the only attribute in this annotation). The value of this attribute is an array of `@NamedQuery` annotations. The `@NamedQuery` annotation has a name attribute, which is used to give it a logical name (by convention, the JPA entity name is used as part of the query name, and we can see in the generated code that the **New Entity Classes from Database** wizard follows this convention), and a `query` attribute, which is used to define a JPQL query to be executed by the named query.

JPQL is a JPA-specific query language; its syntax is similar to SQL. The **New Entity Classes from Database** wizard generates a JPQL query for each field in our entity. When the query is executed, a list containing all instances of our entity that match the criteria in the query will be returned. The following code snippet illustrates this process:

```java
import java.util.List;
import javax.persistence.EntityManager;
import javax.persistence.Query;

public class CustomerDAO {

  public List findCustomerByLastName(String someLastName)
  {
    //code to lookup EntityManager omitted for brevity

    Query query =
        em.createNamedQuery("Customer.findByLastName");
    query.setParameter("lastName", someLastName);
    List resultList = query.getResultList();
    return resultList;
  }
}
```

Here, we see a DAO object that contains a method that will return a list of `Customer` entities for customers whose last name is same as the one provided in the method's parameter. In order to implement this, we need to obtain an instance of an object of type `javax.pesistence.Query`. As we can see in the preceding code snippet, this can be accomplished by invoking the `createNamedQuery()` method in EntityManager and passing the query name (as defined in the `@NamedQuery` annotation) as a parameter. Notice that the named queries generated by the NetBeans wizard contain strings preceded by a colon (`:`). These strings are **named parameters**, which act like placeholders that we can use to substitute for appropriate values.

In our example, we set the `lastName` named parameter in the JPQL query with the `someLastName` argument passed to our method.

Once we have populated all the parameters in our query, we can obtain a list of all matching entities by invoking the `getResultList()` method in our Query object.

Going back to our generated JPA entity, we can see that the wizard automatically placed the `@Id` annotation in the field mapping to the table's primary key. Additionally, each field is decorated with the `@Column` annotation, which allows us to follow standard naming conventions in both the relational database and Java worlds.

Bean Validation

Bean Validation, which comes from Java Specification Request (JSR 303), was introduced in Java EE 6. The Bean Validation specification provides a set of annotations we can use to validate our data. The NetBeans JPA generation wizard takes full advantage of Bean Validation, adding Bean Validation annotations to any appropriate fields, based on the column definitions of the tables we are using to generate our entities.

In our `Customer` entity, we see some Bean Validation annotations. The `customerId` field is decorated with the `@NotNull` annotation, which—as its name implies—prevents the field from accepting a null value.

Several fields in the `Customer` entity are decorated with the `@Size` annotation. This annotation specifies the maximum number of characters a bean's property may accept. Again, the NetBeans wizard obtains this information from the tables used to generate our entity.

Another Bean Validation annotation we can use is the `@Pattern` annotation. This annotation is meant to make sure that the value of the decorated field matches a given regular expression.

Notice that right above the `email` property of the `Customer` annotation, the wizard added the `@Pattern` annotation and commented it out. The reason for this is that the wizard noticed that the name of the table column was `EMAIL` and suspected (but couldn't verify) that this table is meant to store e-mail addresses. Therefore, the wizard added the annotation with a regular expression used to match e-mail addresses. However, since it couldn't be sure that this table is indeed meant to store e-mail addresses, it commented out this line of code. This property is indeed meant to store e-mail addresses, therefore we should uncomment this automatically-generated line.

Entity relationships

There are several annotations we can use in JPA entities to define relationships between them. In the `Customer` entity we discussed, we can see that the wizard detected several one-to-many relationships in the `CUSTOMER` table and automatically added the `@OneToMany` annotation to define these relationships in our entity. Notice that each field annotated with the `@OneToMany` annotation is of the type `java.util.Collection`. The `Customer` entity is one side of the relationship, since a customer can have many orders, many addresses (street, e-mail, and so on), or many telephone numbers (home, work, cell, and so on). Notice that the wizard uses generics to specify the type of objects we can add to each collection. Objects in these collections are the JPA entities mapping to the corresponding tables in our database schema.

Notice that the `@OneToMany` annotation has a `mappedBy` attribute. This attribute is necessary because each of these relationships is bidirectional (we can access all addresses for a customer, and for a given address we can find out which customer it belongs to). The value of this attribute must match the name of the field on the other side of the relationship. Let's take a look at the `Address` entity to illustrate the other side of the customer-address relationship.

```java
package com.ensode.jpa;

import java.io.Serializable;
import javax.persistence.Basic;
import javax.persistence.Column;
import javax.persistence.Entity;
import javax.persistence.Id;
import javax.persistence.JoinColumn;
import javax.persistence.ManyToOne;
import javax.persistence.NamedQueries;
import javax.persistence.NamedQuery;
import javax.persistence.Table;
import javax.validation.constraints.NotNull;
import javax.validation.constraints.Size;

@Entity
@Table(name = "ADDRESS")
@NamedQueries({
    @NamedQuery(name = "Address.findAll",
      query = "SELECT a FROM Address a"),
    @NamedQuery(name = "Address.findByAddressId",
      query = "SELECT a FROM Address a WHERE a.addressId =
:addressId"),
    @NamedQuery(name = "Address.findByAddrLine1",
      query = "SELECT a FROM Address a WHERE a.addrLine1 =
:addrLine1"),
    @NamedQuery(name = "Address.findByAddrLine2",
      query = "SELECT a FROM Address a WHERE a.addrLine2 =
:addrLine2"),
    @NamedQuery(name = "Address.findByCity",
      query = "SELECT a FROM Address a WHERE a.city = :city"),
    @NamedQuery(name = "Address.findByZip",
      query = "SELECT a FROM Address a WHERE a.zip = :zip")})
public class Address implements Serializable {
    private static final long serialVersionUID = 1L;
    @Id
    @Basic(optional = false)
    @NotNull
```

```
@Column(name = "ADDRESS_ID")
private Integer addressId;
@Size(max = 100)
@Column(name = "ADDR_LINE_1")
private String addrLine1;
@Size(max = 100)
@Column(name = "ADDR_LINE_2")
private String addrLine2;
@Size(max = 100)
@Column(name = "CITY")
private String city;
@Size(max = 5)
@Column(name = "ZIP")
private String zip;
@JoinColumn(name = "ADDRESS_TYPE_ID",
   referencedColumnName = "ADDRESS_TYPE_ID")
@ManyToOne
private AddressType addressType;
@JoinColumn(name = "CUSTOMER_ID",
   referencedColumnName = "CUSTOMER_ID")
@ManyToOne
private Customer customer;
@JoinColumn(name = "US_STATE_ID",
   referencedColumnName = "US_STATE_ID")
@ManyToOne
private UsState usState;

//generated methods and constructors omitted for brevity
}
```

Notice that the `Address` entity has a `customer` field. This field is of the type `Customer`, the entity we were just discussing.

Had we left the **Use Column Names in Relationships** checkbox checked in the **Entity Classes from Database** wizard, the generated `customer` field would have been named `customerId`. In most cases, unchecking this checkbox results in saner names for fields used in entity relationships, as was the case here.

Notice that the field is decorated with a @ManyToOne annotation. This annotation marks the *many* side of the one-to-many relationship between Customer and Address. Notice that the field is also decorated with the @JoinColumn annotation. The name attribute of this annotation indicates the column in the database our entity maps to that defines the foreign key constraint between the ADDRESS and CUSTOMER tables (in our case, the CUSTOMER_ID column on the ADDRESS table). The referencedColumnName attribute of @JoinColumn is used to indicate the primary key column of the table on *one* side of the relationship (in our case, the CUSTOMER_ID column in the CUSTOMER table).

In addition to one-to-many and many-to-one relationships, JPA provides annotations to denote many-to-many and one-to-one relationships. In our schema, we have a many-to-many relationship between the CUSTOMER_ORDER and ITEM tables; since an order can have many items, and an item can belong to many orders.

 The table to hold orders was named CUSTOMER_ORDER since the word "order" is a reserved word in SQL.

Let's take a look at the CustomerOrder JPA entity to see how the many-to-many relationship is defined:

```
package com.ensode.jpa;

import java.io.Serializable;
import java.util.Collection;
import javax.persistence.Basic;
import javax.persistence.Column;
import javax.persistence.Entity;
import javax.persistence.Id;
import javax.persistence.JoinColumn;
import javax.persistence.JoinTable;
import javax.persistence.ManyToMany;
import javax.persistence.ManyToOne;
import javax.persistence.NamedQueries;
import javax.persistence.NamedQuery;
import javax.persistence.Table;
import javax.validation.constraints.NotNull;
import javax.validation.constraints.Size;

@Entity
@Table(name = "CUSTOMER_ORDER")
@NamedQueries({
```

```
    @NamedQuery(name = "CustomerOrder.findAll",
       query = "SELECT c FROM CustomerOrder c"),
    @NamedQuery(name = "CustomerOrder.findByCustomerOrderId",
       query = "SELECT c FROM CustomerOrder c WHERE c.customerOrderId =
:customerOrderId"),
    @NamedQuery(name = "CustomerOrder.findByOrderNumber",
       query = "SELECT c FROM CustomerOrder c WHERE c.orderNumber =
:orderNumber"),
    @NamedQuery(name = "CustomerOrder.findByOrderDescription",
       query = "SELECT c FROM CustomerOrder c WHERE c.orderDescription
= :orderDescription")})
public class CustomerOrder implements Serializable {
    private static final long serialVersionUID = 1L;
    @Id
    @Basic(optional = false)
    @NotNull
    @Column(name = "CUSTOMER_ORDER_ID")
    private Integer customerOrderId;
    @Size(max = 10)
    @Column(name = "ORDER_NUMBER")
    private String orderNumber;
    @Size(max = 200)
    @Column(name = "ORDER_DESCRIPTION")
    private String orderDescription;
    @JoinTable(name = "ORDER_ITEM", joinColumns = {
        @JoinColumn(name = "CUSTOMER_ORDER_ID",
          referencedColumnName = "CUSTOMER_ORDER_ID")},
          inverseJoinColumns = {
        @JoinColumn(name = "ITEM_ID",
          referencedColumnName = "ITEM_ID")})
    @ManyToMany
    private Collection<Item> itemCollection;
    @JoinColumn(name = "CUSTOMER_ID", referencedColumnName =
"CUSTOMER_ID")
    @ManyToOne
    private Customer customer;

    //generated constructors and methods omitted for brevity.

}
```

Notice that the `CustomerOrder` entity has a property of type `java.util.Collection` named `itemCollection`. This property holds all items for the order. The field is decorated with the `@ManyToMany` annotation; this annotation is used to declare a many-to-many relationship between the `CustomerOrder` and Item JPA entities. The field is also annotated with the `@JoinTable` annotation; this annotation is necessary since a `join` table is necessary in a database schema whenever there is a many-to-many relationship between tables. Using a `join` table allows us to keep the data in the database normalized.

The `@JoinTable` annotation allows us to specify the table that is used to denote the many-to-many relationship in the schema. The value of the name attribute of `@JoinTable` must match the name of the join table in the schema. The value of the `joinColumns` attribute of `@JoinColumn` must be the foreign key relationship between the join table and the owning side of the relationship. We already discussed the `@JoinColumn` annotation when discussing one-to-many relationships; in this case, its name attribute must match the name of the column in the `join` table that has the foreign key relationship, and its `referencedColumnName` attribute must indicate the name of the primary key column on the owning side of the relationship. The value of the `inverseJoinColumns` attribute of `@JoinTable` has a similar role as its `joinColumns` attribute, except it indicates the corresponding columns for the non-owning side of the relationship.

The side of the many-to-many relationship that contains the above annotations is said to be the owning side of the relationship. Let's look at how the many-to-many relationship is defined in the non-owning side of the relationship, which in our case is the `Item` JPA entity. The code is as follows:

```
package com.ensode.jpa;

import java.io.Serializable;
import java.util.Collection;
import javax.persistence.Basic;
import javax.persistence.Column;
import javax.persistence.Entity;
import javax.persistence.Id;
import javax.persistence.ManyToMany;
import javax.persistence.NamedQueries;
import javax.persistence.NamedQuery;
import javax.persistence.Table;
import javax.validation.constraints.NotNull;
import javax.validation.constraints.Size;

@Entity
@Table(name = "ITEM")
@NamedQueries({
    @NamedQuery(name = "Item.findAll", query = "SELECT i FROM Item
i"),
```

```
    @NamedQuery(name = "Item.findByItemId", query = "SELECT i FROM
Item i WHERE i.itemId = :itemId"),
    @NamedQuery(name = "Item.findByItemNumber", query = "SELECT i FROM
Item i WHERE i.itemNumber = :itemNumber"),
    @NamedQuery(name = "Item.findByItemShortDesc", query = "SELECT i
FROM Item i WHERE i.itemShortDesc = :itemShortDesc"),
    @NamedQuery(name = "Item.findByItemLongDesc", query = "SELECT i
FROM Item i WHERE i.itemLongDesc = :itemLongDesc")})
public class Item implements Serializable {
    private static final long serialVersionUID = 1L;
    @Id
    @Basic(optional = false)
    @NotNull
    @Column(name = "ITEM_ID")
    private Integer itemId;
    @Size(max = 10)
    @Column(name = "ITEM_NUMBER")
    private String itemNumber;
    @Size(max = 100)
    @Column(name = "ITEM_SHORT_DESC")
    private String itemShortDesc;
    @Size(max = 500)
    @Column(name = "ITEM_LONG_DESC")
    private String itemLongDesc;
    @ManyToMany(mappedBy = "itemCollection")
    private Collection<CustomerOrder> customerOrderCollection;

    //generated constructors and methods omitted for brevity
}
```

As we can see, the only thing we need to do on this side of the relationship is to create a `Collection` property, decorate it with the `@ManyToMany` annotation, and specify the property name on the other side of the relationship as the value of its `mappedBy` attribute.

In addition to one-to-many and many-to-many relationships, it is possible to create one-to-one relationships between JPA entities.

The `@OneToOne` annotation is used to indicate a one-to-one relationship between two JPA entities. Our schema doesn't have any one-to-one relationships between tables, therefore this annotation was not added to any of the entities generated by the wizard.

 One-to-one relationships are not very popular in database schemas. Nevertheless, JPA supports one-to-one relationships in case it is necessary.

The procedure to indicate a one-to-one relationship between two entities is similar to what we have already seen. The owning side of the relationship must have a field of the JPA entity type on the other side of the relationship, and this field must be decorated with the @OneToOne and @JoinColumn annotations.

Suppose we had a schema in which a one-to-one relationship was defined between two tables named PERSON and BELLY_BUTTON. This is a one-to-one relationship because each person has one belly button and each belly button belongs to only one person (the reason the schema was modeled this way instead of having the columns relating to the BELLY_BUTTON table in the PERSON table escapes me, but bear with me—I'm having a hard time coming up with a good example!).

```
@Entity
public class Person implements Serializable {
  @JoinColumn(name="BELLY_BUTTON_ID")
  @OneToOne
  private BellyButton bellyButton;

  public BellyButton getBellyButton(){
    return bellyButton;
  }

  public void setBellyButton(BellyButton bellyButton){
    this.bellyButton = bellyButton;
  }
}
```

If the one-to-one relationship is unidirectional (we can only get the belly button from the person), this would be all we had to do. If the relationship is bidirectional, then we need to add the @OneToOne annotation on the other side of the relationship and use its mappedBy attribute to indicate the other side of the relationship. The code is as follows:

```
@Entity
@Table(name="BELLY_BUTTON")
public class BellyButton implements Serializable(
{
  @OneToOne(mappedBy="bellyButton")
  private Person person;

  public Person getPerson(){
    return person;
  }
  public void getPerson(Person person){
    this.person=person;
  }
}
```

As we can see, the procedure to establish one-to-one relationships is very similar to the procedure used to establish one-to-many and many-to-many relationships.

Once we have generated JPA entities from a database, we need to write additional code that contains the business and presentation logic. Alternatively, we can use NetBeans to generate code for these two layers.

Generating JSF applications from JPA entities

One very nice feature of NetBeans is that it allows us to generate JSF applications that will perform Create, Read, Update, and Delete (CRUD) operations from existing JPA entities. This feature, combined with the ability to create JPA entities from an existing database schema as described in the previous section, allows us to write web applications that interact with a database in record time.

To generate JSF pages from existing JPA entities, we need to right-click on **File**, select **New File**, select the **JavaServer Faces** category, and then select the **JSF Pages from Entity Classes** file type.

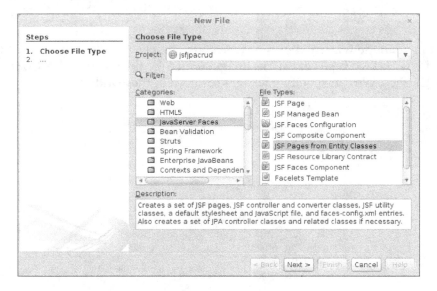

 In order to be able to generate JSF pages from existing JPA entities, the current project must be a **Web Application** project.

After clicking on **Next,** we need to select one or more JPA entities. We would typically want to select all of them, and they can easily be selected by clicking on the **Add All** button.

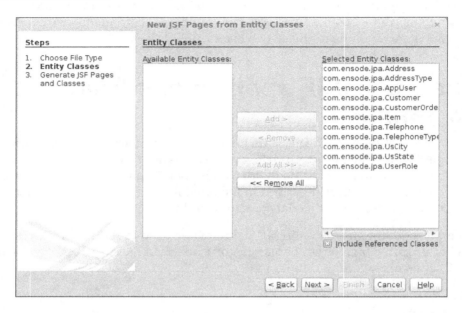

The next page in the wizard allows us to specify a package for newly-created JSF managed beans. Two types of classes are generated by the wizard: **JPA Controllers** and **JSF Classes**. We can specify packages for both of these individually.

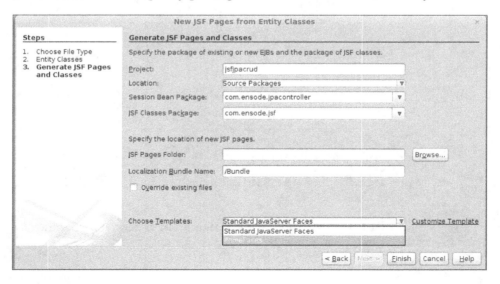

We are also given the opportunity to specify a folder for the JSF pages to be created. If we leave this field blank, pages will be created in our project's **Web Pages** folder.

> The values of the **Session Bean Package** and **JSF Classes Package** text fields default to the package where our JPA entities reside. It is a good idea to modify this default, since placing the JSF managed beans in a different package separates the data access layer classes from the user interface and controller layers of our application.

The wizard also allows us to use two kinds of templates: **Standard JavaServer Faces** or **PrimeFaces**. Selecting **Standard JavaServer Faces** will result in a fairly basic, standard web application that we can use as the base for our application. Selecting **PrimeFaces** will result in a very elegant web application. For our example, we will select **PrimeFaces**, but the procedure is nearly identical when selecting **Standard JavaServer Faces**. We can select the template from the **Choose Templates** dropdown.

> Make sure to add the PrimeFaces 4.0 library to the project when choosing to generate the PrimeFaces templates. Refer to *Chapter 3, JSF Component Libraries*, for details.

After clicking on **Finish**, a complete web application that can perform CRUD operations will be created.

As we can see, NetBeans generates a folder for each of our entities under the **Web Pages** folder of our application. Each of the folders has a **Create**, **Edit**, **List**, and **View** XHTML files. These files are JSF pages that use Facelets as their view technology; since we selected the PrimeFaces template, our pages use PrimeFaces components. The **Create** page will provide functionality to create new entities, the **Edit** page will allow users to update information for a specific entity, the **List** page will display all instances of a specific entity in the database, and the **View** page will display all properties for a JPA entity.

The generated application is a regular JSF application. We can execute it by simply right-clicking on the project and selecting **Run**. Then, the usual things happen: the application server is started if it wasn't already up, the application is deployed, and a browser window opens to display the welcome page for our application.

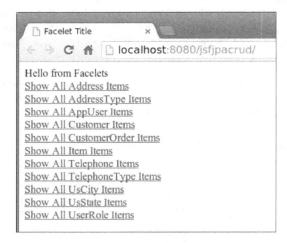

As we can see, the welcome page contains a link corresponding to each of our JPA entities. The links will render a table that displays all the existing instances of our entity in the database. When we click on the **Show All Customer Items** link, the following page is shown:

Since we haven't inserted any data into the database yet, the page displays the message **No records found**. We can insert a customer into the database by clicking on the **Create** button.

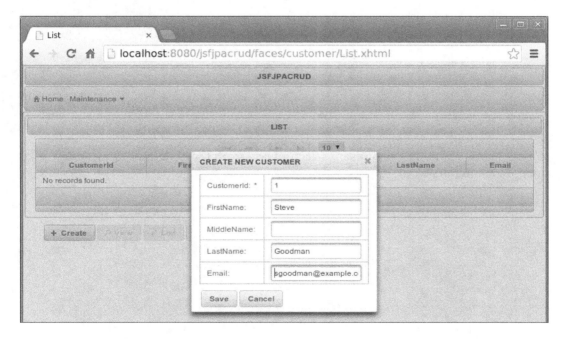

Notice how an input field is generated for each property in our entity, which in turn corresponds to a column in the database table.

 As we can see, an input field was generated for the primary key field of our entity. This field is only generated if the JPA entity does not use a primary key generation strategy.

After entering some information on the page and clicking on the **Save** button, a new row is added to the data table and the message **Customer was successfully created.** is shown.

Notice that the page has buttons to view, edit, and delete the entity.

We can work with other entities by selecting one from the generated **Maintenance** drop-down menu.

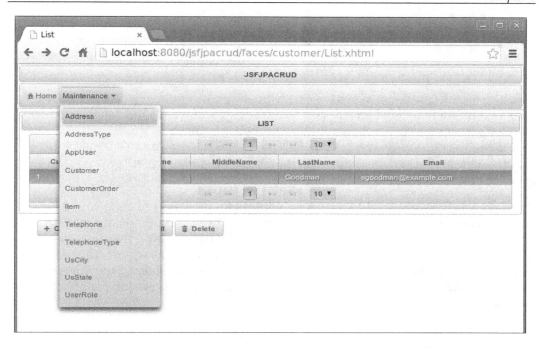

Let's say we want to add an address for our customer. To do so, we simply need to select **Address** from the **Maintenance** drop-down menu and then click on **Create**.

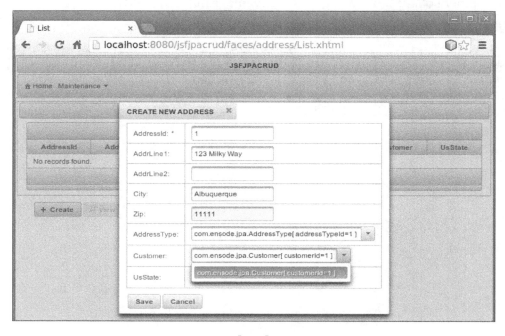

The `Address` entity is at one end of several one-to-many relationships. Notice how a drop-down menu is generated for each one of the entities at the many end. Since we wish to assign this address to the customer we just added, we attempt to select a customer from the **Customer** combobox.

Clicking on the combobox reveals a cryptic and almost undecipherable (from the user's point of view) label for our customer. The reason we see this label is because the labels generated for each item in the combobox come from the `toString()` method of the entities used to populate it. We can work around this issue by modifying the `toString()` method so that it returns a user-friendly string suitable to use as a label.

As we can see, the generated code from NetBeans wizards could certainly use some minor tweaking, such as modifying the `toString()` methods of each JPA entity so that it can be used as a label, or modifying the labels on the generated JSF pages so that they are more user friendly. Nevertheless, as we can see, we can have a fully-working application that is created with a few clicks of the mouse. This functionality certainly saves us a lot of time and effort (just don't tell your boss about it).

Summary

In this chapter, we saw the many ways in which NetBeans can help us speed up the development of applications by taking advantage of JPA.

We saw how NetBeans can generate new JPA classes with all the required annotations already in place. Additionally, we covered how NetBeans can automatically generate code to persist a JPA entity to a database table. We also covered how NetBeans can generate JPA entities from an existing database schema, including the automated generation of JPQL named queries and validation. Finally, we saw how NetBeans can generate a complete, visually appealing JSF application from existing JPA entities.

5
Implementing the Business Tier with Session Beans

Most enterprise applications have a number of common requirements such as transactions, security, scalability, and so on. **Enterprise JavaBeans** (**EJBs**) allow application developers to focus on implementing business logic without worrying about implementing these requirements. There are two types of EJBs: session beans and message-driven beans. In this chapter, we will discuss session beans, which greatly simplify the server-side business logic implementation. In *Chapter 7, Messaging with JMS and Message-driven Beans*, we will discuss message-driven beans, which allow us to easily implement the messaging functionality in our applications.

 Previous versions of J2EE included Entity Beans as well; however, as of Java EE 5, Entity Beans have been deprecated in favor of the JPA.

The following topics will be covered in this chapter:

- Introduction to session beans
- Creating a session bean with NetBeans
- EJB transaction management
- Implementing aspect-oriented programming with Interceptors
- EJB Timer service
- Generating session beans from JPA entities

Introducing session beans

Session beans encapsulate business logic for enterprise applications. It is a good idea to use session beans when developing enterprise applications, since we (as application developers) can focus on developing business logic without worrying about other enterprise application requirements such as scalability, security, transactions, and so on.

 Even though we don't directly implement common enterprise application requirements such as transactions and security, we can configure these services via annotations.

There are three types of session beans: **stateless session beans, stateful session beans**, and **singleton session beans**. Stateful session beans maintain conversational state with their client between method invocations, where stateless session beans do not. There exists only one instance of a singleton session bean in an application, whereas several instances are created by the application server for stateless and stateful session beans.

Creating a session bean in NetBeans

Session beans can be created in three types of NetBeans projects: **Enterprise Application**, **EJB Module**, and **Web Application**. EJB Module projects can contain only EJBs, whereas Enterprise Application projects can contain EJBs along with their clients, which can be web applications or "standalone" Java applications. The ability to add EJBs to web applications was introduced in Java EE 6. Having this ability allows us to simplify packaging and deployment of web applications using EJBs. We can now package the web application code and the EJB code in a single **Web Archive (WAR)** file, whereas with previous versions of Java EE and J2EE, we had to create an **Enterprise Archive (EAR)** file.

When deploying enterprise applications to the GlassFish application server included with NetBeans, it is possible to deploy standalone clients as part of the application to the application server. These standalone clients are then available via Java Web Start (http://www.oracle.com/technetwork/java/javase/javawebstart/index.html); this feature also allows us to more easily access EJBs from the client code by using annotations. "True" standalone clients executing outside the application server require **Java Naming and Directory Interface (JNDI)** lookups to obtain a reference to the EJB. In our first example, we will create both a session bean and a Java Web Start client both deployed to the same enterprise application.

To create an Enterprise Application project, go to **File | New Project...** and select **Enterprise Application** from the **Java EE** category, as shown in the following screenshot:

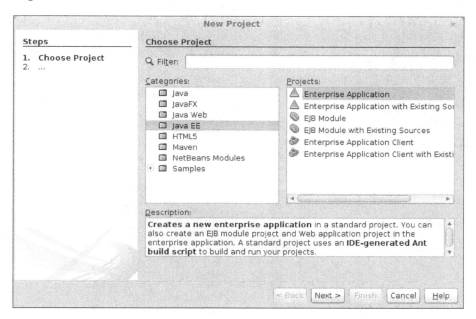

After clicking on **Next**, we need to enter a project name.

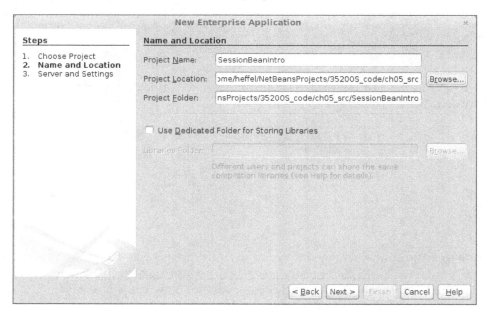

We can optionally select a **Project Location** for our new Enterprise Application project; **Project Folder** will be updated automatically if we do so.

In the next screen, we need to select the modules to be included in our enterprise application. **Create EJB Module** and **Create Web Application Module** are selected by default. In our example, we won't be creating a web application module; therefore, we need to uncheck the **Create Web Application Module** checkbox.

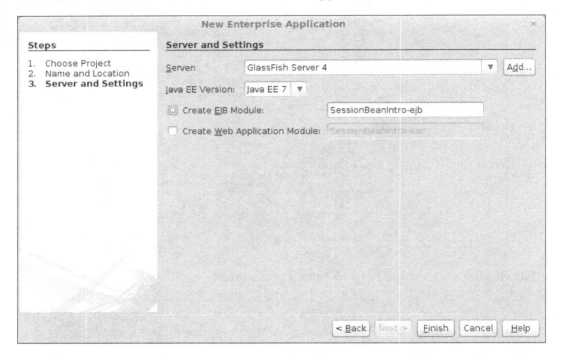

In our example, **SessionBeanIntro** is our Enterprise Application project and **SessionBeanIntro-ejb** is our EJB module.

Before we can continue, we need to create an Enterprise Application Client project that will contain our EJB client code. To do this, we need to select **Enterprise Application Client** from the **Java EE** category in the **New Project** wizard.

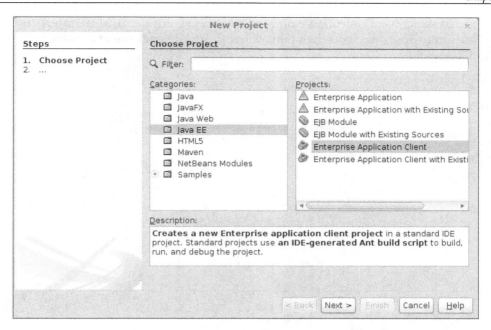

We need to enter a name for **Project Name** and, optionally, a value for **Project Location** for our **Enterprise Application Client** project.

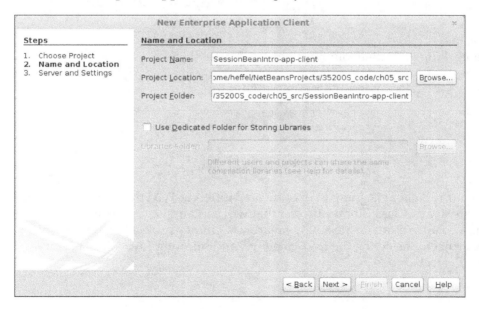

We need to select our Enterprise Application project from the **Add to Enterprise Application** drop-down, and then enter an appropriate package and name for the **Main Class** field.

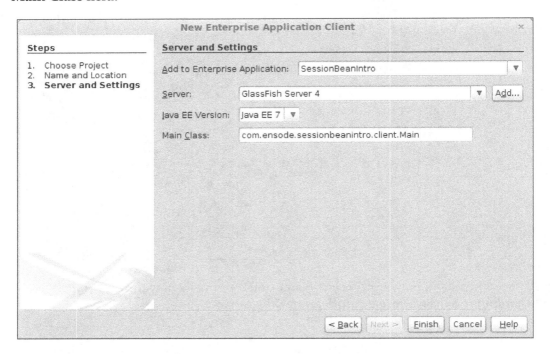

After clicking on **Finish**, our new project is created.

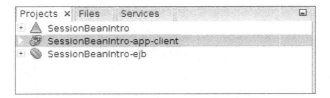

Since our EJB client is going to execute on a different JVM than our EJBs, we need to create a Java Class Library project that will contain the remote interface for our session bean. We can create a new Java Class Library project by going to **File | New Project...**, selecting the **Java** category, and selecting **Java Class Library** under **Projects**.

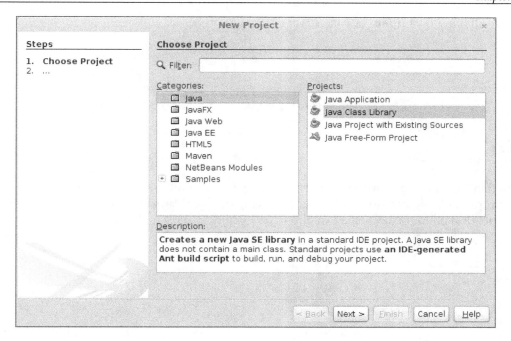

We then need to enter a name for our project, and, optionally, select a value for
Project Location.

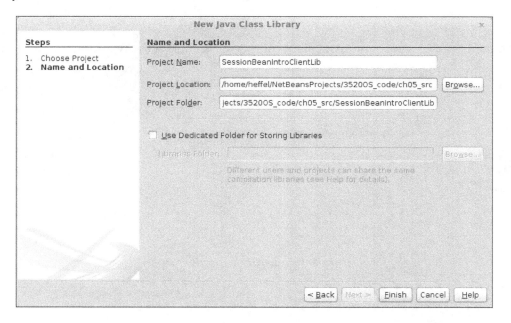

After clicking on **Finish**, our Java class library is created.

We then need to add our Java Class Library project as a library to our application client project. We can do this by right-clicking on the **Libraries** node of the application client project and selecting **Add Project...**.

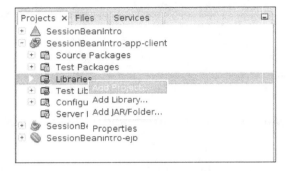

We then need to select our Java Client Library project from the resulting window.

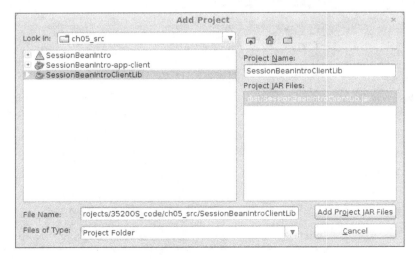

Now that we have set up our projects, it's time to create our first session bean. We can do so by right-clicking on the EJB module, navigating to **New | Other**, and then selecting the **Enterprise JavaBeans** category and the **Session Bean** file type from the **New File** wizard.

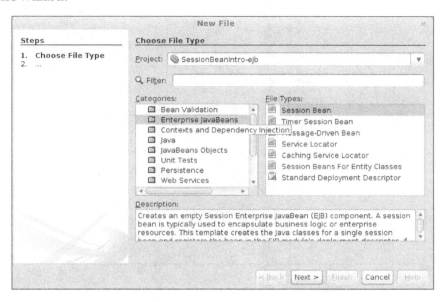

We now need to specify a number of things:

- It is a good idea to override the default name given to our session bean.
- We need to specify the package for our session bean.
- We need to specify the session bean type: stateless, stateful, or singleton.
  - Stateful session beans maintain conversational state with the client (which simply means that the values of any of their member variables are in a consistent state between method calls).
  - Stateless session beans don't maintain conversational state; therefore, they perform better than stateful session beans.
  - Singleton session beans were introduced in Java EE 6. A single instance of each singleton session bean is created when our application is deployed. Singleton session beans are useful to cache frequently read database data.
- We need to specify whether our session bean will have a remote interface, which is used for clients executing in a different JVM than our bean; a local interface, which is meant for clients running in the same JVM as our bean; or both a remote and a local interface.

In early versions of Java EE, local interfaces were required when the EJBs and their clients were on the same JVM. Java EE 6 made local interfaces optional; therefore, it isn't necessary to create any interface for our session beans if they will only be accessed by clients executing in the same JVM.

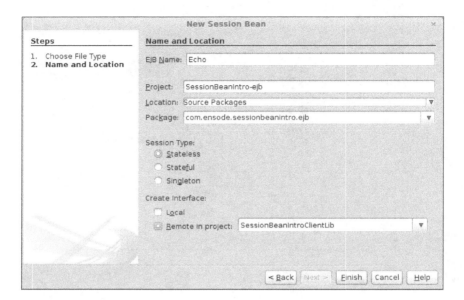

Our example bean does not need to maintain conversational state with its clients; therefore, we should make it a stateless session bean. Its only client will be executing in a different JVM; therefore, we need to create a remote interface and don't need to create a local interface.

When creating a remote interface, NetBeans requires us to specify a client library in which the remote interface will be added. The client library is added as a dependency to both the EJB project and the client project. This is the reason we had to create a Java class library earlier. Our client library is selected by default when we specify that we need to create a remote interface.

After selecting all the appropriate options and clicking on **Finish**, our session bean is created in the EJB module project and the remote interface is created in the client library project.

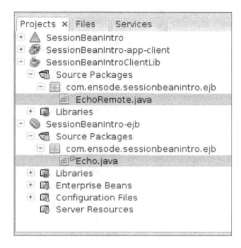

The generated code for our session bean is simply an empty class with the @Stateless annotation already added and the remote interface implemented.

```
7    package com.ensode.sessionbeanintro.ejb;
8
9    import javax.ejb.Stateless;
10
11   /**
12    *
13    * @author heffel
14    */
15   @Stateless
16   public class Echo implements EchoRemote {
17
18       // Add business logic below. (Right-click in editor and choose
19       // "Insert Code > Add Business Method")
20   }
21
```

Notice that our bean implements the remote interface, which at this point is an empty interface with the `@Remote` annotation added. This annotation was added because we chose to create a remote interface.

```java
package com.ensode.sessionbeanintro.ejb;

import javax.ejb.Remote;

/**
 *
 * @author heffel
 */
@Remote
public interface EchoRemote {

}
```

The reason we need to have a remote and/or an optional local interface is because session bean clients never invoke the bean's methods directly; instead, they obtain a reference of a class implementing their remote and/or local interface and invoke the methods on this class. Beginning with Java EE 6, it is no longer necessary to create a local interface; the application server can generate one automatically when the application is deployed.

The remote and/or local interface implementation is created automatically by the EJB container when we deploy our bean. This implementation does some processing before invoking our session bean's method. Since the methods need to be defined both on the interface and our bean, typically we would need to add the method signature to both the bean and its remote and/or local interface. However, when working with session beans in NetBeans, we can simply right-click on the bean's source code and go to **Insert Code | Add Business Method**. This will result in the method being added to both the bean and the remote/local interface.

This results in a window popping up, which prompts us to enter the method name, return type, parameters, and the interface(s) where the method should be added (remote and/or local).

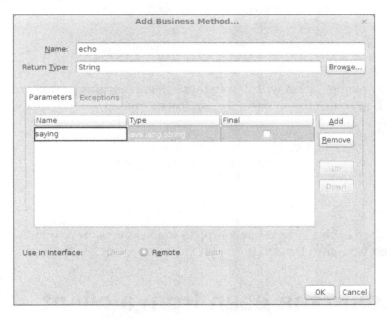

In our example, we will add a method named `echo` that takes a string value as a parameter and returns a string. Since our bean only has a remote interface, the radio buttons for **Local** and **Both** are grayed out.

After entering the appropriate information, the method is added both to the bean and its remote interface.

```
Echo.java ×

Source   History

 8 ⊟ import javax.ejb.Stateless;
 9
10 ⊟ /**
11      *
12      * @author heffel
13      */
14   @Stateless
15   public class Echo implements EchoRemote {
16
17       // Add business logic below. (Right-click in editor and choose
18       // "Insert Code > Add Business Method")
19       @Override
20 ⊟     public String echo(String saying) {
21           return null;
22       }
23   }
24
```

The default implementation will simply return `null`. For this simple example, we will modify it to return the string `echoing:` concatenated with the parameter that was passed.

```
    @Override
    public String echo(String saying) {
        return "echoing: " + saying;
    }
}
```

At this point, we have a simple but complete stateless session bean, which is ready to be accessed from the client code.

Accessing the bean from a client

Now, it's time to focus our attention on the client. For remote clients, the client project needs to use the Java Class Library project containing the remote interface; this is the reason we created a Java Class Library project earlier in the chapter and added it to the client project.

After adding the client library containing the remote interface for our session bean, we are ready to invoke our EJB method. The client code needs to obtain a reference to an instance of a class implementing the remote interface for our bean. When using NetBeans, this is very easy. We simply need to right-click on the client code (`com.ensode.sessionbeanintro.Main` in the application client project in our example) and go to **Insert Code... | Call Enterprise Bean**.

At this point, we are shown a list of all open projects that have EJBs in them; we need to select the bean we wish to access from one of these projects.

If our bean had both a local and remote interface, we would have been given the choice to select the appropriate one. However, since it only has a remote interface, the option to select a local interface is disabled. In our particular example, even if we had the option of selecting a local interface, the correct option would have been to select the remote interface. This is because our client will be executing in a different JVM from the server, and local interfaces are not accessible across JVMs.

At this point, a member variable of type EchoRemote (our bean's remote interface) is added to the client; this variable is annotated with the @EJB annotation. This annotation is used to inject the instance of the remote interface at runtime.

In previous versions of J2EE, it was necessary to perform a JNDI lookup to obtain a reference to the home interface of the bean, and then use the home interface to obtain a reference to the remote or local interface. As we can see, the procedure to obtain a reference to an EJB has been greatly simplified in Java EE.

The generated code shown in the following screenshot:

```
Main.java ×
Source    History

7    package com.ensode.sessionbeanintro.client;
8
9    import com.ensode.sessionbeanintro.ejb.EchoRemote;
10   import javax.ejb.EJB;
11
12   /**
13    *
14    * @author heffel
15    */
16   public class Main {
17       @EJB
18       private static EchoRemote echo;
19
20       /**
21        * @param args the command line arguments
22        */
23       public static void main(String[] args) {
24           // TODO code application logic here
25       }
26
27   }
```

Now we simply need to add a call to the `echo()` method on the remote interface, and our client will be complete.

```
24  □     public static void main(String[] args) {
25             JOptionPane.showMessageDialog(null,
26                 echo.echo("If you don't see this, it didn't work."));
27         }
```

Executing the client

We can execute our client by simply right-clicking on the Enterprise Application project and clicking on **Run**. After a few seconds, we should see an information dialog displaying the output of the session bean's method.

Clients deployed this way take advantage of Java Web Start technology. Java Web Start applications run on the client workstation. However, they can be executed from a URL. The Web Start URL for NetBeans enterprise application client modules defaults to the Enterprise project name, followed by the application client module name. In our example, the URL will be `http://localhost:8080/SessionBeanIntro/SessionBeanIntro-app-client`. We can verify this by pointing the browser to this URL. The application client will be executed after a brief wait.

 At the time of writing, the this procedure does not work with Google Chrome.

Session bean transaction management

As previously mentioned, one of the advantages of EJBs is that they automatically take care of transactions. However, there is still some configuration that we need to do in order to better control transaction management.

Transactions allow us to execute all the steps in a method or, if one of the steps fails (for instance, an exception is thrown), roll back the changes made in that method.

Primarily, what we need to configure is our bean's behavior if one of its methods is called while a transaction is in progress. Should the bean's method become part of the existing transaction? Should the existing transaction be suspended and a new transaction created just for the bean's method? We can configure these behaviors via the `@TransactionAttribute` annotation.

The `@TransactionAttribute` annotation allows us to control how an EJB's methods will behave both when invoked while a transaction is in progress and when invoked when no transaction is in progress. This annotation has a single `value` attribute that we can use to indicate how the bean's method will behave in both of these circumstances.

The following table summarizes the different values that we can assign to the `@TransactionAttribute` annotation:

@TransactionAttribute value	Method invoked when a transaction is in progress	Method invoked when no transaction is in progress
`TransactionAttributeType.MANDATORY`	Method becomes part of the existing transaction	`TransactionRequiredException` is thrown
`TransactionAttributeType.NEVER`	`RemoteException` is thrown	Method is executed without any transaction support
`TransactionAttributeType.NOT_SUPPORTED`	Client transaction is temporarily suspended, the method is executed without transaction support, and then the client transaction is resumed	Method is executed without any transaction support
`TransactionAttributeType.REQUIRED`	Method becomes part of the existing transaction	A new transaction is created for the method
`TransactionAttributeType.REQUIRES_NEW`	Client transaction is temporarily suspended, a new transaction is created for the method, and then the client transaction is resumed	A new transaction is created for the method
`TransactionAttributeType.SUPPORTS`	Method becomes part of the existing transaction	Method is executed without any transaction support

The @TransactionAttribute annotation can be used to decorate the class declaration of our EJB, or it can be used to decorate a single method. If used to decorate the class declaration, the declared transaction behavior will apply to all methods in the bean. If used to decorate a single method, the declared behavior will affect only the decorated method. If a bean has an @TransactionAttribute annotation both at the class level and at the method level, the method-level annotation takes precedence. If no transaction attribute is specified for a method, the TransactionAttributeType.REQUIRED attribute is used by default.

The following example shows how to use the @TransactionAttribute annotation:

```
package com.ensode.sessionbeanintro.ejb;

import javax.ejb.Stateless;
import javax.ejb.TransactionAttribute;
import javax.ejb.TransactionAttributeType;

@Stateless
public class Echo

    @override
    @TransactionAttribute(
        TransactionAttributeType.REQUIRES_NEW)
    public String echo(String.saying) {
        return "echoing: " + saying;
    }
}
```

As we can see, we simply need to decorate the method to be configured with the @TransactionAttribute annotation with the appropriate TransactionAttributeType enumeration constant as a parameter to configure transactions for a single method. As we mentioned before, if we want all of our methods to use the same transaction strategy, we can place the @TransactionAttribute annotation at the class level.

Implementing aspect-oriented programming with interceptors

Sometimes, we wish to execute some logic just before and/or just after a method's main logic executes. For example, we might want to measure the execution time of a method to track down performance problems, or we might want to send a message to a log every time we enter and leave a method, to make it easier to track down bugs or exceptions.

The most common solution to these kinds of problems is to add a little bit of code at the beginning and end of every method, implementing the logic to profile or log in each method. This approach, however, has problems: the logic needs to be implemented several times, and; if we later wish to modify or remove the functionality, we need to modify several methods.

Aspect-oriented programming (AOP) is a programming paradigm that solves the problems mentioned earlier by providing a way to implement the logic to be executed just before and/or just after a method's main logic in a separate class. EJB 3.0 introduced the ability to implement AOP via **interceptors**.

Implementing AOP via interceptors consists of two steps: coding the Interceptor class and decorating the EJBs to be intercepted with the @Interceptors annotation. These steps are described in detail in the next section.

Implementing the Interceptor class

An interceptor is a standard Java class. It must have a single method with the following signature:

```
@AroundInvoke
public Object methodName(InvocationContext invocationContext) throws
Exception
```

Notice that the method must be decorated with the @AroundInvoke annotation, which marks the method as an interceptor method. The InvocationContext parameter can be used to obtain information from the intercepted method, such as its name, parameters, the class that declares it, and more. InvocationContext also has a proceed() method that is used to indicate when to execute the method logic.

The following table summarizes some of the most useful InvocationContext methods. Refer to the Java EE 7 JavaDoc for the complete list (it is accessible within NetBeans by going to **Help | JavaDoc References | Java (TM) EE 7 Specification APIs**).

Method name	Description
getMethod()	This returns an instance of the java.lang.reflect.Method class, which can be used to introspect the intercepted method.
getParameters()	This returns an array of objects containing the parameters passed to the intercepted method.
getTarget()	This returns the object containing the method being invoked. Its return value is java.lang.Object.
proceed()	This invokes the method being intercepted.

The following example illustrates a simple interceptor class:

```java
package com.ensode.sessionbeanintro.ejb;

import java.lang.reflect.Method;
import javax.interceptor.AroundInvoke;
import javax.interceptor.InvocationContext;

public class LoggingInterceptor {

    @AroundInvoke
    public Object logMethodCall(
            InvocationContext invocationContext)
            throws Exception {
        Object interceptedObject =
            invocationContext.getTarget();
        Method interceptedMethod =
            invocationContext.getMethod();

        System.out.println("Entering " +
                interceptedObject.getClass().getName() + "." +
                interceptedMethod.getName() + "()");

        Object o = invocationContext.proceed();

        System.out.println("Leaving   " +
                interceptedObject.getClass().getName() + "." +
                interceptedMethod.getName() + "()");

        return o;
    }
}
```

The preceding example sends a message to the application server log just before and just after an intercepted method is executed. The purpose of implementing something like this would be to aid in debugging applications.

 For simplicity, our example simply uses `System.out.` `println` to output messages to the application server log. A real application more than likely would use a logging API such as the Java Logging API or Log4j.

The first thing that we do in our interceptor method is obtain a reference to the object and method being intercepted. We then output a message to the log indicating the class and method being invoked. This code is executed just before we let the intercepted method execute, which we do by invoking `invocationContext.proceed()`. We store the return value of this method in a variable, and then add some additional logic to be executed just after the method finishes. In our example, we simply send an additional line of text to the application server log. Finally, our method returns the return value of `invocationContext.proceed()`.

Decorating the EJB with the @Interceptors annotations

For an EJB's method to be intercepted, it must be decorated with the `@Interceptors` annotation, which has a single class array attribute. This attribute contains all the interceptors to be executed before and/or after the method call.

The `@Interceptors` annotation can be used at the method level, in which case it applies only to the method it decorates, or at the class level, in which it applies to every method in the bean.

The following example is a new version of our `EchoBean` session bean, which is slightly modified to have its `echo()` method intercepted by the `LoggingInterceptor` class we wrote in the previous section:

```
package com.ensode.sessionbeanintro.ejb;

import javax.ejb.Stateless;
import javax.ejb.TransactionAttribute;
import javax.ejb.TransactionAttributeType;
import javax.interceptor.Interceptors;

@Stateless
public class Echo implements EchoRemote {
    // Add business logic below. (Right-click in editor and choose
    // "Insert Code > Add Business Method")

    @Interceptors({LoggingInterceptor.class})
    @TransactionAttribute(TransactionAttributeType.REQUIRES_NEW)
    public String echo(String saying) {
        return "echoing: " + saying;
    }
}
```

Notice that the only change we had to make to our session bean was to add the @Interceptors annotation to its echo() method. In this particular case, the class array attribute has a single value, which is the LoggingInterceptor class we defined earlier. In our example, we are using a single interceptor for our bean's method. If we need our method to be intercepted by more than one interceptor, we can do that by adding additional interceptor classes between the curly braces in the @Interceptors annotation. The list of interceptors between the curly braces must be separated by commas.

At this point, we are ready to test our interceptor. In NetBeans, we can simply right-click on the project in the **Projects** window and select **Run**. After doing so, we should see the output of the interceptor's logMethodCall() method in NetBean's GlassFish output window.

The EJB Timer service

Stateless session beans and message-driven beans (another type of EJB discussed later in the book) can have a method that is executed automatically at regular intervals. This functionality is useful if we want to execute some logic periodically (once a week, every day, every other hour, and so on) without having to explicitly call any methods. This functionality is achieved by the EJB Timer service.

In order to use the EJB Timer service, we need to use the @Schedule annotation to specify when our method will be called. NetBeans provides a handy wizard that we can use to help us in the process.

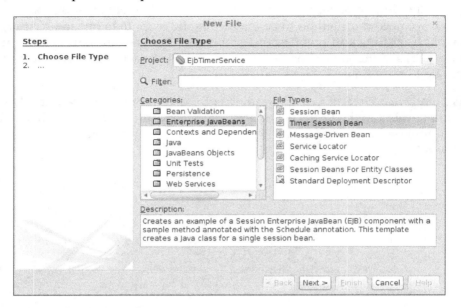

The next step in the wizard allows us to select several options.

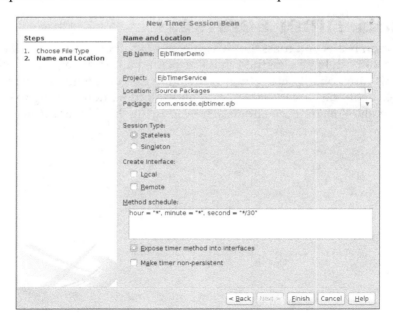

We can implement our bean either as a stateless or as a singleton session bean. We can also choose to create either a local or a remote interface. Local interfaces are optional, and remote interfaces are required only if we need to access our session bean from a different JVM. So, in our example, we choose not to create either one. In the **Method schedule** text area, we need to enter the attributes and values of the @Schedule annotation that will be added to the generated session bean.

 The @Schedule annotation uses a syntax similar to the cron utility commonly found in Unix and Unix-like operating systems such as Linux. Refer to http://www.unixgeeks.org/security/newbie/unix/cron-1.html for a good introduction to cron.

After clicking on **Finish**, our new session bean is generated, as shown in the following code:

```
package com.ensode.ejbtimer.ejb;

import java.util.Date;
import javax.ejb.Schedule;
import javax.ejb.Stateless;
import javax.ejb.LocalBean;

@Stateless
@LocalBean
public class EjbTimerDemo {

    @Schedule(hour = "*", minute = "*", second = "*/30")
    public void myTimer() {
        System.out.println("Timer event: " + new Date());
    }

    // Add business logic below. (Right-click in editor and choose
    // "Insert Code > Add Business Method")
}
```

Notice how the values and attributes of the @Schedule annotation match the values we entered in the wizard. We used the value "*" for its hour attribute to specify that the method should be invoked every hour. We used the value of "*" for the minute attribute as well to specify that the method should be invoked every minute. Finally, we used the value of "*/30" for its second attribute to specify that the method should be invoked every 30 seconds.

After deploying and executing our project in NetBeans, we should see the following output in the output console of GlassFish:

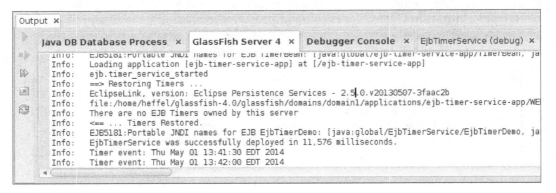

We can see the output of the generated `myTimer()` method in the GlassFish log. This method is being invoked automatically every 30 seconds (as specified in the `@Schedule` annotation) by the EJB Timer service.

Generating session beans from JPA entities

One very nice NetBeans feature is that it allows the generation of stateless session beans from the existing JPA entities. The generated session beans act as **Data Access Objects (DAOs)**. This feature, combined with the ability to generate JPA entities from an existing database schema, allows us to completely generate the data access layers of our application without having to write a single line of Java code.

To take advantage of this functionality, we need to create an EJB project (go to **File | New Project**, select **Enterprise** from the **Categories** list, select **EJB Module** from the **Projects** list), or use the EJB project from an Enterprise Application project and add some JPA entities to it either by manually coding them or by generating them from an existing schema as discussed in *Chapter 4, Interacting with Databases through the Java Persistence API.*

Once we have some JPA entities in the project, we need to go to **File | New File**, select **Persistence** from the categories list, and select **Session Beans For Entity Classes** from the **File Types** list.

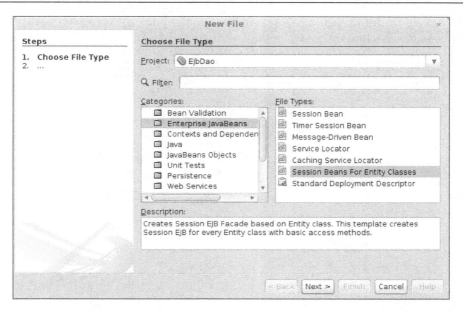

The next screen in the wizard allows us to select for which of the existing JPA entity classes in the project we want to generate session beans; in most cases, they should be generated for all of them by simply clicking on the **Add All** button.

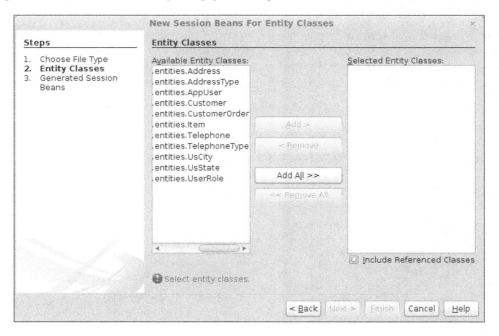

The last screen in the wizard allows us to specify the package for the generated session beans and whether we want to generate local and/or remote interfaces.

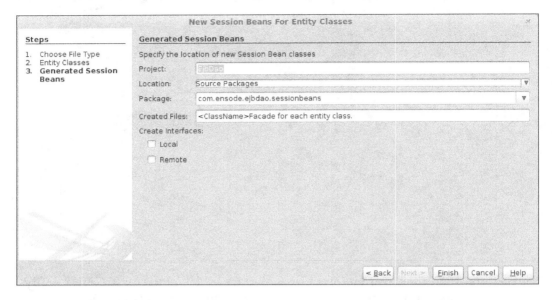

After clicking on **Finish**, the session beans are created and placed in the package we specified.

All of the generated session beans extend `AbstractFacade`, an abstract class that is also generated by the **Session Beans for Entity Classes** wizard. This abstract class contains a number of methods that allow us to perform CRUD (short for Create, Read, Update, and Delete) operations on our entities. The code is as follows:

```
package com.ensode.ejbdao.sessionbeans;

import java.util.List;
import javax.persistence.EntityManager;

public abstract class AbstractFacade<T> {
    private Class<T> entityClass;

    public AbstractFacade(Class<T> entityClass) {
        this.entityClass = entityClass;
    }

    protected abstract EntityManager getEntityManager();
```

```java
    public void create(T entity) {
        getEntityManager().persist(entity);
    }

    public void edit(T entity) {
        getEntityManager().merge(entity);
    }

    public void remove(T entity) {
        getEntityManager().remove(getEntityManager().merge(entity));
    }

    public T find(Object id) {
        return getEntityManager().find(entityClass, id);
    }

    public List<T> findAll() {
        javax.persistence.criteria.CriteriaQuery cq =
            getEntityManager().getCriteriaBuilder().createQuery();
        cq.select(cq.from(entityClass));
        return getEntityManager().createQuery(cq).getResultList();
    }

    public List<T> findRange(int[] range) {
        javax.persistence.criteria.CriteriaQuery cq =
            getEntityManager().getCriteriaBuilder().createQuery();
        cq.select(cq.from(entityClass));
        javax.persistence.Query q = getEntityManager().
createQuery(cq);
        q.setMaxResults(range[1] - range[0] + 1);
        q.setFirstResult(range[0]);
        return q.getResultList();
    }

    public int count() {
        javax.persistence.criteria.CriteriaQuery cq =
            getEntityManager().getCriteriaBuilder().createQuery();
        javax.persistence.criteria.Root<T> rt = cq.from(entityClass);
        cq.select(getEntityManager().getCriteriaBuilder().count(rt));
        javax.persistence.Query q = getEntityManager().
createQuery(cq);
        return ((Long) q.getSingleResult()).intValue();
    }
}
```

As we can see, AbstractFacade is not much more than a facade to EntityManager. Wrapping its calls inside a session bean gives us all of its advantages, such as transaction management and distributed code. The generated create() method is used to create new entities, the edit() method updates an existing entity, and the remove() method deletes existing entities. The find() method finds an entity with the given primary key, and the findAll() method returns a list of all entities in the database. The findRange() method allows us to retrieve a subset of the entities in the database; it takes an array of integers as its sole parameter. The first element in this array should have the index of the first result to retrieve, and the second element should have the index of the last element to retrieve. The count() method returns the number of entities in the database; it is similar to a select count(*) from TABLE_NAME statement in standard SQL.

As we mentioned previously, all of the generated session beans extend AbstractFacade. Let's look at one of these generated EJBs:

```
package com.ensode.ejbdao.sessionbeans;

import com.ensode.ejbdao.entities.Customer;
import javax.ejb.Stateless;
import javax.persistence.EntityManager;
import javax.persistence.PersistenceContext;

@Stateless
public class CustomerFacade extends AbstractFacade<Customer> {
    @PersistenceContext(unitName = "EjbDaoPU")
    private EntityManager em;

    @Override
    protected EntityManager getEntityManager() {
        return em;
    }

    public CustomerFacade() {
        super(Customer.class);
    }
}
```

As we can see, the generated session beans are very simple. They simply include an instance variable of type EntityManager and take advantage of resource injection to initialize it. They also include a getEntityManager() method meant to be called by the parent class so that it has access to this session bean's EntityManager instance. Additionally, the session bean's constructor invokes the parent class' constructor, which via generics initializes the entityClass instance variable on the parent class.

We are, of course, free to add additional methods to the generated session beans. For example, sometimes it is necessary to add a method to find all entities that meet specific criteria, such as finding all customers with the same last name.

 One disadvantage of adding methods to the generated session beans is that, if for any reason they need to be regenerated, we will lose our custom methods and they will need to be added again. In order to avoid this situation, it is a good idea to extend the generated session beans and add additional methods in the child classes; this will prevent our methods from being "wiped out" if we ever need to regenerate our session beans.

Summary

In this chapter, we gave an introduction to session beans, and explained how NetBeans can help us speed up session bean development.

We covered how EJBs in general, and session beans in particular, allow us to easily implement transaction strategies in our enterprise applications. We also covered how we can implement AOP with session beans via interceptors. Additionally, we discussed how session beans can have one of their methods invoked periodically by the EJB container by taking advantage of the EJB Timer service. Lastly, we covered how NetBeans can help speed up the implementation of the data access layer of our applications by generating session beans implementing the Data Access Object (DAO) design pattern automatically.

6
Contexts and Dependency Injection

Contexts and Dependency Injection (CDI) can be used to simplify integrating the different layers of a Java EE application. For example, CDI allows us to use a session bean as a managed bean, so that we can take advantage of the EJB features, such as transactions, directly in our managed beans.

In this chapter, we will cover the following topics:

- Introduction to CDI
- Qualifiers
- Stereotypes
- Interceptor binding types
- Custom scopes

Introduction to CDI

JavaServer Faces (JSF) web applications employing CDI are very similar to JSF applications without CDI; the main difference is that instead of using JSF managed beans for our model and controllers, we use CDI named beans. What makes CDI applications easier to develop and maintain are the excellent dependency injection capabilities of the CDI API.

Just as with other JSF applications, CDI applications use facelets as their view technology. The following example illustrates a typical markup for a JSF page using CDI:

```xml
<?xml version='1.0' encoding='UTF-8' ?>
<!DOCTYPE html PUBLIC "-//W3C//DTD XHTML 1.0 Transitional//EN"
    "http://www.w3.org/TR/xhtml1/DTD/xhtml1-transitional.dtd">
<html xmlns="http://www.w3.org/1999/xhtml"
      xmlns:h="http://xmlns.jcp.org/jsf/html">
    <h:head>
        <title>Create New Customer</title>
    </h:head>
    <h:body>
        <h:form>
            <h3>Create New Customer</h3>
            <h:panelGrid columns="3">
                <h:outputLabel for="firstName" value="First Name"/>
                <h:inputText id="firstName" value="#{customer.
firstName}"/>
                <h:message for="firstName"/>

                <h:outputLabel for="middleName" value="Middle Name"/>
                <h:inputText id="middleName"
                  value="#{customer.middleName}"/>
                <h:message for="middleName"/>

                <h:outputLabel for="lastName" value="Last Name"/>
                <h:inputText id="lastName" value="#{customer.
lastName}"/>
                <h:message for="lastName"/>

                <h:outputLabel for="email" value="Email Address"/>
                <h:inputText id="email" value="#{customer.email}"/>
                <h:message for="email"/>
                <h:panelGroup/>
                <h:commandButton value="Submit"
                    action="#{customerController.
navigateToConfirmation}"/>
            </h:panelGrid>
        </h:form>
    </h:body>
</html>
```

As we can see, the preceding markup doesn't look any different from the markup used for a JSF application that does not use CDI. The page renders as follows (shown after entering some data):

In our page markup, we have JSF components that use Unified Expression Language expressions to bind themselves to CDI named bean properties and methods. Let's take a look at the customer bean first:

```java
package com.ensode.cdiintro.model;

import java.io.Serializable;
import javax.enterprise.context.RequestScoped;
import javax.inject.Named;

@Named
@RequestScoped
public class Customer implements Serializable {

    private String firstName;
    private String middleName;
    private String lastName;
    private String email;

    public Customer() {
    }

    public String getFirstName() {
        return firstName;
    }
```

```java
        public void setFirstName(String firstName) {
            this.firstName = firstName;
        }

        public String getMiddleName() {
            return middleName;
        }

        public void setMiddleName(String middleName) {
            this.middleName = middleName;
        }

        public String getLastName() {
            return lastName;
        }

        public void setLastName(String lastName) {
            this.lastName = lastName;
        }

        public String getEmail() {
            return email;
        }

        public void setEmail(String email) {
            this.email = email;
        }
    }
```

The `@Named` annotation marks this class as a CDI named bean. By default, the bean's name will be the class name with its first character switched to lowercase (in our example, the name of the bean is "customer", since the class name is `Customer`). We can override this behavior if we wish by passing the desired name to the value attribute of the `@Named` annotation, as follows:

```java
@Named(value="customerBean")
```

A CDI named bean's methods and properties are accessible via facelets, just like regular JSF managed beans.

Just like JSF managed beans, CDI named beans can have one of several scopes as listed in the following table. The preceding named bean has a scope of request, as denoted by the @RequestScoped annotation.

Scope	Annotation	Description
Request	@RequestScoped	Request scoped beans are shared through the duration of a single request. A single request could refer to an HTTP request, an invocation to a method in an EJB, a web service invocation, or sending a JMS message to a message-driven bean.
Session	@SessionScoped	Session scoped beans are shared across all requests in an HTTP session. Each user of an application gets their own instance of a session scoped bean.
Application	@ApplicationScoped	Application scoped beans live through the whole application lifetime. Beans in this scope are shared across user sessions.
Conversation	@ConversationScoped	The conversation scope can span multiple requests, and is typically shorter than the session scope.
Dependent	@Dependent	Dependent scoped beans are not shared. Any time a dependent scoped bean is injected, a new instance is created.

As we can see, CDI has equivalent scopes to all JSF scopes. Additionally, CDI adds two additional scopes. The first CDI-specific scope is the **conversation scope**, which allows us to have a scope that spans across multiple requests, but is shorter than the session scope. The second CDI-specific scope is the **dependent scope**, which is a pseudo scope. A CDI bean in the dependent scope is a dependent object of another object; beans in this scope are instantiated when the object they belong to is instantiated and they are destroyed when the object they belong to is destroyed.

Our application has two CDI named beans. We already discussed the customer bean. The other CDI named bean in our application is the controller bean:

```
package com.ensode.cdiintro.controller;

import com.ensode.cdiintro.model.Customer;
import javax.enterprise.context.RequestScoped;
import javax.inject.Inject;
import javax.inject.Named;
```

```
@Named
@RequestScoped
public class CustomerController {

    @Inject
    private Customer customer;

    public Customer getCustomer() {
        return customer;
    }

    public void setCustomer(Customer customer) {
        this.customer = customer;
    }

    public String navigateToConfirmation() {
        //In a real application we would
        //Save customer data to the database here.

        return "confirmation";
    }
}
```

In the preceding class, an instance of the Customer class is injected at runtime; this is accomplished via the @Inject annotation. This annotation allows us to easily use dependency injection in CDI applications. Since the Customer class is annotated with the @RequestScoped annotation, a new instance of Customer will be injected for every request.

The navigateToConfirmation() method in the preceding class is invoked when the user clicks on the **Submit** button on the page. The navigateToConfirmation() method works just like an equivalent method in a JSF managed bean would, that is, it returns a string and the application navigates to an appropriate page based on the value of that string. Like with JSF, by default, the target page's name with an .xhtml extension is the return value of this method. For example, if no exceptions are thrown in the navigateToConfirmation() method, the user is directed to a page named confirmation.xhtml:

```
<?xml version='1.0' encoding='UTF-8' ?>
<!DOCTYPE html PUBLIC "-//W3C//DTD XHTML 1.0 Transitional//EN"
"http://www.w3.org/TR/xhtml1/DTD/xhtml1-transitional.dtd">
<html xmlns="http://www.w3.org/1999/xhtml"
      xmlns:h="http://xmlns.jcp.org/jsf/html">
    <h:head>
```

```
            <title>Success</title>
        </h:head>
        <h:body>
            New Customer created successfully.
            <h:panelGrid columns="2" border="1" cellspacing="0">
                <h:outputLabel for="firstName" value="First Name"/>
                <h:outputText id="firstName" value="#{customer.
firstName}"/>

                <h:outputLabel for="middleName" value="Middle Name"/>
                <h:outputText id="middleName"
                  value="#{customer.middleName}"/>

                <h:outputLabel for="lastName" value="Last Name"/>
                <h:outputText id="lastName" value="#{customer.lastName}"/>

                <h:outputLabel for="email" value="Email Address"/>
                <h:outputText id="email" value="#{customer.email}"/>

            </h:panelGrid>
        </h:body>
    </html>
```

Again, there is nothing special we need to do to access the named beans properties from the preceding markup. It works just as if the bean was a JSF managed bean. The preceding page renders as follows:

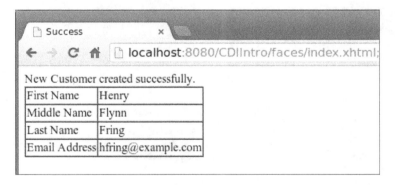

As we can see, CDI applications work just like JSF applications. However, CDI applications have several advantages over JSF, for example (as we mentioned previously) CDI beans have additional scopes not found in JSF. Additionally, using CDI allows us to decouple our Java code from the JSF API. Also, as we mentioned previously, CDI allows us to use session beans as named beans.

Qualifiers

In some instances, the type of bean we wish to inject into our code may be an interface or a Java superclass, but we may be interested in injecting a subclass or a class implementing the interface. For cases like this, CDI provides qualifiers we can use to indicate the specific type we wish to inject into our code.

A CDI qualifier is an annotation that must be decorated with the `@Qualifier` annotation. This annotation can then be used to decorate the specific subclass or interface. In this section, we will develop a `Premium` qualifier for our customer bean; premium customers could get perks that are not available to regular customers, for example, discounts.

Creating a CDI qualifier with NetBeans is very easy; all we need to do is go to **File | New File**, select the **Contexts and Dependency Injection** category, and select the **Qualifier Type** file type.

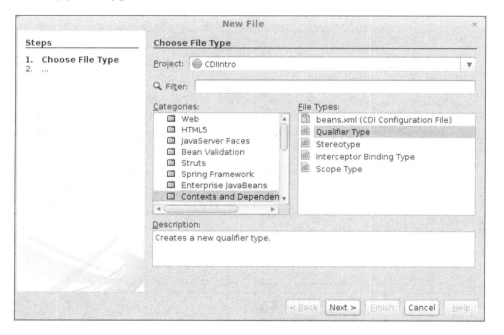

In the next step in the wizard, we need to enter a name and a package for our qualifier.

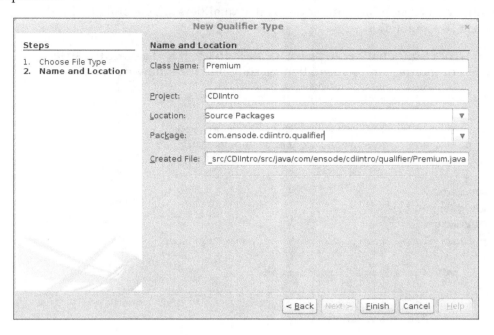

After these two simple steps, NetBeans generates the code for our qualifier:

```
package com.ensode.cdiintro.qualifier;

import static java.lang.annotation.ElementType.TYPE;
import static java.lang.annotation.ElementType.FIELD;
import static java.lang.annotation.ElementType.PARAMETER;
import static java.lang.annotation.ElementType.METHOD;
import static java.lang.annotation.RetentionPolicy.RUNTIME;
import java.lang.annotation.Retention;
import java.lang.annotation.Target;
import javax.inject.Qualifier;

@Qualifier
@Retention(RUNTIME)
@Target({METHOD, FIELD, PARAMETER, TYPE})
public @interface Premium {
}
```

Qualifiers are standard Java annotations. Typically, they have retention of runtime and can target methods, fields, parameters, or types. The only difference between a qualifier and a standard annotation is that qualifiers are decorated with the @Qualifier annotation.

Once we have our qualifier in place, we need to use it to decorate the specific subclass or interface implementation, as shown in the following code:

```
package com.ensode.cdiintro.model;

import com.ensode.cdiintro.qualifier.Premium;
import javax.enterprise.context.RequestScoped;
import javax.inject.Named;

@Named
@RequestScoped
@Premium
public class PremiumCustomer extends Customer {

    private Integer discountCode;

    public Integer getDiscountCode() {
        return discountCode;
    }

    public void setDiscountCode(Integer discountCode) {
        this.discountCode = discountCode;
    }
}
```

Once we have decorated the specific instance we need to qualify, we can use our qualifiers in the client code to specify the exact type of dependency we need:

```
package com.ensode.cdiintro.controller;

import com.ensode.cdiintro.model.Customer;
import com.ensode.cdiintro.model.PremiumCustomer;
import com.ensode.cdiintro.qualifier.Premium;

import java.util.logging.Level;
import java.util.logging.Logger;
import javax.enterprise.context.RequestScoped;
import javax.inject.Inject;
import javax.inject.Named;
```

```
@Named
@RequestScoped
public class PremiumCustomerController {

    private static final Logger logger = Logger.getLogger(
            PremiumCustomerController.class.getName());
    @Inject
    @Premium
    private Customer customer;

    public String saveCustomer() {

        PremiumCustomer premiumCustomer =
          (PremiumCustomer) customer;

        logger.log(Level.INFO, "Saving the following information \n"
                + "{0} {1}, discount code = {2}",
                new Object[]{premiumCustomer.getFirstName(),
                    premiumCustomer.getLastName(),
                    premiumCustomer.getDiscountCode()});

        //If this was a real application, we would have code to save
        //customer data to the database here.

        return "premium_customer_confirmation";
    }
}
```

Since we used our `@Premium` qualifier to decorate the customer field, an instance of the `PremiumCustomer` class is injected into that field. This is because this class is also decorated with the `@Premium` qualifier.

As far as our JSF pages go, we simply access our named bean as usual using its name, as shown in the following code;

```
<?xml version='1.0' encoding='UTF-8' ?>
<!DOCTYPE html PUBLIC "-//W3C//DTD XHTML 1.0 Transitional//EN"
"http://www.w3.org/TR/xhtml1/DTD/xhtml1-transitional.dtd">
<html xmlns="http://www.w3.org/1999/xhtml"
      xmlns:h="http://xmlns.jcp.org/jsf/html">
    <h:head>
        <title>Create New Premium Customer</title>
    </h:head>
    <h:body>
        <h:form>
```

```
            <h3>Create New Premium Customer</h3>
            <h:panelGrid columns="3">
                <h:outputLabel for="firstName" value="First Name"/>
                <h:inputText id="firstName"
                    value="#{premiumCustomer.firstName}"/>
                <h:message for="firstName"/>

                <h:outputLabel for="middleName" value="Middle Name"/>
                <h:inputText id="middleName"
                    value="#{premiumCustomer.middleName}"/>
                <h:message for="middleName"/>

                <h:outputLabel for="lastName" value="Last Name"/>
                <h:inputText id="lastName"
                    value="#{premiumCustomer.lastName}"/>
                <h:message for="lastName"/>

                <h:outputLabel for="email" value="Email Address"/>
                <h:inputText id="email"
                    value="#{premiumCustomer.email}"/>
                <h:message for="email"/>

                <h:outputLabel for="discountCode" value="Discount
Code"/>
                <h:inputText id="discountCode"
                    value="#{premiumCustomer.discountCode}"/>
                <h:message for="discountCode"/>

                <h:panelGroup/>
                <h:commandButton value="Submit"
                    action="#{premiumCustomerController.
saveCustomer}"/>
            </h:panelGrid>
        </h:form>
    </h:body>
</html>
```

In this example, we are using the default name for our bean, which is the class name with the first letter switched to lowercase.

Now, we are ready to test our application:

After submitting the page, we can see the confirmation page.

Stereotypes

A CDI stereotype allows us to create new annotations that bundle up several CDI annotations. For example, if we need to create several CDI named beans with a scope of session, we would have to use two annotations in each of these beans, namely `@Named` and `@SessionScoped`. Instead of having to add two annotations to each of our beans, we could create a stereotype and annotate our beans with it.

To create a CDI stereotype in NetBeans, we simply need to create a new file by selecting the **Contexts and Dependency Injection** category and the **Stereotype** file type.

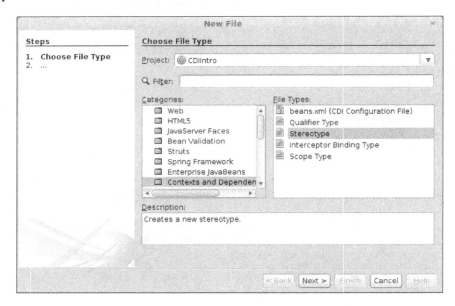

Then, we need to enter a name and package for our new stereotype.

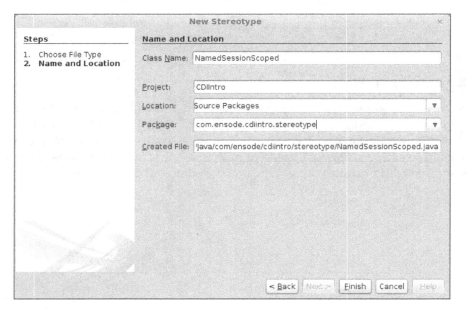

At this point, NetBeans generates the following code:

```
package com.ensode.cdiintro.stereotype;

import static java.lang.annotation.ElementType.TYPE;
import static java.lang.annotation.ElementType.FIELD;
import static java.lang.annotation.ElementType.METHOD;
import static java.lang.annotation.RetentionPolicy.RUNTIME;
import java.lang.annotation.Retention;
import java.lang.annotation.Target;
import javax.enterprise.inject.Stereotype;

@Stereotype
@Retention(RUNTIME)
@Target({METHOD, FIELD, TYPE})
public @interface NamedSessionScoped {
}
```

Now, we simply need to add the CDI annotations that we want the classes annotated with our stereotype to use. In our case, we want them to be named beans and have a scope of session; therefore, we add the @Named and @SessionScoped annotations as shown in the following code:

```
package com.ensode.cdiintro.stereotype;

import static java.lang.annotation.ElementType.TYPE;
import static java.lang.annotation.ElementType.FIELD;
import static java.lang.annotation.ElementType.METHOD;
import static java.lang.annotation.RetentionPolicy.RUNTIME;
import java.lang.annotation.Retention;
import java.lang.annotation.Target;
import javax.enterprise.context.SessionScoped;
import javax.enterprise.inject.Stereotype;
import javax.inject.Named;

@Named
@SessionScoped
@Stereotype
@Retention(RUNTIME)
@Target({METHOD, FIELD, TYPE})
public @interface NamedSessionScoped {
}
```

Now we can use our stereotype in our own code:

```
package com.ensode.cdiintro.beans;
```

```
import com.ensode.cdiintro.stereotype.NamedSessionScoped;
import java.io.Serializable;

@NamedSessionScoped
public class StereotypeClient implements Serializable {

    private String property1;
    private String property2;

    public String getProperty1() {
        return property1;
    }

    public void setProperty1(String property1) {
        this.property1 = property1;
    }

    public String getProperty2() {
        return property2;
    }

    public void setProperty2(String property2) {
        this.property2 = property2;
    }
}
```

We annotated the `StereotypeClient` class with our `NamedSessionScoped` stereotype, which is equivalent to using the `@Named` and `@SessionScoped` annotations.

Interceptor binding types

One of the advantages of EJBs is that they allow us to easily perform **aspect-oriented programming (AOP)** via interceptors. CDI allows us to write interceptor binding types; this lets us bind interceptors to beans and the beans do not have to depend on the interceptor directly. Interceptor binding types are annotations that are themselves annotated with `@InterceptorBinding`.

Creating an interceptor binding type in NetBeans involves creating a new file, selecting the **Contexts and Dependency Injection** category, and selecting the **Interceptor Binding Type** file type.

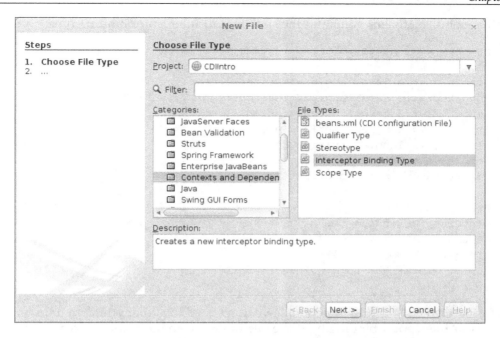

Then, we need to enter a class name and select or enter a package for our new interceptor binding type.

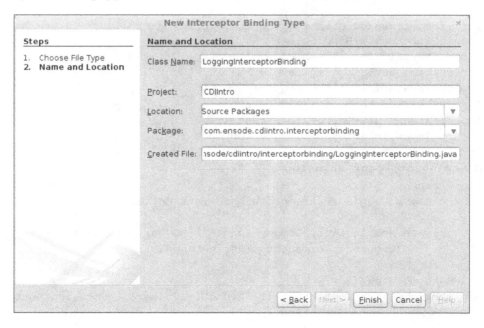

At this point,, NetBeans generates the code for our interceptor binding type:

```
package com.ensode.cdiintro.interceptorbinding;

import static java.lang.annotation.ElementType.TYPE;
import static java.lang.annotation.ElementType.METHOD;
import static java.lang.annotation.RetentionPolicy.RUNTIME;
import java.lang.annotation.Inherited;
import java.lang.annotation.Retention;
import java.lang.annotation.Target;
import javax.interceptor.InterceptorBinding;

@Inherited
@InterceptorBinding
@Retention(RUNTIME)
@Target({METHOD, TYPE})
public @interface LoggingInterceptorBinding {
}
```

The generated code is fully functional; we don't need to add anything to it. In order to use our interceptor binding type, we need to write an interceptor and annotate it with our interceptor binding type, as shown in the following code:

```
package com.ensode.cdiintro.interceptor;

import com.ensode.cdiintro.interceptorbinding.
LoggingInterceptorBinding;
import java.io.Serializable;
import java.util.logging.Level;
import java.util.logging.Logger;
import javax.interceptor.AroundInvoke;
import javax.interceptor.Interceptor;
import javax.interceptor.InvocationContext;

@LoggingInterceptorBinding
@Interceptor
public class LoggingInterceptor implements Serializable{

    private static final Logger logger = Logger.getLogger(
            LoggingInterceptor.class.getName());

    @AroundInvoke
    public Object logMethodCall(InvocationContext invocationContext)
            throws Exception {
```

```
logger.log(Level.INFO, new StringBuilder("entering ").append(
        invocationContext.getMethod().getName()).append(
        " method").toString());

Object retVal = invocationContext.proceed();

logger.log(Level.INFO, new StringBuilder("leaving ").append(
        invocationContext.getMethod().getName()).append(
        " method").toString());

        return retVal;
    }
}
```

As we can see, other than being annotated with our interceptor binding type, the preceding class is a standard interceptor similar to the ones we use with EJB session beans (refer to *Chapter 5, Implementing the Business Tier with Session Beans*, for details).

In order for our interceptor binding type to work properly, we need to add a CDI configuration file (beans.xml) to our project.

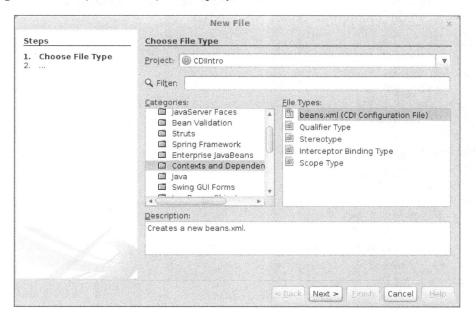

Then, we need to register our interceptor in beans.xml as follows:

```
<?xml version="1.0" encoding="UTF-8"?>
<beans xmlns="http://xmlns.jcp.org/xml/ns/javaee"
        xmlns:xsi="http://www.w3.org/2001/XMLSchema-instance"
        xsi:schemaLocation="http://xmlns.jcp.org/xml/ns/javaee
        http://xmlns.jcp.org/xml/ns/javaee/beans_1_1.xsd"
        bean-discovery-mode="all">
    <interceptors>
      <class>
        com.ensode.cdiintro.interceptor.LoggingInterceptor
      </class>
    </interceptors>
</beans>
```

To register our interceptor, we need to set bean-discovery-mode to all in the generated beans.xml and add the <interceptor> tag in beans.xml, with one or more nested <class> tags containing the fully qualified names of our interceptors.

The final step before we can use our interceptor binding type is to annotate the class to be intercepted with our interceptor binding type:

```
package com.ensode.cdiintro.controller;

import com.ensode.cdiintro.interceptorbinding.
LoggingInterceptorBinding;
import com.ensode.cdiintro.model.Customer;
import com.ensode.cdiintro.model.PremiumCustomer;
import com.ensode.cdiintro.qualifier.Premium;
import java.util.logging.Level;
import java.util.logging.Logger;
import javax.enterprise.context.RequestScoped;
import javax.inject.Inject;
import javax.inject.Named;


@LoggingInterceptorBinding
@Named
@RequestScoped
public class PremiumCustomerController {

    private static final Logger logger = Logger.getLogger(
            PremiumCustomerController.class.getName());
    @Inject
    @Premium
```

```
    private Customer customer;

    public String saveCustomer() {

        PremiumCustomer premiumCustomer = (PremiumCustomer) customer;

        logger.log(Level.INFO, "Saving the following information \n"
                + "{0} {1}, discount code = {2}",
                new Object[]{premiumCustomer.getFirstName(),
                    premiumCustomer.getLastName(),
                    premiumCustomer.getDiscountCode()});

        //If this was a real application, we would have code to save
        //customer data to the database here.

        return "premium_customer_confirmation";
    }
}
```

Now, we are ready to use our interceptor. After executing the preceding code and examining the GlassFish log, we can see our interceptor binding type in action.

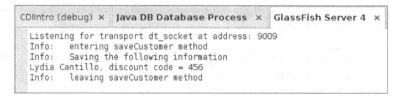

The lines `entering saveCustomer method` and `leaving saveCustomer method` were added to the log by our interceptor, which was indirectly invoked by our interceptor binding type.

Custom scopes

In addition to providing several prebuilt scopes, CDI allows us to define our own custom scopes. This functionality is primarily meant for developers building frameworks on top of CDI, not for application developers. Nevertheless, NetBeans provides a wizard for us to create our own CDI custom scopes.

To create a new CDI custom scope, we need to go to **File | New File**, select the **Contexts and Dependency Injection** category, and select the **Scope Type** file type.

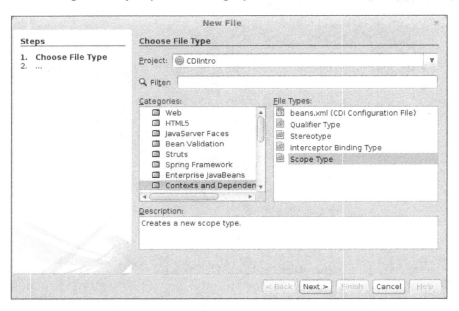

Then, we need to enter a package and a name for our custom scope.

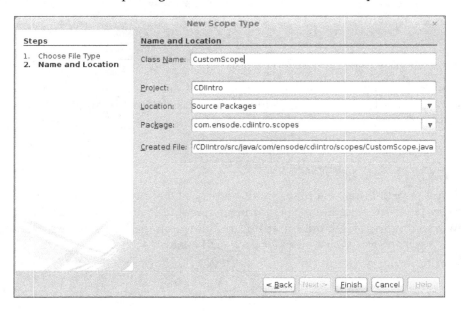

After clicking on **Finish**, our new custom scope is created, as shown in the following code:

```
package com.ensode.cdiintro.scopes;

import static java.lang.annotation.ElementType.TYPE;
import static java.lang.annotation.ElementType.FIELD;
import static java.lang.annotation.ElementType.METHOD;
import static java.lang.annotation.RetentionPolicy.RUNTIME;
import java.lang.annotation.Inherited;
import java.lang.annotation.Retention;
import java.lang.annotation.Target;
import javax.inject.Scope;

@Inherited
@Scope // or @javax.enterprise.context.NormalScope
@Retention(RUNTIME)
@Target({METHOD, FIELD, TYPE})
public @interface CustomScope {
}
```

To actually use our scope in our CDI applications, we would need to create a custom context which, as mentioned previously, is primarily a concern for framework developers and not for Java EE application developers. Therefore, it is beyond the scope of this chapter. Interested readers can refer to *JBoss Weld CDI for Java Platform, Ken Finnigan, Packt Publishing*. (JBoss Weld is a popular CDI implementation and it is included with GlassFish.)

Summary

In this chapter, we covered NetBeans support for CDI, a new Java EE API introduced in Java EE 6. We provided an introduction to CDI and explained additional functionality that the CDI API provides over standard JSF. We also covered how to disambiguate CDI injected beans via CDI Qualifiers. Additionally, we covered how to group together CDI annotations via CDI stereotypes. We also saw how CDI can help us with AOP via interceptor binding types. Finally, we covered how NetBeans can help us create custom CDI scopes.

Messaging with JMS and Message-driven Beans

7

Java Message Service (JMS) is a standard Java EE messaging API that allows loosely coupled, asynchronous communication between Java EE components.

NetBeans includes good support to aid us in creating applications that take advantage of the JMS API, generating most of the JMS-specific code and allowing us to focus on the business logic of our application.

We will cover the following topics in this chapter:

- Introduction to JMS
- Creating JMS resources from NetBeans
- Implementing a JMS message producer
- Consuming JMS messages with message-driven beans

Introduction to JMS

JMS is a standard Java EE API that allows loosely coupled, asynchronous communication between Java EE components. Applications that take advantage of JMS do not interact with each other directly; instead, JMS message producers send messages to a destination (JMS queue or topic) and JMS consumers receive messages from those destinations.

There are two messaging domains that can be used when working with JMS: point-to-point (PTP) messaging, in which a JMS message is processed by only one message receiver, and **publish/subscribe (pub/sub)** messaging, in which all message receivers subscribed to a specific topic receive and process each message for said topic. JMS applications that use the PTP messaging domains use message queues as their JMS destinations, whereas applications that use pub/sub use message topics.

Creating JMS resources from NetBeans

Before we can send and receive JMS messages, we need to add a JMS destination (queue or topic) in our application server. When using GlassFish as our application server, we can create JMS destinations directly from any Java EE project in NetBeans.

 Older versions of Java EE required the creation of a JMS connection factory in addition to JMS destinations. The Java EE 7 specification requires all compliant application servers to supply a default JMS connection factory; therefore, this step is no longer necessary.

JMS destinations are an intermediate location where JMS producers place messages and JMS consumers retrieve them. When using the PTP messaging domain, JMS destinations are message queues, whereas with the pub/sub messaging domain, the destination is a message topic.

In our example, we will use the PTP messaging domain. Therefore, we need to create a message queue; the procedure to create a message topic is almost identical.

First, we need to create a new Java EE project; for our example, we will create a **Web Application** project:

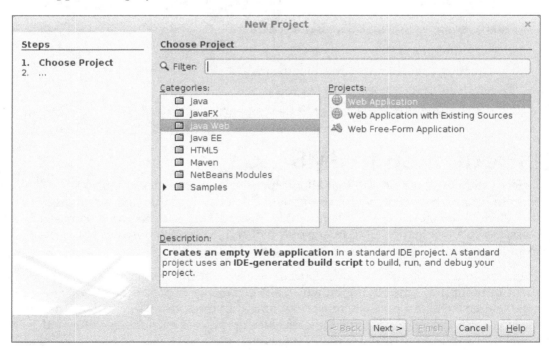

In the next step in the wizard, name the project `JMSIntro`.

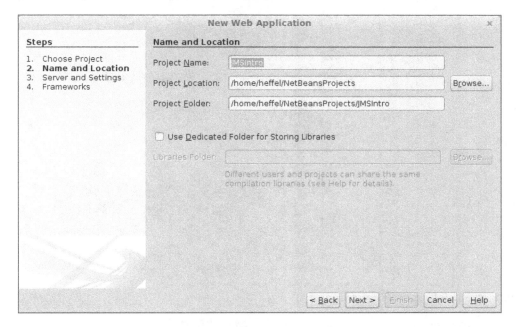

Accept all the default values in the next step in the wizard.

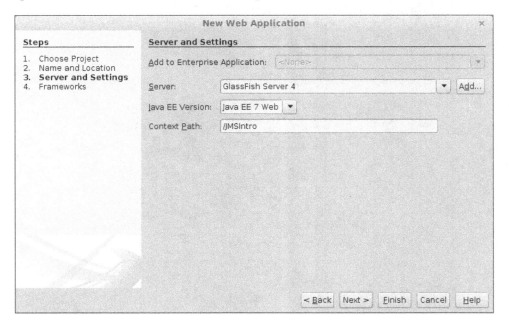

Select the **JavaServer Faces** framework in the next step in the wizard.

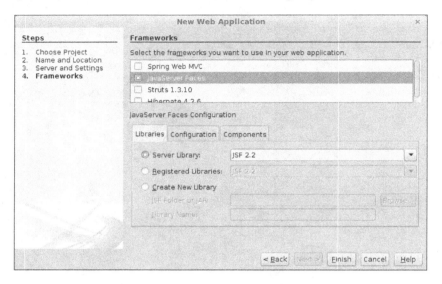

Click on **Finish** to create the project.

In order to create a message queue, we need to go to **File | New File**, select **GlassFish** from the **Categories** list, and select **JMS Resource** from the **File Types** list. This is shown in the following screenshot:

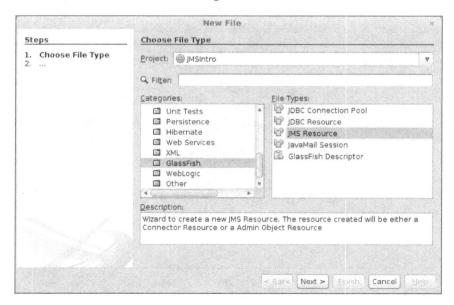

Then, we need to enter a JNDI name for our queue; in our example, we simply picked the default name jms/MyQueue and accepted the default resource type **javax.jms.Queue**.

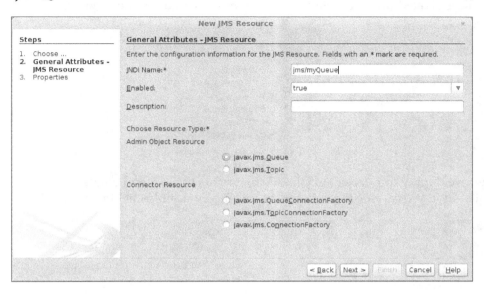

JMS message queues require a Name property; in our example, we simply chose to use the JNDI name of our queue (without the jms/ prefix) as the value of this property.

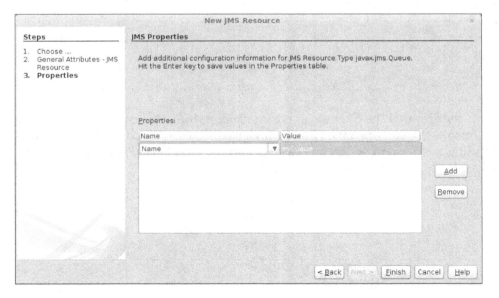

So, we have created a JMS queue to act as a JMS destination for our application.

NetBeans adds the GlassFish resources we created to a file called `sun-resources.xml`. This file is created under the **Server Resources** node in the **Projects** view.

When we deploy our project to GlassFish, it reads this file and creates the resources defined in it. We can see the contents of this file by double-clicking on it.

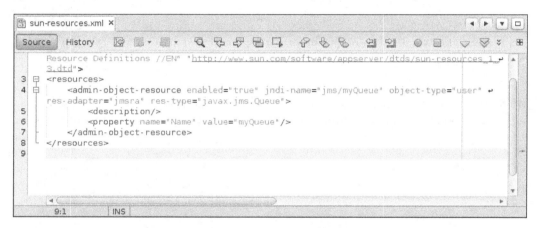

We can confirm that the queue was created successfully by inspecting the GlassFish web console. We can open the GlassFish web console by clicking on the **Services** tab, expanding the **Servers** node, then right-clicking on the **GlassFish Server 4** node, and finally selecting **View Domain Admin Console**.

After a few seconds, a browser window will open automatically to display the GlassFish web-based administration console.

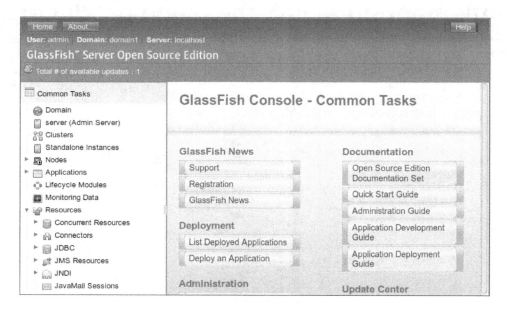

We can verify that our queue was created successfully by expanding the **JMS Resources** node on the left-hand side, expanding the **Destination Resources** node, and verifying that our queue is listed.

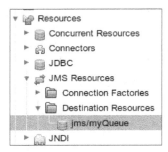

Now that we have verified that our queue was created successfully, it is time to write some code to send a JMS message.

Implementing a JMS message producer

In this section, we will develop a simple JSF application. One of the CDI managed beans in our application will produce a JMS message and send it to the queue we configured in the previous section.

Let's create a new Java class named `JmsMessageModel`. This class will store the message text that will be sent to the queue.

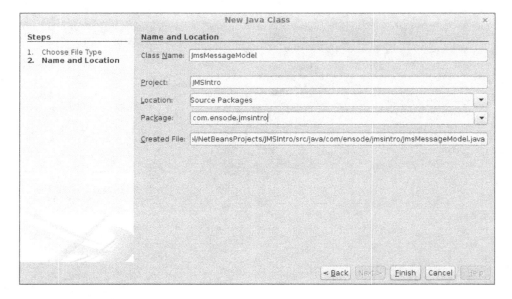

We should then annotate the class with the `@Named` annotation to make the class a CDI named bean. We should also annotate the class with the `@RequestScoped` annotation to give it a scope of request.

We should add a private variable named `msgText` of type String, along with its corresponding getter and setter methods.

 Generating getter and setter methods
Getter and setter methods can be automatically generated by pressing *Alt + Insert*, and then selecting Getter and Setter

When finished, our class should look like this:

```
package com.ensode.jmsintro;

import javax.enterprise.context.RequestScoped;
import javax.inject.Named;

@Named
@RequestScoped
public class JmsMessageModel {

    private String msgText;

    public String getMsgText() {
        return msgText;
    }

    public void setMsgText(String msgText) {
        this.msgText = msgText;
    }

}
```

We now turn our attention to the controller, which will actually send the JMS message to the queue we created in the previous section. Using the NetBeans wizard, let's create a new Java class named `JmsMessageController` and annotate it with the `@Named` and `@RequestScoped` annotations.

Now, our class should look like this:

```
package com.ensode.jmsintro;

import javax.enterprise.context.RequestScoped;
import javax.inject.Named;

@Named
@RequestScoped
public class JmsMessageController {

}
```

We need to add some code to send a JMS message. NetBeans can aid us in this task. All we need to do is click on *Alt + Insert* and select **Send JMS Message...**:

Now, a dialog window appropriately titled **Send JMS Message** pops up. We need to select the **Server Destinations** radio button and select **jms/myQueue** from the corresponding dropdown (this is the queue we created in the previous section).

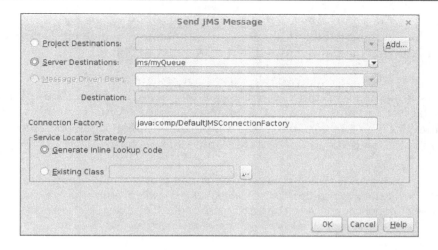

When we click on **OK**, NetBeans automatically generates the code to send the JMS message:

```
package com.ensode.jmsintro;

import javax.annotation.Resource;
import javax.enterprise.context.RequestScoped;
import javax.inject.Inject;
import javax.inject.Named;
import javax.jms.JMSConnectionFactory;
import javax.jms.JMSContext;
import javax.jms.Queue;

@Named
@RequestScoped
public class JmsMessageController {
    @Resource(mappedName = "jms/myQueue")
    private Queue myQueue;
    @Inject
    @JMSConnectionFactory("java:comp/DefaultJMSConnectionFactory")
    private JMSContext context;

    private void sendJMSMessageToMyQueue(String messageData) {
        context.createProducer().send(myQueue, messageData);
    }

}
```

NetBeans generates a private variable called `myQueue` of the type `javax.jms.Queue`. This variable is annotated with the `@Resource` annotation, which binds the `myQueue` variable to the JMS queue we created in the previous section.

NetBeans also adds a private variable named `context` of the type `JMSContext`. This variable is annotated with the `@Inject` annotation, which results in the application server (GlassFish, in our case) injecting an instance of `JMSContext` to this variable at runtime. The `context` variable is also annotated with `@JMSConnectionFactory`, which binds the context variable to a JMS connection factory.

 In previous versions of Java EE, we had to create a JMS connection factory in addition to a JMS destination. Java EE 7 introduces a default connection factory that we can use in our JMS code. The NetBeans generated code takes advantage of this new Java EE 7 feature.

Finally, NetBeans adds a method to actually send the JMS message to the queue. The name of the generated method depends on the name of the queue. In our case, we named our queue `myQueue`; therefore, NetBeans named the method `sendJMSMessageToMyQueue()`.

This method uses the simplified JMS 2.0 API added in Java EE 7. The body of the method invokes the `createProducer()` method of the generated `JMSContext` instance. This method returns an instance of `javax.jms.JMSProducer`. Then, the method invokes the `send()` method of `JMSProducer`; this method sends the message to the queue. The first parameter of the `send()` method is the JMS destination that will receive the message; the second parameter is a string that contains the message.

There are several message types we can send to a JMS queue (all standard JMS message types are described later in the chapter). The most common message type is `javax.jms.TextMessage`. In previous versions of the JMS API, we had to explicitly use this interface to send JMS messages containing simple strings. The new JMS 2.0 API generates an instance of a class implementing this interface behind the scenes when we send a string as a message; this simplifies our work as application developers.

After generating the JMS code with a few simple clicks, we need to add a few simple modifications to our code. To do this, simply invoke the generated code with the message we wish to send:

```
package com.ensode.jmsintro;

import javax.annotation.Resource;
import javax.enterprise.context.RequestScoped;
import javax.inject.Inject;
import javax.inject.Named;
```

```
import javax.jms.JMSConnectionFactory;
import javax.jms.JMSContext;
import javax.jms.Queue;

@Named
@RequestScoped
public class JmsMessageController {

    @Inject
    private JmsMessageModel jmsMessageModel;

    @Resource(mappedName = "jms/myQueue")
    private Queue myQueue;
    @Inject
    @JMSConnectionFactory("java:comp/DefaultJMSConnectionFactory")
    private JMSContext context;

    public String sendMsg() {
        sendJMSMessageToMyQueue(jmsMessageModel.getMsgText());
        return "confirmation";
    }

    private void sendJMSMessageToMyQueue(String messageData) {
        context.createProducer().send(myQueue, messageData);
    }

}
```

As we can see, all we had to do was to inject an instance of the JmsMessageModel class we developed earlier and add a simple method that will invoke the generated sendJMSMessageToMyQueue() method, passing the message text as a parameter.

Next, we need to modify the generated index.xhtml file to add a form binding the msgText variable of JmsMessageModel to a text field and a command button that invokes the sendMsg() method when it is clicked. The code is as follows:

```
<?xml version='1.0' encoding='UTF-8' ?>
<!DOCTYPE html PUBLIC "-//W3C//DTD XHTML 1.0 Transitional//EN"
"http://www.w3.org/TR/xhtml1/DTD/xhtml1-transitional.dtd">
<html xmlns="http://www.w3.org/1999/xhtml"
      xmlns:h="http://xmlns.jcp.org/jsf/html">
    <h:head>
        <title>Send JMS Message</title>
    </h:head>
    <h:body>
```

```
<h:form>
    <h:panelGrid columns="2">
        <h:outputLabel for="msgText" value="Enter Message
Text:"/>
        <h:inputText id="msgText"
            value="#{jmsMessageModel.msgText}"/>
        <h:panelGroup/>
        <h:commandButton value="Submit"
            action="#{jmsMessageController.sendMsg()}"/>
    </h:panelGrid>
</h:form>
</h:body>
</html>
```

The `<h:inputText>` tag binds user input to the `msgText` variable of `JMSMessageModel` via its Unified Expression Language value binding expression (`#{jmsMessageModel.msgText}`).

As is evident from the value of its `action` attribute, the `<h:commandButton>` tag passes control to the `sendMsg()` method of `JmsMessageController` when the user clicks on the rendered button. As we discussed in the chapter, `JmsMessageController.sendMsg()` takes the value of `JmsMessageModel.msgText` and puts it in a message queue. The `JmsMessageController.sendMsg()` method also directs the user to a simple confirmation page. The code is as follows:

```
<?xml version='1.0' encoding='UTF-8' ?>
<!DOCTYPE html PUBLIC "-//W3C//DTD XHTML 1.0 Transitional//EN"
"http://www.w3.org/TR/xhtml1/DTD/xhtml1-transitional.dtd">
<html xmlns="http://www.w3.org/1999/xhtml"
    xmlns:h="http://xmlns.jcp.org/jsf/html">
    <h:head>
        <title>JMS message sent</title>
    </h:head>
    <h:body>
        JMS message sent successfully.
    </h:body>
</html>
```

As we can see, the confirmation page for our example is very simple. It simply displays the message **JMS message sent successfully** on the browser.

Now that we are done producing a message and placing it in a JMS queue, we will see how to develop code that will retrieve the message from the queue.

Consuming JMS messages with message-driven beans

The most common way of implementing JMS message consumers is by developing message-driven beans. Message-driven beans are a special type of Enterprise JavaBean (EJB) whose purpose is to listen to JMS messages on a message queue or topic. Message-driven beans provide EJB features such as transactions and scalability.

 In real systems, JMS message producers and JMS message consumers will be developed in separate NetBeans projects, as these are usually completely different systems. For simplicity, we will develop both the JMS producer and consumer in the same NetBeans project.

We can develop message-driven beans in NetBeans by going to **File | New File**, selecting the **Enterprise JavaBeans** category, and selecting the **Message-Driven Bean** file type.

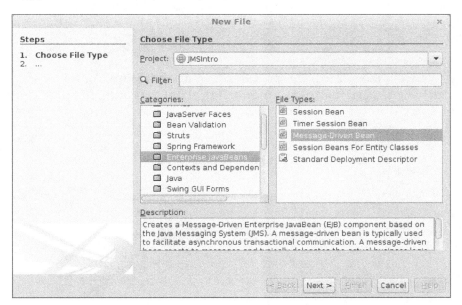

Then, we need to enter an **EJB Name** and select an appropriate value for the **Project Destinations** or **Server Destinations** fields; in our example, we need to select the server destination we created earlier in the chapter.

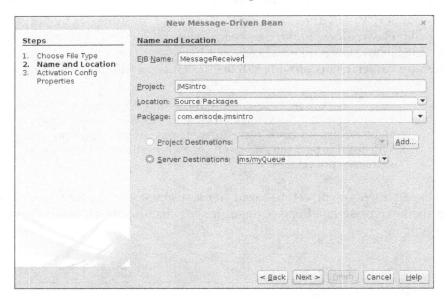

In the next step in the wizard, we can select several **Activation Config Properties** that are used to provide information about the configuration of our message-driven bean.

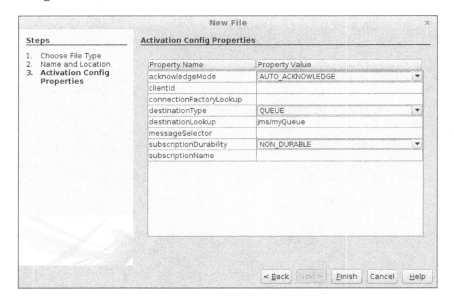

The following table explains the different activation configuration properties:

Activation configuration property	Valid values	Description
acknowledgeMode	AUTO_ACKNOWLEDGE or DUPS_OK_ACKNOWLEDGE	When set to AUTO_ACKNOWLEDGE, the application server acknowledges the message immediately after it is received. When set to DUPS_OK_ACKNOWLEDGE, the application server acknowledges the message at any time after it has received the message.
clientId	Free form	This is the client ID for durable subscribers. This is only used when using the pub/sub messaging domains (that is, topics instead of queues).
connectionFactoryLookup	Free form	This is the JNDI name of the JMS connection factory, and the default value is the JNDI name of the default connection factory.
destinationType	QUEUE or TOPIC	This defines whether the destination type is a queue (for the point-to-point messaging domain) or topic (for the pub/sub messaging domain).
destinationLookup	Free form	This is the JNDI name of the destination (queue or topic).
messageSelector	Free form	This allows message-driven beans to be selective about which messages they process.

Activation configuration property	Valid values	Description
subscriptionDurability	NON_DURABLE or DURABLE	This specifies whether a subscription is durable or nondurable. Durable subscriptions survive an application server restart or crash and they are only used for JMS topics (pub/sub messaging domain).
subscriptionName	Free form	This sets the subscription name for durable subscriptions.

For our example, we simply need to accept all of the default values and click on the **Finish** button. The following code shows the generated message-driven bean:

```
package com.ensode.jmsintro;

import javax.ejb.ActivationConfigProperty;
import javax.ejb.MessageDriven;
import javax.jms.Message;
import javax.jms.MessageListener;

@MessageDriven(activationConfig = {
    @ActivationConfigProperty(propertyName =
    "destinationLookup", propertyValue = "jms/myQueue"),
    @ActivationConfigProperty(propertyName = "destinationType",
    propertyValue = "javax.jms.Queue")
})
public class MessageReceiver implements MessageListener {

    public MessageReceiver() {
    }

    @Override
    public void onMessage(Message message) {
    }

}
```

The `@MessageDriven` annotation marks our class as a message-driven bean. Its `activationConfig` attribute accepts an array of `@ActivationConfigProperty` annotations, each of which specifies a JMS property name and value. Both the `@MessageDriven` annotation and the corresponding `@ActivationConfig` annotations are generated automatically from the values we pick on the last page of the NetBeans **New Message-Driven Bean** wizard.

Notice that the generated class implements the `javax.jms.MessageListener` interface. This is a requirement for message-driven beans. This interface defines a single method, the `onMessage()` method, which takes an instance of a class implementing `javax.jms.Message` as its sole parameter and returns void. This method is invoked automatically when a message is received in the JMS destination where the message-driven bean is listening. We need to add our custom processing to this method to handle the received message, as shown in the following code:

```
@Override
public void onMessage(Message message) {
    TextMessage textMessage = (TextMessage) message;
    try {
        System.out.println("received message: " +
            textMessage.getText());
    } catch (JMSException ex) {
        Logger.getLogger(MessageReceiver.class.getName()).log(
            Level.SEVERE, null, ex);
    }
}
```

All JMS message types extend the `javax.jms.Message` interface. In order to process the message, we need to cast it to the specific `Message` subinterface. In our case, the message we received is an instance of `javax.jms.TextMessage`.

In our simple example, we simply sent the message content to the application server log by invoking `System.out.println()` and passing the value `textMessage.getText()` as a parameter. The `getText()` method of `javax.jms.TextMessage` returns a string containing the message text. In a real application, we would do something more substantial, such as populating database tables from the message contents or rerouting the message to another JMS destination based on the contents of the message.

Last but not least, the `getText()` method of `javax.jms.TextMessage` can potentially throw a `JMSException`; therefore, we need to add a `catch` block to handle the exception.

Seeing our messaging application in action

Now that we have finished developing our application, it is time to see it in action; we can deploy it and run it in one shot by right-clicking on the project and selecting **Run Project**.

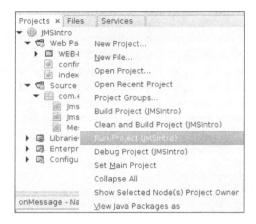

After a brief wait, the browser will automatically pop up to display the index page of our application.

After entering some text in the text field and clicking on **Submit**, we can see the output of the onMessage() method on our message-driven bean on the application server log.

As we can see, developing messaging applications using the JMS 2.0 API is very simple, and it is made even simpler by employing NetBeans features such as code generation and wizards.

In our example, we discussed only one message type, namely `javax.jms.TextMessage`. In the following table, we briefly describe all JMS message types:

Subinterface	Description
BytesMessage	This is used to send an array of bytes as a message.
MapMessage	This is used to send name-value pairs as messages. The names must be string objects and the values must be either primitive types or Java objects.
ObjectMessage	This is used to send serializable objects as messages. A serializable object is an instance of any class that implements `java.io.Serializable`.
StreamMessage	This is used to send a stream of Java primitive types as a message.
TextMessage	This is used to send a string as a message.

Summary

In this chapter, we covered an introduction to JMS and messaging systems in general. We talked about the two JMS messaging domains, namely the PTP messaging domain, in which a single listener processes a message, and the pub/sub messaging domain, in which all subscribed message listeners process the message.

Then, we covered how to create JMS resources such as message queues quickly and easily by taking advantage of the NetBeans **JMS Resource** wizard.

We also covered how to send JMS messages using JMS 2.0 included in Java EE 7, and we saw how NetBeans can generate most of the JMS boilerplate code.

Then, we turned our attention to developing code to receive and process JMS messages, specifically how to develop message-driven beans via the NetBeans **Message-Driven Bean** wizard.

Java API for JSON Processing

8

JSON (short for JavaScript Object Notation) is a lightweight data interchange format. JSON's primary advantage over other data interchange formats such as XML is that JSON is both easy for humans to read and easy for computers to generate and parse. It is commonly used in many modern web applications.

Java EE 7 introduces the Java API for **JSON Processing (JSON-P)**, which is a standard Java EE API to parse and generate JSON data.

JSON-P provides two ways to both parse and generate JSON data: the object model API and the streaming API.

In this chapter, we will cover the following topics:

- The JSON-P object model API:
    - Generating JSON data with the JSON-P object model API
    - Parsing JSON data with the JSON-P object model API

- The JSON-P streaming API:
    - Generating JSON data with the JSON-P streaming API
    - Parsing JSON data with the JSON-P streaming API

The JSON-P object model API

The JSON-P model API allows us to generate an in-memory tree structured representation of a JSON object. The JSON-P API uses the builder pattern, which allows us as application developers to easily create a JSON representation of a Java object.

Generating JSON data with the JSON-P object model API

When using the JSON-P object model API, we typically start by invoking the add() method of an implementation of the JsonObjectBuilder interface. This method returns an instance of another JsonObjectBuilder interface implementation. We can chain invocations of JsonObject.add() together, allowing us to easily create a JSON representation from a Java object. The following example illustrates this process:

```java
package com.ensode.jsonpmodelapi;

//imports omitted

@Named
@RequestScoped
public class JsonPModelApiBean {

    @Inject
    private Person person;
    private String jsonStr;

    public String generateJson() {
        JsonObjectBuilder jsonObjectBuilder =
            Json.createObjectBuilder();

        JsonObject jsonObject = jsonObjectBuilder.
                add("firstName", person.getFirstName()).
                add("middleName", person.getMiddleName()).
                add("lastName", person.getLastName()).
                add("gender", person.getGender()).
                add("age", person.getAge()).
                build();

        StringWriter stringWriter = new StringWriter();

        try (JsonWriter jsonWriter = Json.createWriter(stringWriter))
        {

            jsonWriter.writeObject(jsonObject);
        }
        setJsonStr(stringWriter.toString());

        //JSF Dynamic navigation
        return "generated_json";
    }

    //other methods omitted
}
```

This example part of a JSF application, specifically a CDI named bean. We are only showing code that is relevant to the discussion.

In this example, we are generating a JSON representation of a simple `Person` Java class containing a few simple properties such as `firstName`, `middleName`, `lastName`, and so on, along with the corresponding getter and setter methods.

The first thing we do in our example is obtain an instance of a class implementing the `JsonObjectBuilder` interface by invoking the static `createObjectBuilder()` method on the `Json` class. This method returns an instance of a class implementing the `JsonObjectBuilder` interface, which we can use as a starting point to generate a JSON representation of a Java object.

Once we obtain an instance of `JsonObjectBuilder`, we need to invoke one of its overloaded `add()` methods, all of which accept a string as their first parameter and a value as its second parameter. This method returns another instance of `JsonObjectBuilder`, as seen in our example. We can chain invocations of the `add()` method to quickly and easily generate the final JSON representation we need. What we are seeing here is the builder pattern in action.

In our example, we used two versions of the `JsonObjectBuilder.add()` method, one accepting a string as its second parameter and another one accepting an integer as its second parameter. (In our example, we passed an `Integer` object to this method. Java unboxing takes care of converting our parameter to an `int` primitive) There are several other overloaded versions of `JsonObjectBuilder.add()`. This allows great flexibility when building JSON representations of Java objects via the JSON-P object model API. The following table describes all overloaded versions of `JsonObjectBuilder.add()`; in all cases, the first parameter corresponds to the name of the JSON property on the generated JSON object, and the second parameter is the corresponding value in the generated JSON.

add method	Description
`add(String name, BigDecimal value)`	This adds a `JsonNumber` representation of a `BigDecimal` value to the generated JSON object
`add(String name, BigInteger value)`	This adds a `JsonNumber` representation of a `BigInteger` value to the generated JSON object
`add(String name, boolean value)`	This adds either a `JsonValue.TRUE` or `JsonValue.FALSE` value to the generated JSON object, depending on the Boolean value passed as a parameter

add method	Description
add(String name, double value)	This adds a JsonNumber representation of a double value to the generated JSON object
add(String name, int value)	This adds a JsonNumber representation of an int value to the generated JSON object
add(String name, JsonArrayBuilder builder)	This adds an array of JSON objects to the generated JSON object
add(String name, JsonObjectBuilder builder)	This adds another JSON object to the generated JSON object
add(String name, JsonValue value)	This adds an implementation of the JsonValue interface to the generated JSON object
add(String name, long value)	This adds a JsonNumber representation of a long value to the generated JSON object
add(String name, String value)	This adds a string value to the generated JSON object

Lets go back to our example. After invoking the chain of add() methods, we invoke the build() method on the resulting JsonObjectBuilder implementation. This method invocation returns an instance of a class implementing JsonObject.

Once we have a JsonObject implementation, typically we would want to convert it to its string representation. To convert a JsonObject implementation to a JSON string, we need to invoke the static createWriter() method on the Json class, passing a new instance of StringWriter as a parameter. This method returns an instance of a class implementing the JsonWriter interface. Now, we need to invoke the writeObject() method of JsonWriter, passing the JsonObject instance we previously created as a parameter. This method invocation populates the StringWriter object we used to create our JsonWriter interface. We can obtain the JSON string representation of our object by simply invoking the toString() method of our StringWriter object.

Our example in action

Our example consists of a simple web application that uses JSF to populate a CDI named bean and generates a JSON string from this bean. The markup for our simple JSF page populating the CDI named bean is as follows:

```
<?xml version='1.0' encoding='UTF-8' ?>
<!DOCTYPE html PUBLIC "-//W3C//DTD XHTML 1.0 Transitional//EN"
"http://www.w3.org/TR/xhtml1/DTD/xhtml1-transitional.dtd">
<html xmlns="http://www.w3.org/1999/xhtml"
      xmlns:h="http://xmlns.jcp.org/jsf/html">
```

```
    <h:head>
        <title>Object to JSON With the JSON-P Object Model API</title>
    </h:head>
    <h:body>
        <h:form>
            <h:panelGrid columns="2">
                <h:outputLabel for="firstName" value="First Name"/>
                <h:inputText id="firstName" value="#{person.
firstName}"/>
                <h:outputLabel for="middleName" value="Middle Name"/>
                <h:inputText id="middleName"
                    value="#{person.middleName}"/>
                <h:outputLabel for="lastName" value="Last Name"/>
                <h:inputText id="lastName" value="#{person.
lastName}"/>
                <h:outputLabel for="gender" value="Gender"/>
                <h:inputText id="gender" value="#{person.gender}"/>
                <h:outputLabel for="age" value="Age"/>
                <h:inputText id="age" value="#{person.age}"/>
                <h:panelGroup/>
                <h:commandButton value="Submit"
                    action="#{jsonPModelApiBean.generateJson()}"/>
            </h:panelGrid>
        </h:form>
    </h:body>
</html>
```

As we can see, the preceding markup is very simple. It consists of a form with
several input text fields bound to properties in the `Person` CDI named bean. There is
also a command button that transfers control to the `generateJson()` method of the
`JsonPModelApiBean` class we discussed in the previous section.

Here is the source code for the `Person` bean:

```
package com.ensode.jsonpmodelapi;

import java.io.Serializable;
import javax.enterprise.context.SessionScoped;
import javax.inject.Named;

@Named
@SessionScoped
public class Person implements Serializable {
```

```
    private String firstName;
    private String middleName;
    private String lastName;
    private String gender;
    private Integer age;

    public String getFirstName() {
        return firstName;
    }

    public void setFirstName(String firstName) {
        this.firstName = firstName;
    }

    public String getMiddleName() {
        return middleName;
    }

    public void setMiddleName(String middleName) {
        this.middleName = middleName;
    }

    public String getLastName() {
        return lastName;
    }

    public void setLastName(String lastName) {
        this.lastName = lastName;
    }

    public String getGender() {
        return gender;
    }

    public void setGender(String gender) {
        this.gender = gender;
    }

    public Integer getAge() {
        return age;
    }

    public void setAge(Integer age) {
        this.age = age;
    }

}
```

Again, there is nothing special about the `Person` class; it's just a simple CDI named bean with private properties and corresponding setter and getter methods.

We can execute our application as usual by right-clicking on the project and selecting **Run**.

After a few seconds, the browser should pop up and render our JSF page.

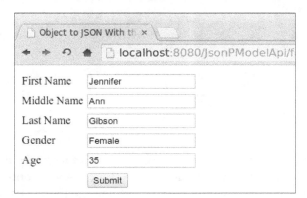

When we click on the **Submit** button, control goes to the controller we discussed in the previous section. Then, we navigate to the JSF page displaying the JSON representation of the `Person` object.

Here is the markup of the JSF page displaying the JSON string:

```
<?xml version='1.0' encoding='UTF-8' ?>
<!DOCTYPE html PUBLIC "-//W3C//DTD XHTML 1.0 Transitional//EN"
"http://www.w3.org/TR/xhtml1/DTD/xhtml1-transitional.dtd">
<html xmlns="http://www.w3.org/1999/xhtml"
      xmlns:h="http://xmlns.jcp.org/jsf/html">
```

```
<h:head>
    <title>Generated JSON with the JSON-P Object Model API</title>
</h:head>
<h:body>
    <h:form>
        <h:panelGrid columns="2">
            <h:outputLabel for="parsedJson" value="Parsed JSON"/>
            <h:inputTextarea
                value="#{jsonPModelApiBean.jsonStr}" rows="4"/>
            <h:panelGroup/>
            <h:commandButton value="Submit"
                action="#{jsonPModelApiBean.parseJson()}"/>
        </h:panelGrid>
    </h:form>
</h:body>
</html>
```

It simply displays a text area that contains the JSON representation of the Person object, as shown in the following screenshot:

Notice how the property names match the ones we used to create the JSON object in the previous section, and all the values match the values we entered on the input page we just discussed. At this point, we can modify the JSON string displayed in the text area (making sure that it is still properly formatted JSON). When the user clicks on the **Submit** button, the Person object will be repopulated from the updated JSON string.

Parsing JSON data with the JSON-P object model API

Now that we know how to generate JSON from Java objects, let's focus our attention on the opposite functionality, populating Java objects from JSON strings.

The following code illustrates how to do this:

```java
package com.ensode.jsonpmodelapi;

//imports omitted

@Named
@RequestScoped
public class JsonPModelApiBean {

    @Inject
    private Person person;
    private String jsonStr;

    public String generateJson() {
        //body omitted for brevity
    }

    public String parseJson() {
        JsonObject jsonObject;

        try (JsonReader jsonReader = Json.createReader(
            new StringReader(jsonStr))) {
            jsonObject = jsonReader.readObject();
        }

        person.setFirstName(jsonObject.getString("firstName"));
        person.setMiddleName(jsonObject.getString(
            "middleName"));
        person.setLastName(jsonObject.getString("lastName"));
        person.setGender(jsonObject.getString("gender"));
        person.setAge(jsonObject.getInt("age"));

        return "display_populated_obj";
    }

    public String getJsonStr() {
        return jsonStr;
    }

    public void setJsonStr(String jsonStr) {
        this.jsonStr = jsonStr;
    }

}
```

The first thing we need to do is create a new instance of `java.io.StringReader` from our JSON string. We do this by passing a string containing our JSON data to the constructor of `StringReader`. Then, we pass the resulting `StringReader` instance to the static `createReader()` method of JSON-P's `javax.json.Json` class. This method invocation returns an implementation of the `javax.json.JsonReader` interface, which we then use to obtain an implementation of `javax.json.JsonObject`.

The JSON object contains several *get* methods we can use to obtain data from the JSON string. These methods take the JSON property name as a parameter and return the corresponding value. In our example we used two of these methods, namely `getString()` and `getInt()`, and we used them to populate an instance of our `Person` object. The following table summarizes all of the available get methods:

get method	Description
`getBoolean(String name)`	This returns the value of the specified property as a Boolean.
`getInt(String name)`	This returns the value of the specified property as an integer.
`getJsonArray(String name)`	This returns the value of the specified property as an array in the form of a `JsonArray` implementation.
`getJsonNumber(String name)`	This returns the value of the specified numeric property as a `JsonNumber` implementation. The value can then be converted to int, long, or double by invoking `intValue()`, `longValue()`, or `doubleValue()`, respectively.
`getJsonObject(String name)`	This returns the value of the specified property as a `JsonObject` implementation.
`getJsonString(String name)`	This returns the value of the specified property as a `JsonString` implementation.
`getString(String name)`	This returns the value of the specified property as a string.

Let's go back to our example. You can see that the `parseJson()` method of our `JsonModelApiBean` controller class returns the string `display_populated_obj`. Therefore, based on JSF conventions, we know that it will navigate to a JSF page named `display_populated_obj.xhtml`. The markup for this page is as follows:

```
<?xml version='1.0' encoding='UTF-8' ?>
<!DOCTYPE html PUBLIC "-//W3C//DTD XHTML 1.0 Transitional//EN"
"http://www.w3.org/TR/xhtml1/DTD/xhtml1-transitional.dtd">
<html xmlns="http://www.w3.org/1999/xhtml"
      xmlns:h="http://xmlns.jcp.org/jsf/html">
    <h:head>
        <title>Java Object Properties Populated from JSON</title>
```

```
            </h:head>
            <h:body>
                <table>
                    <tr>
                        <td>
                            First Name:
                        </td>
                        <td>
                            #{person.firstName}
                        </td>
                    </tr>
                    <tr>
                        <td>
                            Middle Name:
                        </td>
                        <td>
                            #{person.middleName}
                        </td>
                    </tr>
                    <tr>
                        <td>
                            Last Name:
                        </td>
                        <td>
                            #{person.lastName}
                        </td>
                    </tr>
                    <tr>
                        <td>
                            Gender:
                        </td>
                        <td>
                            #{person.gender}
                        </td>
                    </tr>
                    <tr>
                        <td>
                            Age:
                        </td>
                        <td>
                            #{person.age}
                        </td>
                    </tr>
                </table>
            </h:body>
        </html>
```

As we can see, all it does is display all of the `Person` object properties via the Unified Expression Language. The object properties are repopulated from the JSON string that was displayed on the previous page, which is bound to the `jsonStr` property of `JsonPModelApiBean`.

As we can see, populating and parsing JSON using JSON-P's object model API is fairly straightforward and intuitive. It works great when we are dealing with smaller amounts of data. It might be possible, however, to run into performance problems when dealing with large amounts of data. In such instances, we can use JSON-P's streaming API.

The JSON-P streaming API

The JSON-P streaming API allows us to read and write JSON data to and from a stream (a subclass of `java.io.OutputStream` or a subclass of `java.io.Writer`). The JSON-P streaming API has better performance and better memory efficiency than the JSON-P object model API. These performance and efficiency gains, however, come with some limitations. The JSON-P streaming API only allows JSON data to be read sequentially; we can't access JSON properties directly like we can with the object model API. In general, we should use the streaming API if we need to handle large amount of JSON data; otherwise, the simpler object model API should be used.

In the following sections, we will reimplement the example from the previous section using the JSON-P streaming API.

 Since the examples on this section mirror the functionality we implemented in the previous sections, we will not show any screenshots of our sample application in action. They will be identical to the ones we saw earlier on this chapter.

Generating JSON data with the JSON-P streaming API

When using the JSON-P streaming API, we generate JSON data via the `JsonGenerator` class, invoking one or more of its several overloaded `write()` methods to add JSON properties and corresponding values to the JSON data.

The following example illustrates how to generate data via the JSON-P streaming API:

```
package com.ensode.jsonpstreamingapi;

//imports omitted

@Named
@RequestScoped
public class JsonPStreamingApiBean {

    @Inject
    private Person person;
    private String jsonStr;

    public String generateJson() {
        StringWriter stringWriter = new StringWriter();
        try (JsonGenerator jsonGenerator
                = Json.createGenerator(stringWriter)) {
                    jsonGenerator.writeStartObject().
                    write("firstName", person.getFirstName()).
                    write("middleName", person.getMiddleName()).
                    write("lastName", person.getLastName()).
                    write("gender", person.getGender()).
                    write("age", person.getAge()).
                    writeEnd();
        }

        setJsonStr(stringWriter.toString());
        return "generated_json";
    }
}
```

 This example is part of a JSF application, specifically a CDI named bean, and we are only showing code that is relevant to our discussion.

To generate JSON data using the JSON-P streaming API, first we need to invoke a call to the static `Json.createGenerator()` method. This method returns an instance of a class implementing `javax.json.stream.JsonGenerator`. There are two overloaded versions of the `Json.createGenerator()` method, one takes an instance of `java.io.OutputStream` (or one of its subclasses) as a parameter and the other one takes an instance of `java.io.Writer` (or one of its subclasses) as a parameter. In our example we chose the second version, passing an instance of `java.io.StringWriter` to `Json.createGenerator()`.

Once we obtain an instance of `JsonGenerator`, we need to invoke the `writeStartObject()` method on it. This method writes the start object character of JSON (the opening curly brace {) to the `OutputStream` or `Writer` we passed to `Json.createGenerator()`. The `writeStartObject()` method returns another instance of `JsonGenerator`, allowing us to immediately invoke the `write()` method on the resulting `JsonGenerator`.

The `write()` method of `JsonGenerator` adds a JSON property to our JSON data. Its first parameter is a string containing the property value, and its second parameter is the corresponding value. There are several overloaded versions of the `write()` method, one for each corresponding supported JSON value type (either `String` or a numeric type such as `BigInteger` or `double`). In our example, we are only adding properties of the type `String` and `Integer`, therefore we used the corresponding versions of the `write()` methods. The following table lists all of the existing versions of the `write()` method:

write() method	Description
`write(String name, BigDecimal value)`	Adds a numeric property of type `BigDecimal` to our JSON data
`write(String name, BigInteger value)`	Adds a numeric property of type `BigInteger` to our JSON data
`write(String name, JsonValue value)`	Adds a property of type `JsonValue` or one of its subinterfaces (`JsonArray`, `JsonNumber`, `JsonObject`, `JsonString` or `JsonStructure`) to our JSON data
`write(String name, String value)`	Adds a property of type `String` to our JSON data
`write(String name, boolean value)`	Adds a `boolean` property to our JSON data
`write(String name, double value)`	Adds a numeric property of type `double` to our JSON data
`write(String name, int value)`	Writes a numeric property of type `int` to our JSON data
`write(String name, long value)`	Writes a numeric property of type `long` to our JSON data

Once we are done adding properties to our JSON data, we need to invoke the `writeEnd()` method of `JsonGenerator`, which adds the JSON end object character (represented by a closing curly brace }) to our JSON string.

At this point, the `Writer` or `OutputStream` we passed to `Json.createGenerator()` contains a complete JSON object. What we do with it depends on our application requirements; in our example we simply invoke the `toString()` method of the `StringWriter` instance we used and assign its return value to the `jsonStr` variable.

Parsing JSON data with the JSON-P streaming API

The following example illustrates how we can parse JSON data using the JSON-P streaming API:

```
package com.ensode.jsonpstreamingapi;

//imports omitted

@Named
@RequestScoped
public class JsonPStreamingApiBean {

    @Inject
    private Person person;
    private String jsonStr;

    public String parseJson() {
        StringReader stringReader = new StringReader(jsonStr);

        JsonParser jsonParser = Json.createParser(stringReader);

        Map<String, Object> jsonMap = new HashMap<>();
        String jsonKeyNm = null;
        Object jsonVal = null;

        while (jsonParser.hasNext()) {
            JsonParser.Event event = jsonParser.next();

            if (event.equals(Event.KEY_NAME)) {
                jsonKeyNm = jsonParser.getString();
            } else if (event.equals(Event.VALUE_STRING)) {
                jsonVal = jsonParser.getString();
```

```
        } else if (event.equals(Event.VALUE_NUMBER)) {
            jsonVal = jsonParser.getInt();
        }

        jsonMap.put(jsonKeyNm, jsonVal);
    }

    person.setFirstName((String) jsonMap.get("firstName"));
    person.setMiddleName((String) jsonMap.get("middleName"));
    person.setLastName((String) jsonMap.get("lastName"));
    person.setGender((String) jsonMap.get("gender"));
    person.setAge((Integer) jsonMap.get("age"));

    return "display_populated_obj";
    }

}
```

In order to read and parse JSON data using the JSON-P streaming API, we need to obtain an implementation of the `JsonParser` interface. The `Json` class has two overloaded versions of a `createParser()` method we can use to obtain a `JsonParser` implementation. One version of `Json.createParser()` takes an instance of `java.io.InputStream` (or one of its subclasses) as its sole parameter, and the other version takes an instance of `java.io.Reader` (or one of its subclasses) as its sole parameter. In our example, we use the second version, passing an instance of `java.io.StringReader` (which extends `java.io.Reader`) that contains our JSON string as a parameter.

Once we obtain a reference to `JsonParser`, we invoke its `hasNext()` method in a while loop. The `JsonParser.hasNext()` method returns `true` if there are more property names or values to read from the JSON string, otherwise it returns `false`.

Inside the `while` loop, we invoke `JsonParser.next()`. This method returns an instance of the `JsonParser.Event` enum. The specific value of the `JsonParser.Event` enum we get from `JsonParser.next()` lets us know what type of data we are reading (key name, string value, numeric value, and so on). In our example, our JSON string contains only string and numeric values, so we only check for those two value types by comparing the `JsonParser.Event` instance we got from `JsonParser.next()` against `Event.VALUE_STRING` and `Event.VALUE_NUMBER`, respectively. We also check for a JSON key name by comparing the obtained value against `Event.KEY_NAME`. Once we have read a key/value pair combination from our JSON string, what we do with it depends on our application requirements. In our example, we simply populate a hash map using the corresponding values from our JSON string.

We only saw three of the possible values we can obtain when sequentially reading JSON data by invoking `JsonParser.next()`. The following table lists all of the possible values:

Event enum Value	Description
Event.START_OBJECT	Indicates the beginning of a JSON object
Event.END_OBJECT	Indicates the end of a JSON object
Event.KEY_NAME	Indicates the name of a JSON property
Event.VALUE_STRING	Indicates a `String` value was read
Event.VALUE_NUMBER	Indicates a numeric value was read
Event.VALUE_TRUE	Indicates a Boolean `true` value was read
Event.VALUE_FALSE	Indicates a Boolean `false` value was read
Event.VALUE_NULL	Indicates that a `null` value was read
Event.VALUE_START_ARRAY	Indicates that the start of an array was read
EVENT.VALUE_END_ARRAY	Indicates that the end of an array was read

Summary

In this chapter we covered JSON-P, which is a new addition to the Java EE specification. We covered how to generate and parse data using the simple JSON-P object model API, and then we switched our attention to the more performant and memory-efficient JSON-P streaming API, covering JSON data manipulation with this JSON-P API as well.

9
Java API for WebSocket

Traditionally, web applications consist of a request/response model. That is, the browser sends an HTTP request to the server and the server sends back an HTTP response. WebSocket is a new HTML5 technology that allows two-way, full-duplex communication between the client (typically a web browser) and the server. In other words, it allows the server to send data to the browser in real time, without having to wait for an HTTP request. Java EE 7 includes full support for developing WebSocket applications, and NetBeans includes some features that make developing WebSocket Java EE applications easier.

In this chapter, we will cover the following topics:

- Examining WebSocket code using samples included with NetBeans
- Developing a Java EE application using WebSocket

Examining the WebSocket code using samples included with NetBeans

NetBeans includes a lot of example projects that we can use as the basis for our own projects. One particularly useful sample included with NetBeans is an Echo application that uses WebSockets to output some server data on the browser.

To create the sample project, go to **File | New Project**, select **Java EE** under **Samples** from **Categories**, and select **Echo WebSocket (Java EE 7)** from **Projects**.

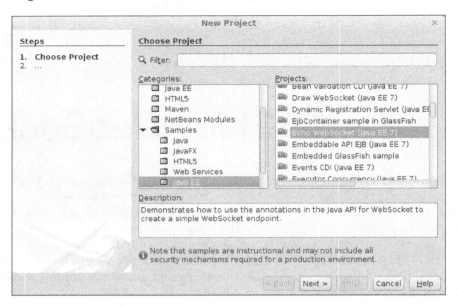

In the next screen of the wizard, select a project location or accept the default location.

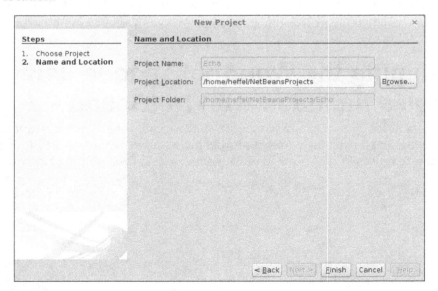

Click on **Finish** and the project is created.

The sample Echo application in action

Before looking at the generated source code, let's take a quick look at the sample Echo application in action. We can run it as usual by right-clicking on the project and selecting **Run**.

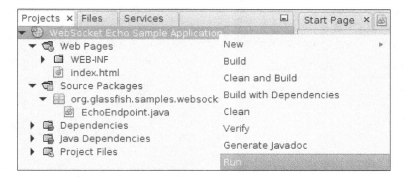

A few seconds after clicking on **Run**, the browser pops up and automatically runs the application.

The text **Hello WebSocket!** Is automatically prepopulated on the text input field. Clicking on the button labeled **Press me** sends the text to a WebSocket server endpoint, which simply sends the text back to the client. We can see the results of this at the bottom of the preceding screenshot.

The sample project consists of two files: an `index.html` file containing JavaScript functions that generate WebSocket events and a corresponding Java class that processes these events. We'll discuss the Java class first, and briefly cover the client-side JavaScript.

Examining the generated Java code

The following code snippet lists the Java source code for the generated WebSocket server endpoint:

```
package org.glassfish.samples.websocket.echo;

import javax.websocket.OnMessage;
import javax.websocket.server.ServerEndpoint;

@ServerEndpoint("/echo")
public class EchoEndpoint {

    @OnMessage
    public String echo(String message) {
        return message;
    }
}
```

A Java class that processes WebSocket requests on the server side is called a server endpoint. As we can see, developing a WebSocket server endpoint using the Java API for WebSocket requires very little code.

We can designate a Java class as a server endpoint by annotating it with the @ServerEndPoint annotation. Its value attribute indicates the Uniform Resource Identifier (URI) of the server endpoint, and clients (typically client-side web applications) access the server endpoint via this URI.

Any method annotated with the @OnMessage annotation is invoked automatically any time a client sends a message to the WebSocket server endpoint. Methods annotated with this annotation and expecting textual data must take a string argument, which will contain the contents of the message sent from the client. The contents of the message can be anything; however, it is a common practice for the clients to send JSON-formatted data. In the NetBeans sample application, a simple string is passed to the echo() method.

The value returned by the @OnMessage annotated method is sent back to the client. A typical use case is to send a JSON-formatted string; however, in this simple example, the string that was received as an argument is sent back to the client.

Examining the generated JavaScript code

The other file in the Echo WebSocket sample included with NetBeans is an HTML
file that contains embedded JavaScript used to communicate with the Java server
endpoint. Take a look at the following code:

```html
<html>
<head>
    <meta http-equiv="content-type"
        content="text/html; charset=ISO-8859-1">
</head>

<body>
<meta charset="utf-8">
<title>Web Socket JavaScript Echo Client</title>
<script language="javascript" type="text/javascript">
    var wsUri = getRootUri() + "/websocket-echo/echo";

    function getRootUri() {
        return "ws://" + (document.location.hostname == "" ?
"localhost" :
            document.location.hostname) + ":" +
                (document.location.port == "" ? "8080" :
                document.location.port);
    }

    function init() {
        output = document.getElementById("output");
    }

    function send_echo() {

        websocket = new WebSocket(wsUri);
        websocket.onopen = function (evt) {
            onOpen(evt)
        };
        websocket.onmessage = function (evt) {
            onMessage(evt)
        };
        websocket.onerror = function (evt) {
            onError(evt)
        };

    }
```

```
    function onOpen(evt) {
        writeToScreen("CONNECTED");
        doSend(textID.value);

    }

    function onMessage(evt) {
        writeToScreen("RECEIVED: " + evt.data);
    }

    function onError(evt) {
        writeToScreen('<span style="color: red;">ERROR:</span> ' +
            evt.data);
    }

    function doSend(message) {
        writeToScreen("SENT: " + message);
        websocket.send(message);
    }

    function writeToScreen(message) {
        var pre = document.createElement("p");
        pre.style.wordWrap = "break-word";
        pre.innerHTML = message;
        //alert(output);
        output.appendChild(pre);
    }

    window.addEventListener("load", init, false);

</script>

<h2 style="text-align: center;">WebSocket Echo Client</h2>

<br></br>

<div style="text-align: center;">
    <form action="">
        <input onclick="send_echo()" value="Press me" type="button">
        <input id="textID" name="message" value="Hello WebSocket!"
                    type="text"><br>
    </form>
</div>
<div id="output"></div>
</body>
</html>
```

What we are interested in here is the embedded JavaScript code between the `<script>` tags. You can see that the send_echo() JavaScript function creates a new JavaScript WebSocket object then assigns the onopen, onmessage, and onerror functions of the WebSocket object to the onOpen(), onMessage(), and onError() functions that are embedded in the code. Now, our onOpen() function will be automatically invoked when a WebSocket connection is opened, our onMessage() function will be called whenever a WebSocket message is received from the server, and our onError() function will be automatically called whenever there is a WebSocket error.

The Echo sample project simply updates the div with the ID of output with the message received from the server. This is done in the writeToScreen() function, which is invoked from the onMessage() function whenever a WebSocket message is received from the server.

The Echo sample project is a great way to understand how to write our own applications using the Java API for WebSocket. In the next section, we will write our own application, shamelessly borrowing as much as possible from the sample Echo application to make our job easier.

Building our own WebSocket applications

In the previous section, we saw how NetBeans provides sample WebSocket applications we can use as a base for our own projects. In this section, we will build a web application that contains a WebSocket server endpoint that will populate a form with default values.

To build a WebSocket application, create a web application project by going to **File | New Project,** selecting the **Java Web** option from the **Categories** list, and selecting **Web Application** from the **Projects** list.

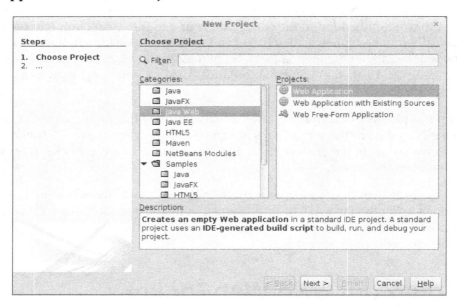

Then, we pick a name and location as usual.

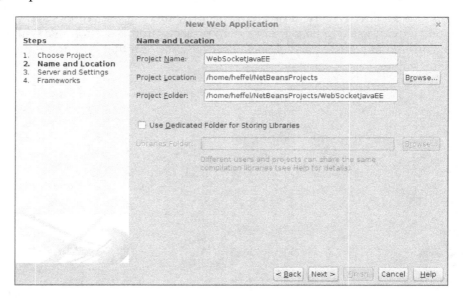

The Java API for WebSocket was introduced in Java EE 7; therefore, we must select this Java EE version if we want to develop WebSocket applications. The default values in this step of the wizard are sensible and can be used as they are:

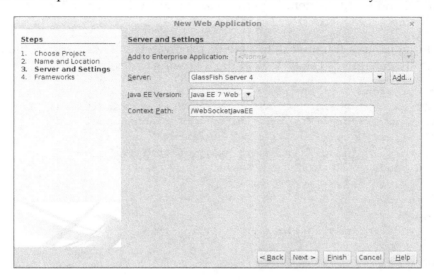

In our example, we will be using JSF for the user interface. Therefore, we need to select **JavaServer Faces** from the **Frameworks** list.

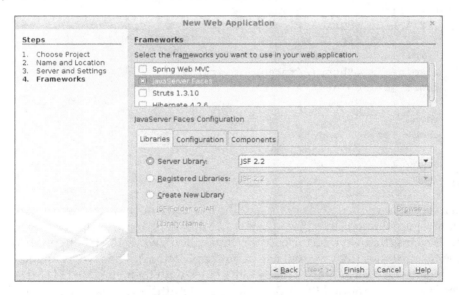

Now, we are ready to develop our WebSocket application.

Developing the user interface

Before developing the WebSocket-specific code, let's develop the user interface using JSF 2.2 and HTML5-friendly markup as explained in *Chapter 2, Developing Web Applications Using JavaServer Faces 2.2.*

When adding JSF as a framework to a NetBeans project, an `index.xhtml` file is automatically generated. Take a look at the following code:

```
<?xml version='1.0' encoding='UTF-8' ?>
<!DOCTYPE html PUBLIC "-//W3C//DTD XHTML 1.0 Transitional//EN"
"http://www.w3.org/TR/xhtml1/DTD/xhtml1-transitional.dtd">
<html xmlns="http://www.w3.org/1999/xhtml"
      xmlns:h="http://xmlns.jcp.org/jsf/html">
    <h:head>
        <title>Facelet Title</title>
    </h:head>
    <h:body>
        Hello from Facelets
    </h:body>
</html>
```

The generated markup uses JSF-specific tags. We need to make a few small changes to modify it to use HTML5-friendly markup. Take a look at the following code:

```
<?xml version='1.0' encoding='UTF-8' ?>
<!DOCTYPE html PUBLIC "-//W3C//DTD XHTML 1.0 Transitional//EN"
"http://www.w3.org/TR/xhtml1/DTD/xhtml1-transitional.dtd">
<html xmlns="http://www.w3.org/1999/xhtml"
      xmlns:jsf="http://xmlns.jcp.org/jsf">
    <head jsf:id="head">
        <title>Facelet Title</title>
    <head>
    <body jsf:id="body">
        Hello from Facelets
    </body>
</html>
```

The main change we made was to replace the `xmlns:h=http://xmlns.jcp.org/jsf/html` namespace with `xhmlns:jsf=http://xmlns.jsp.org/jsf`; the former specifies JSF-specific tags (that we won't use in our application), while the latter specifies JSF-specific attributes (that we will use in our applications). Then, we changed the JSF-specific `<h:head>` and `<h:body>` attributes with their standard HTML counterparts, and we added the JSF-specific `jsf:id` attribute to both tags. Recall from *Chapter 2, Developing Web Applications Using JavaServer Faces 2.2,* that to make JSF interpret HTML tags, we need to add at least one JSF-specific attribute to the tags.

Then, we need to add a form and a couple of simple input fields. Later, we will use the Java API for WebSocket to populate these fields with default values.

After making the previously mentioned modifications, our markup now looks like this:

```
<?xml version='1.0' encoding='UTF-8' ?>
<!DOCTYPE html PUBLIC "-//W3C//DTD XHTML 1.0 Transitional//EN"
"http://www.w3.org/TR/xhtml1/DTD/xhtml1-transitional.dtd">
<html xmlns="http://www.w3.org/1999/xhtml"
      xmlns:jsf="http://xmlns.jcp.org/jsf">
    <head jsf:id="head">
        <title>WebSocket and Java EE</title>
    </head>
    <body jsf:id="body">
        <form method="POST" jsf:prependId="false">
            <table>
                <tr>
                    <td>First Name</td>
                    <td>
                        <input type="text" jsf:id="firstName"
                                jsf:value="#{person.firstName}"/>
                    </td>
                </tr>
                <tr>
                    <td>Last Name</td>
                    <td>
                        <input type="text" jsf:id="lastName"
                                jsf:value="#{person.lastName}"/>
                    </td>
                </tr>
                <tr>
                    <td></td>
                    <td>
                      <input type="submit" value="Submit"
                        jsf:action="confirmation"/>
                    </td>
                </tr>
            </table>
        </form>
    </body>
</html>
```

We just added some simple HTML to the markup and used JSF-specific attributes so that the HTML tags are treated like their equivalent JSF-specific tags.

Note that the input fields in our markup are bound to properties of a CDI named bean with a name of person. The `Person` bean looks like this:

```java
package com.ensode.websocket;

import javax.enterprise.context.RequestScoped;
import javax.inject.Named;

@Named
@RequestScoped
public class Person {

    private String firstName;
    private String lastName;

    public String getFirstName() {
        return firstName;
    }

    public void setFirstName(String firstName) {
        this.firstName = firstName;
    }

    public String getLastName() {
        return lastName;
    }

    public void setLastName(String lastName) {
        this.lastName = lastName;
    }

}
```

As we can see, the `Person` bean is a simple request scoped CDI named bean.

Now that we have a simple JSF application that uses HTML5-friendly markup, the next step is to modify it to take advantage of the Java API for WebSocket.

Developing the WebSocket server endpoint

Once we have our JSF code in place, we can add a WebSocket server endpoint to our project by going to **File** | **New File**, selecting the **Web** category, and selecting **WebSocket Endpoint** as the file type.

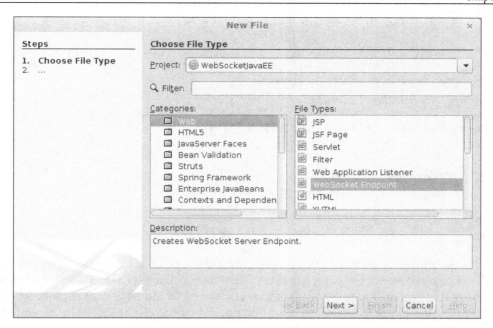

We need to give our endpoint a name and specify the value for **WebSocket URI**.

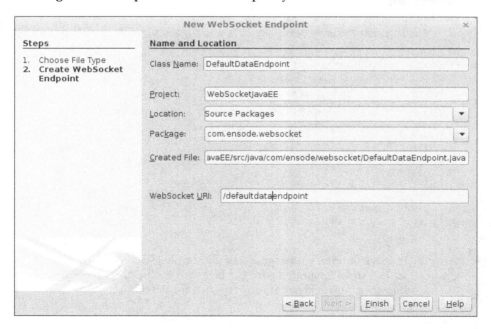

After clicking on **Finish**, NetBeans generates a WebSocket server endpoint for us:

```java
package com.ensode.websocket;

import javax.websocket.OnMessage;
import javax.websocket.server.ServerEndpoint;

@ServerEndpoint("/defaultdataendpoint")
public class DefaultDataEndpoint {

    @OnMessage
    public String onMessage(String message) {
        return null;
    }
}
```

Notice how the value attribute of the `@ServerEndpoint` annotation matches the value we entered when creating the class with the wizard. NetBeans also generates a dummy method annotated with `@OnMessage` for us to modify. We will modify this method to return a JSON string that will be parsed by the client side. The modified `onMessage()` method looks like this:

```java
@OnMessage
public String onMessage(String message) {
    String retVal;

    if (message.equals("get_defaults")) {
        retVal = new StringBuilder("{").
                append("\"firstName\":\"Auto\",").
                append("\"lastName\":\"Generated\"").
                append("}").toString();
    } else {
        retVal = "";
    }

    return retVal;
}
```

 In this example, we are generating a simple JSON string by hand. JSON can be generated with the Java API for JSON-P. Refer to *Chapter 8, Java API for JSON Processing*, for details.

The `message` parameter of the `onMessage()` method represents the value of the message that will be sent from the client. If our `onMessage()` method receives the `get_defaults` string from the client, it generates a JSON string with default values that will be used to populate the form.

 Typically, messages sent from clients are JSON-formatted strings. In our simple example, we are just using an arbitrary string.

The JSON string will then need to be parsed by JavaScript on the client side. In order to implement this last piece of the puzzle, we need to add some JavaScript to our JSF markup.

Implementing WebSocket functionality on the client

Now, we need add JavaScript code to our markup to interact with our WebSocket server endpoint. Take a look at the following code:

```xml
<?xml version='1.0' encoding='UTF-8' ?>
<!DOCTYPE html PUBLIC "-//W3C//DTD XHTML 1.0 Transitional//EN"
"http://www.w3.org/TR/xhtml1/DTD/xhtml1-transitional.dtd">
<html xmlns="http://www.w3.org/1999/xhtml"
      xmlns:jsf="http://xmlns.jcp.org/jsf">
    <head jsf:id="head">
        <title>WebSocket and Java EE</title>
        <script language="javascript" type="text/javascript">
            var wsUri = getRootUri() +
                "/WebSocketJavaEE/defaultdataendpoint";

            function getRootUri() {
                return "ws://" + (document.location.hostname == "" ?
                    "localhost" : document.location.hostname) + ":" +
                    (document.location.port == "" ? "8080" :
                    document.location.port);
            }

            function init() {
                websocket = new WebSocket(wsUri);
                websocket.onopen = function (evt) {
                    onOpen(evt)
                };
```

```
            websocket.onmessage = function (evt) {
                onMessage(evt)
            };
            websocket.onerror = function (evt) {
                onError(evt)
            };
        }

        function onOpen(evt) {
            console.log("CONNECTED");

        }

        function onMessage(evt) {
            console.log("RECEIVED: " + evt.data);

            var json = JSON.parse(evt.data);

             document.getElementById('firstName').value=
                json.firstName;
            document.getElementById('lastName').value=
                json.lastName;
        }

        function onError(evt) {
            console.log('ERROR: ' + evt.data);
        }

        function doSend(message) {
            console.log("SENT: " + message);
            websocket.send(message);
        }

        window.addEventListener("load", init, false);

    </script>

</head>
<body jsf:id="body">
    <form method="POST" jsf:prependId="false">
        <input type="button" value="Get Defaults"
            onclick="doSend('get_defaults')"/>
        <table>
            <tr>
```

```
                <td>First Name</td>
                <td>
                    <input type="text" jsf:id="firstName"
                            jsf:value="#{person.firstName}"/>
                </td>
            </tr>
            <tr>
                <td>Last Name</td>
                <td>
                    <input type="text" jsf:id="lastName"
                            jsf:value="#{person.lastName}"/>
                </td>
            </tr>
            <tr>
                <td></td>
                <td>
                    <input type="submit" value="Submit"
                        jsf:action="confirmation"/>
                </td>
            </tr>
        </table>
    </form>
  </body>
</html>
```

We based the JavaScript code in this example on the Echo sample application included with NetBeans and discussed this earlier in this chapter. The first change we made was to change the value of the `wsUri` variable to match the URI of our WebSocket server endpoint. The URI of the WebSocket endpoints we develop will always consist of the context root of our application followed by the value of the `value` attribute of the `@ServerEndpoint` annotation (in our example, `/defaultdataendpoint`).

 The context root of a Java EE application is the part of the URL that we type right after the port; by default, the context root matches the name of our WAR file.

For example, our application's URL is `http://localhost:8080/WebSocketJavaEE`. Therefore, the context root of our application is `WebSocketJavaEE`.

In the original Echo sample application, a new WebSocket connection was created every time we clicked on the button labeled **Press me**. We modified the JavaScript code to establish the connection only once when the page loads for the first time. We added the necessary calls to the `init()` JavaScript function. In this function, we bind some of our JavaScript functions to react to certain WebSocket events. Our `onOpen()` function will be called when a connection is made to our WebSocket server endpoint. The `onMessage()` function will be invoked when the client receives a message from the WebSocket server endpoint, and `onError()` will be invoked if there is an error while communicating with the WebSocket server endpoint.

Our `onOpen()` and `onError()` JavaScript functions are slightly modified versions of the corresponding functions in the Echo sample message; in our case, we modified them to simply display a message on the browser log.

[In most browsers, the browser console can be seen by hitting *F12* and clicking on the **Console** tab.]

Our `onMessage()` function parses the JSON string sent by our WebSocket server endpoint and populates our form with the appropriate values.

As far as the actual markup goes, we added a button labeled **Get Defaults** that invokes our `doSend()` JavaScript function, passing the `get_defaults` string as a parameter. The `doSend()` function, in turn, passes this string to our WebSocket server endpoint via the `send()` function of the JavaScript WebSocket object. Our WebSocket server endpoints returns a JSON string with default values when it gets this exact string as a parameter.

The following screenshot shows our application in action:

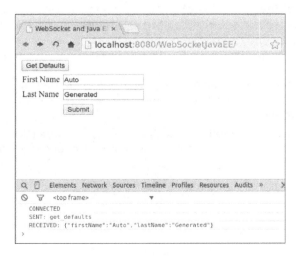

Our screenshot shows what happens after we click on the button labeled **Get Defaults**. Text fields are populated with the values we got from the JSON-formatted string we got from the server. At the bottom of the screenshot, we can see the output of the values we sent to the browser log.

Summary

In this chapter, we covered how to develop Java EE applications using the new WebSocket protocol. First, we examined a sample application using WebSocket provided by NetBeans, examining its source code to better understand how to write our own applications. We then applied that knowledge to develop our own WebSocket application via the new Java API for WebSocket introduced in Java EE 7, taking full advantage of NetBeans wizards to aid us in the creation of our application.

10
RESTful Web Services with JAX-RS

Representational State Transfer (REST) is an architectural style in which web services are viewed as resources and can be identified by Uniform Resource Identifiers (URI).

Web services developed using the REST style are known as RESTful web services. Java EE 6 added support to RESTful web services through the addition of the Java API for RESTful Web Services (JAX-RS). JAX-RS has been available as a standalone API for a while, but it became part of Java EE in version 6 of the specification.

One very common use of RESTful web services is to act as a frontend to a database, that is, RESTful web service clients can use a RESTful web service to perform CRUD (short for create, read, update, and delete) operations in a database. Since this is such a common use case, NetBeans includes outstanding support for this—allowing us to create RESTful web services that act as a database frontend with a few simple mouse clicks.

Here are some of the topics we will cover in this chapter:

- Generating RESTful web services from an existing database
- Testing RESTful web services using tools provided by NetBeans
- Generating RESTful Java client code for our RESTful web services
- Generating RESTful JavaScript clients for our RESTful web services

Generating a RESTful web service from an existing database

To create a RESTful web service from an existing database, we simply need to go to **File | New** in a web application project, then select the **Web Services** category, and select the **RESTful Web Services From Database** file type:

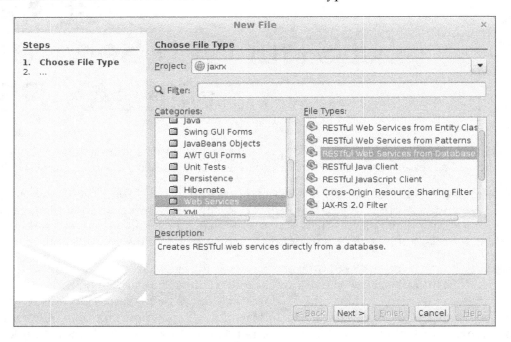

In the next step in the wizard, we need to pick a data source and select one or more tables to use to generate our web service. In our example, we will generate a web service for the CUSTOMER table of the sample database included in NetBeans.

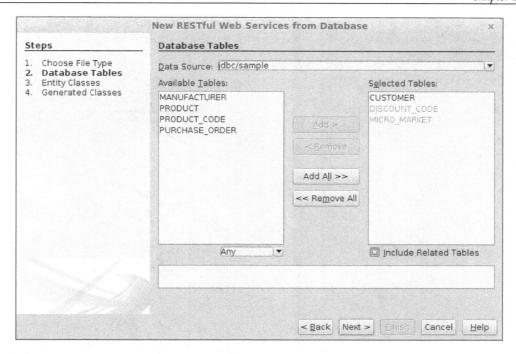

Now, we need to enter a package for our web service code.

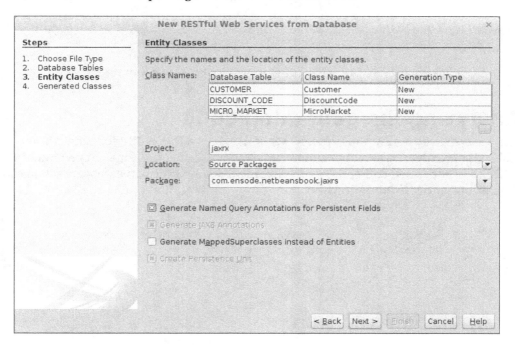

Then, we need to pick a **Resource Package** or simply accept the default value of service. It is a good idea to enter a package name that follows standard package naming conventions.

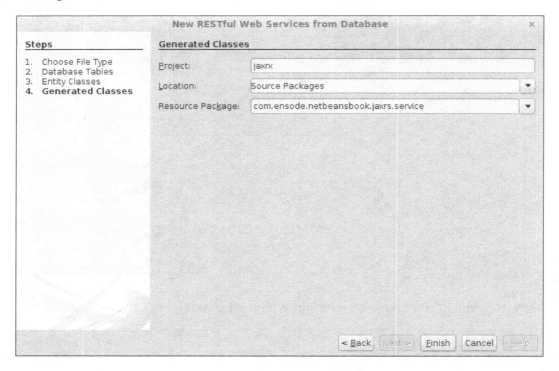

When we click on **Finish**, our RESTful web service code is generated.

Analyzing the generated code

The wizard discussed in the previous section creates a JPA entity for each chosen table, along with an AbstractFacade class and a Facade class for each generated JPA entity. The generated code follows the Facade design pattern; in essence, each Facade class is a wrapper for the JPA code.

See http://en.wikipedia.org/wiki/Facade_pattern for more information on the Facade design pattern.

The generated Facade classes are deployed as RESTful web services and can be accessed as such.

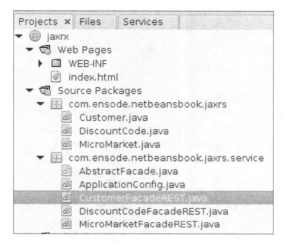

The AbstractFacade class serves as a parent class for all other Facade classes, as shown in the following code:

```java
package com.ensode.netbeansbook.jaxrs.service;

import java.util.List;
import javax.persistence.EntityManager;

public abstract class AbstractFacade<T> {
    private Class<T> entityClass;

    public AbstractFacade(Class<T> entityClass) {
        this.entityClass = entityClass;
    }

    protected abstract EntityManager getEntityManager();

    public void create(T entity) {
        getEntityManager().persist(entity);
    }

    public void edit(T entity) {
        getEntityManager().merge(entity);
    }
```

```java
    public void remove(T entity) {
        getEntityManager().remove(getEntityManager().merge(entity));
    }

    public T find(Object id) {
        return getEntityManager().find(entityClass, id);
    }

    public List<T> findAll() {
        javax.persistence.criteria.CriteriaQuery cq =
            getEntityManager().getCriteriaBuilder().createQuery();
        cq.select(cq.from(entityClass));
        return getEntityManager().createQuery(cq).getResultList();
    }

    public List<T> findRange(int[] range) {
        javax.persistence.criteria.CriteriaQuery cq =
            getEntityManager().getCriteriaBuilder().createQuery();
        cq.select(cq.from(entityClass));
        javax.persistence.Query q = getEntityManager().
createQuery(cq);
        q.setMaxResults(range[1] - range[0] + 1);
        q.setFirstResult(range[0]);
        return q.getResultList();
    }

    public int count() {
        javax.persistence.criteria.CriteriaQuery cq =
            getEntityManager().getCriteriaBuilder().createQuery();
        javax.persistence.criteria.Root<T> rt = cq.from(entityClass);
        cq.select(getEntityManager().getCriteriaBuilder().count(rt));
        javax.persistence.Query q = getEntityManager().
createQuery(cq);
        return ((Long) q.getSingleResult()).intValue();
    }

}
```

As we can see, AbstractFacade has an entityClass variable that gets set to the appropriate type via generics by its child classes. Also, it has methods to create, edit, remove, find, and count entities. The body of these methods is standard JPA code and should be familiar to you by now.

As we mentioned earlier, the wizard generates a facade for each generated JPA entity. In this example, we picked a single table (CUSTOMER); therefore, a JPA entity was created for this table (along with two related tables). The Facade class for the Customer JPA entity is called CustomerFacadeREST. The code is as follows:

```java
package com.ensode.netbeansbook.jaxrs.service;

import com.ensode.netbeansbook.jaxrs.Customer;
import java.util.List;
import javax.ejb.Stateless;
import javax.persistence.EntityManager;
import javax.persistence.PersistenceContext;
import javax.ws.rs.Consumes;
import javax.ws.rs.DELETE;
import javax.ws.rs.GET;
import javax.ws.rs.POST;
import javax.ws.rs.PUT;
import javax.ws.rs.Path;
import javax.ws.rs.PathParam;
import javax.ws.rs.Produces;

@Stateless
@Path("com.ensode.netbeansbook.jaxrs.customer")
public class CustomerFacadeREST extends AbstractFacade<Customer> {
    @PersistenceContext(unitName = "jaxrxPU")
    private EntityManager em;

    public CustomerFacadeREST() {
        super(Customer.class);
    }

    @POST
    @Override
    @Consumes({"application/xml", "application/json"})
    public void create(Customer entity) {
        super.create(entity);
    }

    @PUT
    @Path("{id}")
    @Consumes({"application/xml", "application/json"})
    public void edit(@PathParam("id") Integer id, Customer entity) {
        super.edit(entity);
    }
```

```
@DELETE
@Path("{id}")
public void remove(@PathParam("id") Integer id) {
    super.remove(super.find(id));
}

@GET
@Path("{id}")
@Produces({"application/xml", "application/json"})
public Customer find(@PathParam("id") Integer id) {
    return super.find(id);
}

@GET
@Override
@Produces({"application/xml", "application/json"})
public List<Customer> findAll() {
    return super.findAll();
}

@GET
@Path("{from}/{to}")
@Produces({"application/xml", "application/json"})
public List<Customer> findRange(@PathParam("from") Integer from,
  @PathParam("to") Integer to) {
    return super.findRange(new int[]{from, to});
}

@GET
@Path("count")
@Produces("text/plain")
public String countREST() {
    return String.valueOf(super.count());
}

@Override
protected EntityManager getEntityManager() {
    return em;
}

}
```

As evident from the `@Stateless` annotation, the generated class is a stateless session bean. The `@Path` annotation is used to identify the Uniform Resource Identifier (URI) that our class will serve requests for. As we can see, several of the methods in our class are annotated with the `@POST`, `@PUT`, `@DELETE` and `@GET` annotations. These methods will be automatically invoked when our web service responds to the corresponding HTTP requests. Notice that several of the methods are annotated with the `@Path` annotation as well; this is because some of these methods require a parameter. For example, when we need to delete an entry from the CUSTOMER table, we need to pass the primary key of the corresponding rows as a parameter. The format of the value attribute of the `@Path` annotation is `"{varName}"`, where the text between the curly braces is known as a **path parameter**. Notice that the method has corresponding parameters that are annotated with the `@PathParam` annotation.

Testing our RESTful web service

Once we deploy our project, we can make sure that the web service was deployed successfully by expanding the **RESTful Web Services** node on our project, right-clicking on our RESTful web service, and selecting **Test Resource Uri**:

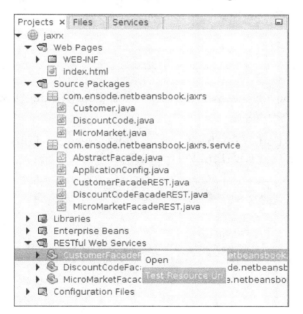

This action will invoke the `findAll()` method in our service (since it is the only method that doesn't require a parameter), and the generated XML response will automatically be opened in the browser.

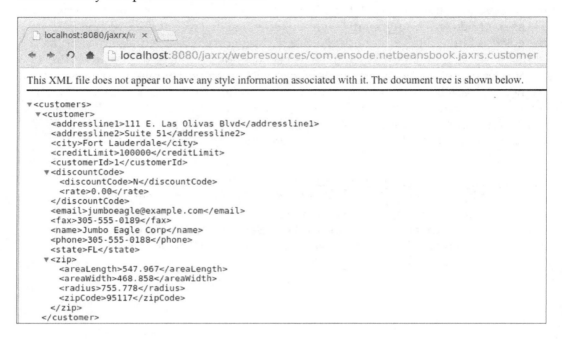

The XML response for our web service displays the data in the CUSTOMER table in the database in an XML format.

We can also easily test other methods in our web service by right-clicking on the project and selecting **Test RESTful Web Services**:

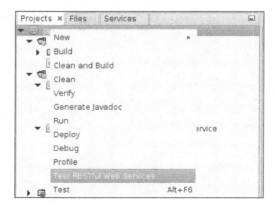

Now, the following popup window will show up:

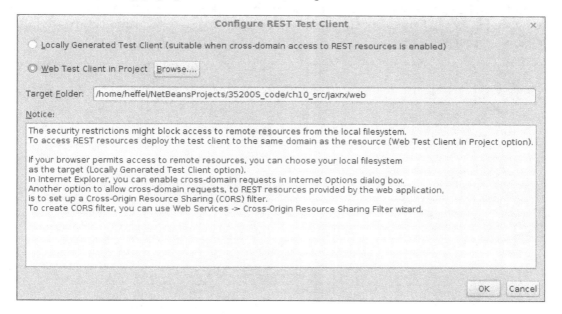

In most cases, we should accept the default **Web Test Client** from the **Project** option, since it works with most browsers and operating systems.

Now, a page similar to the following will automatically open in the browser:

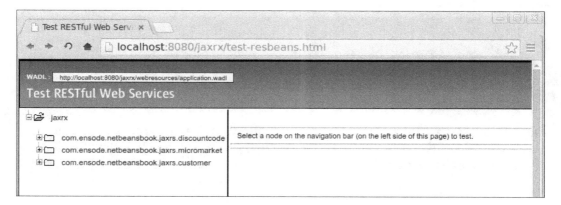

Expand any node from the left and click on a web service, select **GET(application/json)** from the dropdown labeled **Choose method to test**, and click on **Test**. Now, an HTTP GET request being sent to the RESTful web service and returns a JSON response.

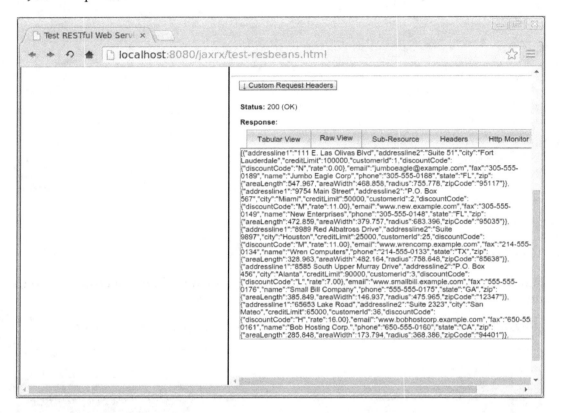

Now, the page displays a JSON-formatted representation of the data in the CUSTOMER table.

Our RESTful web service can produce or consume either XML or JSON (short for JavaScript Object Notation); this can be seen in the values for each of the @Produces and @Consumes annotations in our code.

If we want to see the XML representation of the result of the `findAll()` method, all
we need to do is select **GET(application/xml)** and click on the **Test** button.

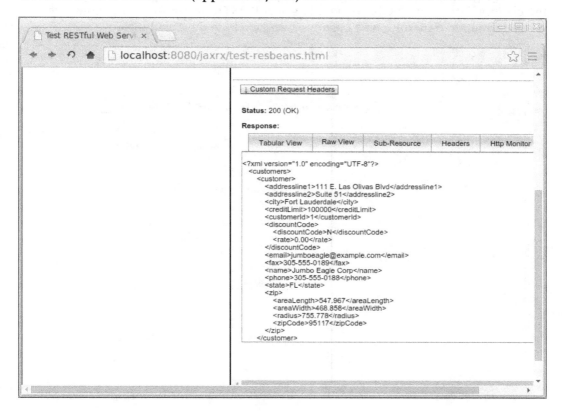

We can also insert a single record by selecting the POST method from the dropdown and passing either XML or JSON-formatted data. For example, if we want to test the post method using JSON, we would select **POST(application/json)**, enter the JSON-formatted data for a new customer, and click on the **Test** button.

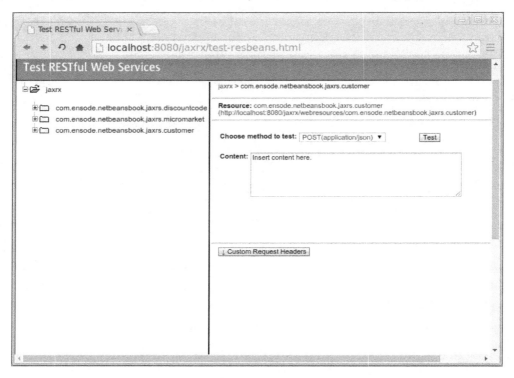

Now that we have verified that our RESTful web service was deployed successfully, the next step is to implement a client application that uses our service. However, before doing so, let's take a look at the ApplicationConfig class generated by NetBeans.

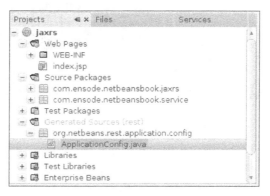

The source code for this class looks like this:

```java
package com.ensode.netbeansbook.jaxrs.service;

import java.util.Set;
import javax.ws.rs.core.Application;

@javax.ws.rs.ApplicationPath("webresources")
public class ApplicationConfig extends Application {

    @Override
    public Set<Class<?>> getClasses() {
        Set<Class<?>> resources = new java.util.HashSet<>();
        addRestResourceClasses(resources);
        return resources;
    }

    /**
     * Do not modify addRestResourceClasses() method.
     * It is automatically populated with
     * all resources defined in the project.
     * If required, comment out calling this method in getClasses().
     */
    private void addRestResourceClasses(Set<Class<?>> resources) {
        resources.add(
com.ensode.netbeansbook.jaxrs.service.CustomerFacadeREST.class
            );
        resources.add(
com.ensode.netbeansbook.jaxrs.service.DiscountCodeFacadeREST.class
            );
        resources.add(
com.ensode.netbeansbook.jaxrs.service.MicroMarketFacadeREST.class
            );
    }
}
```

The purpose of this class is to configure JAX-RS. The only requirement is that the class should extend `javax.ws.rs.core.Application` and should be annotated with the `@javax.ws.rs.ApplicationPath` annotation. This annotation is used to specify the base URI of all paths specified by the `@Path` annotation in our RESTful web services classes. By default, NetBeans uses a path named `webresources` for all RESTful web services.

NetBeans overrides the `getClasses()` method of `javax.ww.rs.core.Application` and makes it return a set of classes containing all of the RESTful web services in our application (classes annotated with the `@Path` annotation). NetBeans automatically adds all of our RESTful web services in the `addRestResourceClasses()` method, and invokes this method from the generated `getClasses()` method.

Generating RESTful Java client code

NetBeans provides a wizard that can automatically generate client Java code that invokes our RESTful web service methods via the corresponding HTTP requests.

To generate this client code in a Java application project, we simply need to go to **File | New File**, select the **Web Services** category, and select **RESTful Java Client** as the file type.

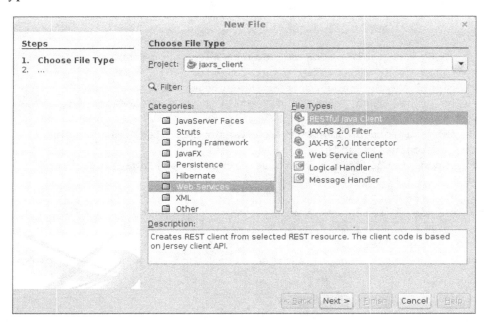

In the next step in the wizard, we need to enter a class name and a package name for our JAX-RS client.

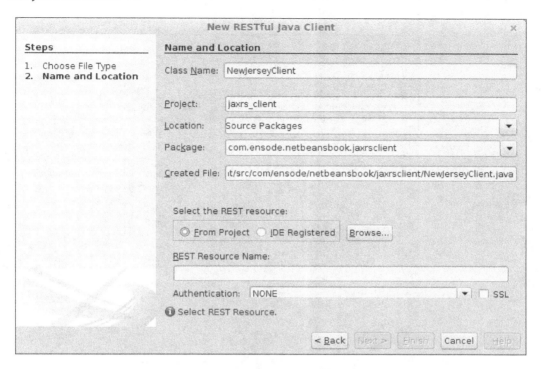

Jersey is the JAX-RS implementation included with GlassFish. Since we are using the GlassFish application server included with NetBeans, NetBeans uses a default name **NewJerseyClient** for the **Class Name** field; this default class name will suffice for our purposes.

Then, we need to select the RESTful web service that our client will consume. In
our case, we need to select the **From Project** radio button under **Select the REST
resource** and click on the button labeled **Browse**.

Then, we simply need to select the RESTful web service we developed earlier.

At this point, NetBeans generates the following code:

```
/*
 * To change this license header, choose License Headers in Project
Properties.
 * To change this template file, choose Tools | Templates
 * and open the template in the editor.
 */
package com.ensode.netbeansbook.jaxrsclient;

import javax.ws.rs.ClientErrorException;
import javax.ws.rs.client.Client;
import javax.ws.rs.client.WebTarget;
```

```
/**
 * Jersey REST client generated for REST resource:CustomerFacadeREST
 * [com.ensode.netbeansbook.jaxrs.customer]<br>
 * USAGE:
 * <pre>
 *         NewJerseyClient client = new NewJerseyClient();
 *         Object response = client.XXX(...);
 *         // do whatever with response
 *         client.close();
 * </pre>
 *
 */
public class NewJerseyClient {
    private WebTarget webTarget;
    private Client client;
    private static final String BASE_URI = "http://localhost:8080/
jaxrx/webresources";
    public NewJerseyClient() {
        client = javax.ws.rs.client.ClientBuilder.newClient();
        webTarget = client.target(BASE_URI).path(
          "com.ensode.netbeansbook.jaxrs.customer");
    }
    public String countREST() throws ClientErrorException {
        WebTarget resource = webTarget;
        resource = resource.path("count");
        return resource.request(
            javax.ws.rs.core.MediaType.TEXT_PLAIN).get(String.class);
    }
    public void edit_XML(Object requestEntity, String id) throws
ClientErrorException {
        webTarget.path(
          java.text.MessageFormat.format("{0}", new Object[]
            {id})).request(
            javax.ws.rs.core.MediaType.APPLICATION_XML)
            .put(javax.ws.rs.client.Entity.entity(requestEntity,
            javax.ws.rs.core.MediaType.APPLICATION_XML));
    }
    public void edit_JSON(Object requestEntity, String id)
      throws ClientErrorException {
        webTarget.path(
          java.text.MessageFormat.format("{0}", new Object[]
          {id})).request(
```

```
            javax.ws.rs.core.MediaType.APPLICATION_JSON)
            .put(javax.ws.rs.client.Entity.entity(requestEntity,
            javax.ws.rs.core.MediaType.APPLICATION_JSON));
    }
    public <T> T find_XML(Class<T> responseType, String id)
       throws ClientErrorException {
        WebTarget resource = webTarget;
        resource = resource.path(java.text.MessageFormat.format(
        "{0}", new Object[]{id}));
        return resource.request(
           javax.ws.rs.core.MediaType.APPLICATION_XML).
get(responseType);
    }
    public <T> T find_JSON(Class<T> responseType, String id)
       throws ClientErrorException {
        WebTarget resource = webTarget;
        resource = resource.path(java.text.MessageFormat.format("{0}",
           new Object[]{id}));
        return resource.request(
           javax.ws.rs.core.MediaType.APPLICATION_JSON).
           get(responseType);
    }
    public <T> T findRange_XML(Class<T> responseType, String from,
       String to) throws ClientErrorException {
        WebTarget resource = webTarget;
        resource = resource.path(java.text.MessageFormat.format("{0}/
{1}",
           new Object[]{from, to}));
        return
           resource.request(javax.ws.rs.core.MediaType.APPLICATION_
XML).
           get(responseType);
    }
    public <T> T findRange_JSON(Class<T> responseType, String from,
       String to) throws ClientErrorException {
        WebTarget resource = webTarget;
        resource = resource.path(java.text.MessageFormat.format("{0}/
{1}",
           new Object[]{from, to}));
        return resource.request(
           javax.ws.rs.core.MediaType.APPLICATION_JSON).
get(responseType);
    }
```

```
    public void create_XML(Object requestEntity) throws
      ClientErrorException  {
    webTarget.request(javax.ws.rs.core.MediaType.APPLICATION_XML).
    post(javax.ws.rs.client.Entity.entity(requestEntity,
    javax.ws.rs.core.MediaType.APPLICATION_XML));
    }
    public void create_JSON(Object requestEntity) throws
      ClientErrorException {
      webTarget.request(javax.ws.rs.core.MediaType.APPLICATION_JSON).
      post(javax.ws.rs.client.Entity.entity(requestEntity,
      javax.ws.rs.core.MediaType.APPLICATION_JSON));
    }
    public <T> T findAll_XML(Class<T> responseType) throws
      ClientErrorException {
        WebTarget resource = webTarget;
        return
          resource.request(javax.ws.rs.core.MediaType.APPLICATION_
XML).
          get(responseType);
    }
    public <T> T findAll_JSON(Class<T> responseType) throws
      ClientErrorException {
        WebTarget resource = webTarget;
        return resource.request(
          javax.ws.rs.core.MediaType.APPLICATION_JSON).
get(responseType);
    }
    public void remove(String id) throws ClientErrorException {
        webTarget.path(java.text.MessageFormat.format("{0}",
          new Object[]{id})).request().delete();
    }
    public void close() {
        client.close();
    }
}
```

The generated Java client code uses the JAX-RS client API introduced in JAX-RS 2.0.

As we can see, NetBeans generates wrapper methods for each of the methods in our RESTful web service. NetBeans generates two versions of each method: one that produces and/or consumes XML and another one that produces and/or consumes JSON. Each method uses generics so that we can set the return type of these methods at run time.

The easiest and most straightforward way of using these methods is to use strings. For example, we can invoke the `find_JSON(Class<T> responseType, String id)` as follows:

```
public class Main {
    public static void main(String[] args) {
        NewJerseyClient newJerseyClient = new NewJerseyClient();
        String response = newJerseyClient.find_JSON(
            String.class, "1");

        System.out.println("response is: " + response);

        newJerseyClient.close();
    }

}
```

The preceding invocation will return a string containing a JSON representation of the values in the row with an ID of 1 in the database. On executing the code, we should see the following output:

```
response is: {"addressline1":"111 E. Las Olivas
Blvd","addressline2":"Suite 51","city":"Fort Lauderdale","creditLimit"
:100000,"customerId":1,"discountCode":{"discountCode":"N","rate":0.00
},"email":"jumboeagle@example.com","fax":"305-555-0189","name":"Jumbo
Eagle Corp","phone":"305-555-0188","state":"FL","zip":{"areaLength":54
7.967,"areaWidth":468.858,"radius":755.778,"zipCode":"95117"}}
```

We can then parse and manipulate the JSON response as usual.

Additionally, we can send data to our web service in JSON or XML format; all we need to do is create a string with the appropriate JSON or XML and pass it to one of the generated methods. For example, we could insert a row into the database by using the following code:

```
package com.ensode.netbeansbook.jaxrsclient;

import javax.ws.rs.ClientErrorException;

public class Main1 {
    public static void main(String[] args) {
        String json = "{\"addressline1\":\"123 Icant Dr.\","
                + "\"addressline2\":\"Apt 42\",\"city\":"
                + "\"Springfield\",\"creditLimit\":1000,"
```

```
           +  "\"customerId\":999,\"discountCode\":"
           +  "{\"discountCode\":\"N\",\"rate\":0.00},"
           +  "\"email\":\"customer@example.com\","
           +  "\"fax\":\"555-555-1234\",\"name\":"
           +  "\"Customer Name\",\"phone\":"
           +  "\"555-555-2345\",\"state\":"
           +  "\"AL\",\"zip\":{\"areaLength\":"
           +  "547.967,\"areaWidth\":468.858,\""
           +  "radius\":755.778,"
           +  "\"zipCode\":\"12345\"}}";

        NewJerseyClient newJerseyClient = new NewJerseyClient();

        newJerseyClient.create_JSON(json);

        newJerseyClient.close();
    }
}
```

In the preceding client code, we generate JSON-formatted data so that our RESTful web service can understand it, and pass it to the create_JSON() method in the generated client class. This class in turn invokes our web service, which inserts a row in the database.

Generating RESTful JavaScript clients for our RESTful web services

In the previous section, we saw how to generate Java clients for our RESTful web services. A common scenario is to develop RESTful web services in Java and RESTful web service clients in JavaScript running in the browser. Just as NetBeans can generate Java clients, it can also generate JavaScript clients for our RESTful web services.

To generate JavaScript clients for our RESTful web services, go to **File** | **New** in a web application project, select the **Web Services** category, and select the **RESTful JavaScript Client** file type:

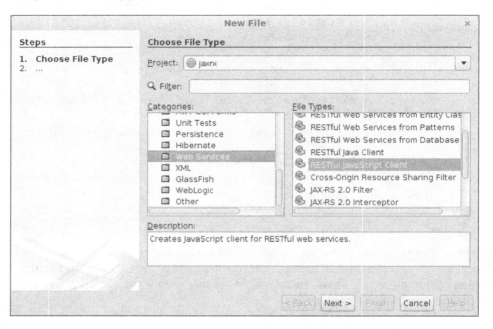

In the next step in the wizard, select **Tablesorter UI** from the **Choose resulting UI** dropdown to generate a complete CRUD application. The generated web application uses the `Backbone.js` JavaScript library. Checking the **Add Backbone.js to project sources** checkbox does exactly what is expected; if we don't click it, then backbone will be loaded from `http://cdnjs.com`, a popular Content Delivery Network (CDN) containing several popular JavaScript libraries.

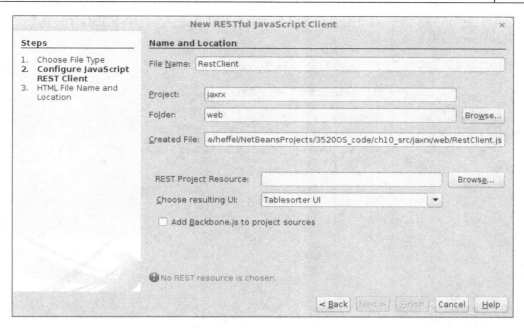

Now, we need to select a REST project resource by clicking on the **Browse** button:

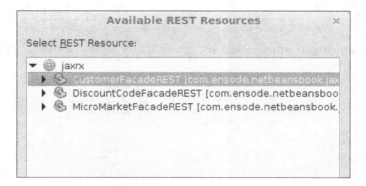

In this example, we pick the `CustomerFacadeREST` web service we developed earlier in this chapter.

In the next step in the wizard, we need to select a filename for the HTML file that will be generated.

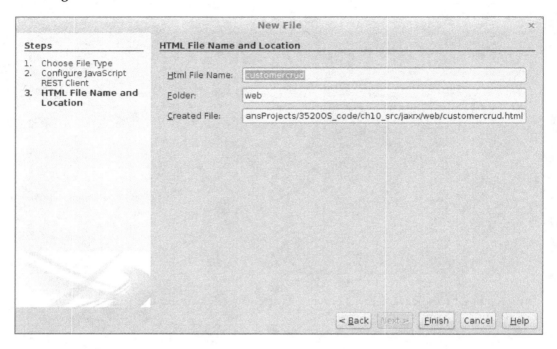

Now, we can deploy our application and point the browser to the generated page.

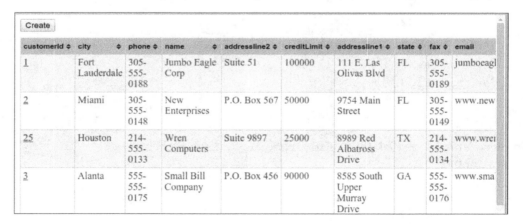

Clicking on the **Create** button in the top-left corner allows us to insert a new row to the database; input fields will be displayed at the bottom of the page. Moreover, clicking on the ID or any row will allow us to modify the data for that particular customer.

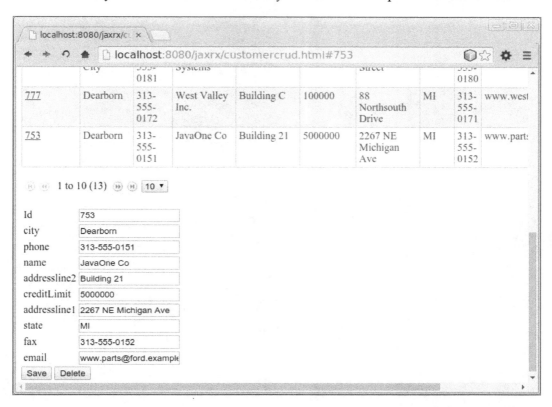

As we can see, NetBeans generated a complete JavaScript RESTful web service client without us having to write a single line of code.

Summary

In this chapter, we covered some of the powerful RESTful web service generation capabilities that NetBeans offers. We saw how NetBeans allows us to easily generate a RESTful web service from an existing database schema. We also saw how we can easily test our web services using tools provided by NetBeans and GlassFish.

Additionally, we saw how to generate a Java RESTful web service client with a few clicks of the mouse and how we can generate JavaScript web service clients with very little effort.

11
SOAP Web Services with JAX-WS

Web Services allow us to develop functionality that can be accessed across a network. What makes web services different from other similar technologies such as EJBs or **Remote Method Invocation** (**RMI**) is that they are language and platform independent, for example, a web service developed in Java might be accessed by clients written in other languages and vice versa.

In this chapter, we will cover the following topics:

- Introduction to web services
- Creating a simple web service
- Creating a web service client
- Exposing EJBs as web services

Introduction to web services

Web services allow us to write functionality that can be accessed across a network in a language- and platform-independent way.

There are two different approaches that are frequently used to develop web services: the first approach is to use the Simple Object Access Protocol (SOAP) and the second approach is to use the Representational State Transfer (REST) protocol. NetBeans supports creating web services using either approach. SOAP web services are covered in this chapter. RESTful web services were covered in the previous chapter.

When using the SOAP protocol, web service operations are defined in an XML document called a **Web Services Definition Language** (**WSDL**) file. After creating the WSDL file, an implementation of web services is performed in a proper programming language such as Java. The process of creating a WSDL is complex and error-prone; fortunately, when working with Java EE, a WSDL file can be automatically generated from a web service written in Java when this web service is deployed to the application server. Additionally, if we have a WSDL file available and need to implement the web service operations in Java, NetBeans can automatically generate most of the Java code for the implementation—creating a class with method stubs for each web service operation. All we need to do is to implement the actual logic for each method; all the "plumbing" code is automatically generated.

Creating a simple web service

In this section, we will develop a web service that performs a conversion of units of length. Our web service will have an operation that will convert inches to centimeters and another operation to do the opposite conversion (centimeters to inches).

In order to create a web service, we need to create a new web application project; in our example, the project name is UnitConversion. We can create the web service by right-clicking on our project, going to **File | New File**, then selecting the **Web Services** category, and finally selecting **Web Service** as our file type.

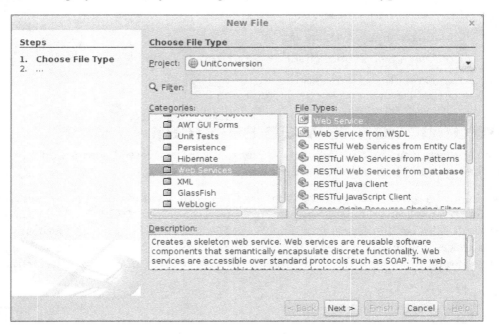

After clicking on **Next**, we need to enter a name and package for our web service in the following window:

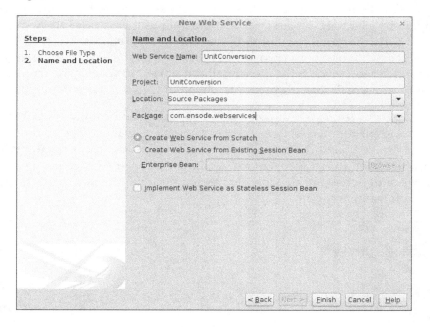

After clicking on **Finish**, our web service is created. The source code for our web service is automatically opened, as shown in the following screenshot:

```java
package com.ensode.webservices;

import javax.jws.WebService;
import javax.jws.WebMethod;
import javax.jws.WebParam;

@WebService(serviceName = "UnitConversion")
public class UnitConversion {

    /**
     * This is a sample web service operation
     */
    @WebMethod(operationName = "hello")
    public String hello(@WebParam(name = "name") String txt) {
        return "Hello " + txt + " !";
    }
}
```

As you can see, NetBeans automatically generates a simple "Hello World" web service. The class-level `@WebService` annotation marks our class as a web service. The method-level `@WebMethod` annotation marks the annotated method as a web service operation; its `operationName` attribute defines the name of the web service operation. This is the name to be used by the web service clients. The `@WebParam` annotation is used to define the properties of the web service operation parameters. In the generated web service, the `name` attribute is used to specify the name of the parameter in the WSDL that is generated when the web service is deployed.

NetBeans allows us to modify our web services via a graphical interface. We can simply add and/or remove web service operations and parameters by pointing and clicking on them, and the corresponding method stubs and annotations are automatically added to our web service's code. To access the graphical web service designer, we simply need to click on the **Design** button in the top-right corner of the web service source code.

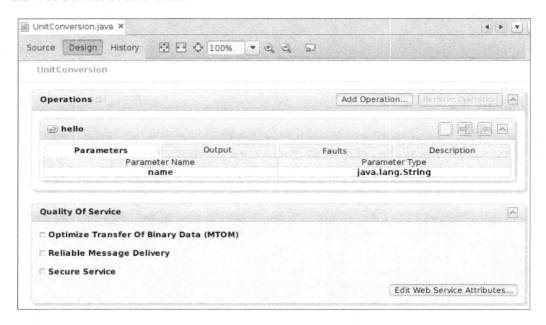

The first thing we need to do is to remove the automatically generated operation; to accomplish this, click on the **hello** operation and then click on the **Remove Operation** button.

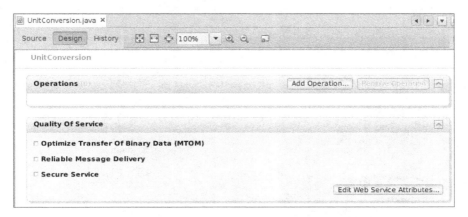

To add a web service operation, we simply need to click on the **Add Operation** button and fill in the blanks in the resulting window.

Our web service will have two operations: one to convert from inches to centimeters and another one to convert centimeters to inches. Both of these operations will take a single parameter of type double and return a double value. After clicking on the **Add Operation** button, we can enter the required information for the inchesToCentimeters operation.

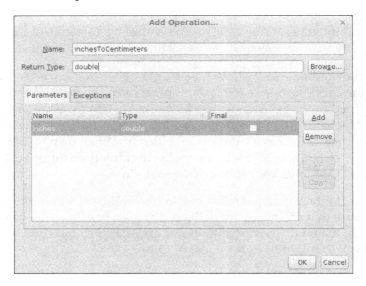

Then, we need to do the same for the `centimetersToInches` operation (not shown here). After doing so, our design window will show the newly added operations.

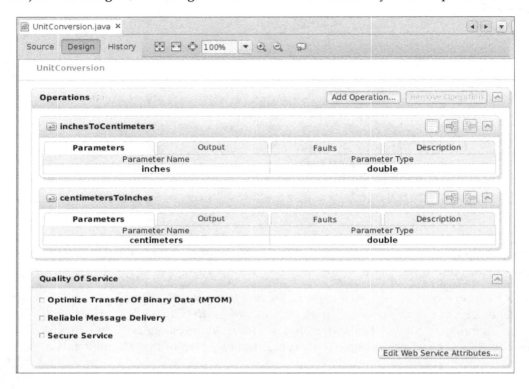

In addition to adding operations to our web service, we can control the quality of service settings by simply selecting or deselecting checkboxes in the design window.

Web services transmit data as XML text messages between the web service and its client. Sometimes, it is necessary to transmit binary data such as images. Binary data is normally inlined in the SOAP message by using MTOM (Message Transmission Optimization Mechanism); binary data is sent as an attachment to the message. This makes the transmission of binary data more efficient. When using NetBeans, we can indicate that we wish to use MTOM by simply checking the **Optimize Transfer Of Binary Data (MTOM)** checkbox in the design window.

Checking the **Reliable Message Delivery** checkbox allows us to indicate that we want to make sure that messages are delivered at least once and not more than once. Enabling reliable message delivery allows our applications to recover from situations where our messages might have been lost in transit.

Clicking on the **Secure Service** checkbox results in security features, such as encrypting messages between the client and server and requiring client authentication to be enabled for our web service.

We can see the generated method stubs by clicking on the **Source** tab:

```java
package com.ensode.webservices;

import javax.jws.WebService;
import javax.jws.WebMethod;
import javax.jws.WebParam;

@WebService(serviceName = "UnitConversion")
public class UnitConversion {

    /**
     * Web service operation
     */
    @WebMethod(operationName = "inchesToCentimeters")
    public double inchesToCentimeters(@WebParam(name = "inches") double inches) {
        //TODO write your implementation code here:
        return 0.0;
    }

    /**
     * Web service operation
     */
    @WebMethod(operationName = "centimetersToInches")
    public double centimetersToInches(@WebParam(name = "centimeters") double centimeters) {
        //TODO write your implementation code here:
        return 0.0;
    }
}
```

Now, all we need to do is to replace the generated body of the methods in the class with the real bodies, deploy our application, and our web service will be good to go. In our case, all we need to do is multiply the inches by 2.54 to convert from inches to centimeters and divide the centimeters by 2.54 to convert them to inches.

Once we have replaced the method bodies with the actual required functionality, we are ready to deploy our web service. This can be done by right-clicking on our project and selecting **Deploy**.

Testing our web service

At this point, we should notice a **Web Services** node in our **Projects** window. If we expand it, we should see our newly developed web service.

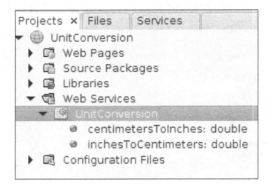

If we deployed our web service to the GlassFish application server included with NetBeans, we can test it by simply right-clicking on it in the **Projects** window and selecting **Test Web Service**.

 If you see the following error in the GlassFish log: **Failed to read schema document 'xjc.xsd', because 'bundle' access is not allowed due to restriction set by the accessExternalSchema property**, then create a file named `jaxp.properties` that contains the following line: `javax.xml.accessExternalSchema=all`.

Place the file under (path to JDK): `/jre/lib`.

Here, we can test our web service's methods by simply entering some values in the text fields and clicking on the appropriate button. For example, entering 2.54 in the second text field and clicking on the button labeled **centimetersToInches** displays the following page in the browser:

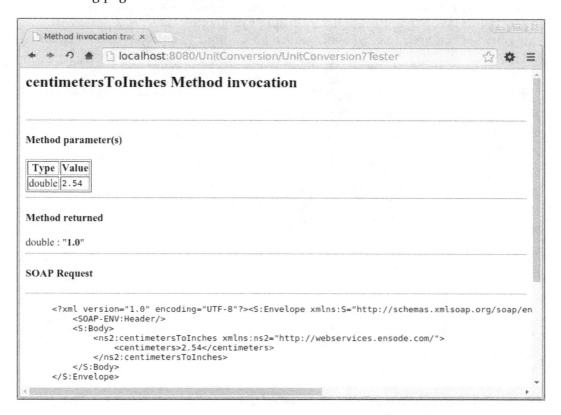

At the top of the page, we can see the parameters that were passed to the method, along with the return value. At the bottom of the page, we can see the "raw" SOAP request and response.

Developing a client for our web service

Now that we have developed our web service and tested it to verify that it works properly, we are going to create a simple client that will invoke our web service. A web services client can be any kind of Java project, such as a standard Java application, a Java ME application, a web application or an enterprise project. To keep our client code simple, we will create a Java application project for our client.

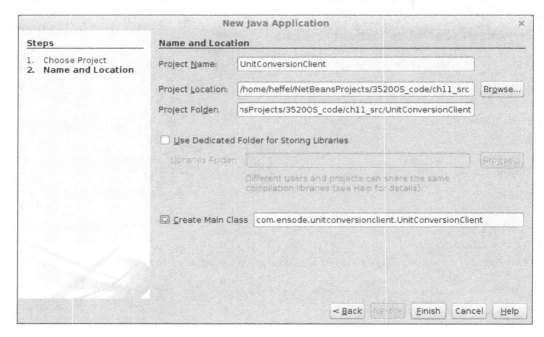

Once we have created our project, we need to create a new web service client by creating a new file, selecting the **Web Services** category, and selecting the **Web Service Client** file type.

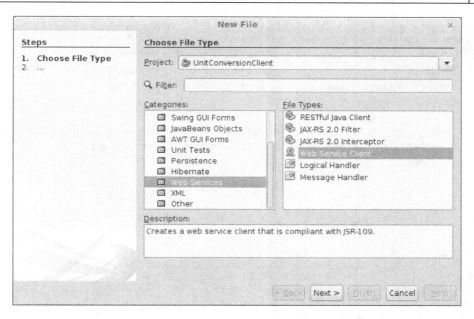

In the next step in the wizard, we need to select the radio button labeled **Project** if it is not selected already, then click on **Browse**, and finally select one of the web services we created in our web services project. The URL for the generated WSDL file for the web service we selected will automatically be added to the corresponding text field.

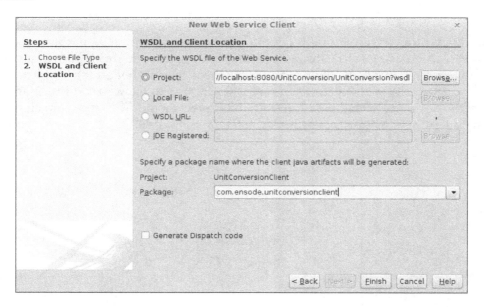

Notice that we can develop web service clients for web services we didn't develop ourselves. In order to do this, we simply select the **Local File** radio button to use a WSDL file in our hard drive or the **WSDL URL** radio button to use a WSDL that is published online. NetBeans also comes preconfigured to use several publicly available web services. To develop a client for one of these, click on the **IDE Registered** radio button.

At this point, a new node labeled **Web Service References** is added to our project. Expanding this node all the way reveals the operations we defined in our web services project.

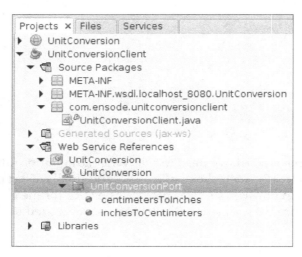

Typically, writing a web services client involves some amount of boilerplate code. However, when using NetBeans, we can simply drag the web service operation we wish to invoke to our code. This generates all the necessary boilerplate code and we just need to specify which parameters we want to send to the web service. Dragging the **inchesToCentimeters** operation from the **Projects** window to the main class of our web services client project generates the following code:

```
      UnitConversionClient.java ×

   Source  History    ⟦⟧  ⟦⟧ ▾ ⟦⟧ ▾    ⟦⟧ ⟦⟧ ⟦⟧ ⟦⟧ ⟦⟧    ⟦⟧ ⟦⟧ ⟦⟧    ⟦⟧ ⟦⟧   ⟦⟧ ⟦⟧    ⟦⟧ ⟦⟧

    1     package com.ensode.unitconversionclient;
    2
    3     public class UnitConversionClient {
    4
    5  ⊟      /**
    6            * @param args the command line arguments
    7            */
    8  ⊟      public static void main(String[] args) {
    9              // TODO code application logic here
   10          }
   11
   12  ⊟      private static double inchesToCentimeters(double inches) {
   13              com.ensode.unitconversionclient.UnitConversion_Service service
   14                  = new com.ensode.unitconversionclient.UnitConversion_Service();
   15              com.ensode.unitconversionclient.UnitConversion port
   16                  = service.getUnitConversionPort();
   17              return port.inchesToCentimeters(inches);
   18          }
   19
   20     }
```

As we can see, a method called `inchesToCentimeters()` (the name of the web service operation we dragged to the source code) is automatically added. This method in turn invokes a couple of methods in a class called `UnitConversion_Service`. This class (along with several others) is automatically generated when we drag the web service operation to our code. We can see the generated classes by expanding the **Generated Sources (jax-ws)** node in our project window:

The `getUnitConversionPort()` method of `UnitConversion_Service` returns an instance of the `UnitConversion` class that is generated from the WSDL and is similar to the identically named class we wrote in our web service project. The method generated when we drag the web service operation to our code invokes this method, and then invokes the `inchesToCentimeters()` method on the `UnitConversion` instance that is returned. All we need to do is invoke the generated method from the main method in our code. After making this simple modification, our code now looks like this:

```
UnitConversionClient.java ×

Source   History

 1    package com.ensode.unitconversionclient;
 2
 3    public class UnitConversionClient {
 4
 5        /**
 6         * @param args the command line arguments
 7         */
 8        public static void main(String[] args) {
 9            System.out.println("Result = " + inchesToCentimeters(1));
10        }
11
12        private static double inchesToCentimeters(double inches) {
13            com.ensode.unitconversionclient.UnitConversion_Service service
14                    = new com.ensode.unitconversionclient.UnitConversion_Service();
15            com.ensode.unitconversionclient.UnitConversion port
16                    = service.getUnitConversionPort();
17            return port.inchesToCentimeters(inches);
18        }
19
20    }
```

At this point, we are ready to execute our web services client code. We should see the following output in the console:

```
t ×  Search Results

ava DB Database Process  ×  GlassFish Server 4  ×  UnitConversionClient (run)  ×

ant -f /home/heffel/NetBeansProjects/35200S_code/ch11_src/UnitConversionClient -Dnb.internal.action.name=run run
init:
Deleting: /home/heffel/NetBeansProjects/35200S_code/ch11_src/UnitConversionClient/build/built-jar.properties
deps-jar:
Updating property file: /home/heffel/NetBeansProjects/35200S_code/ch11_src/UnitConversionClient/build/built-jar.
wsimport-init:
wsimport-client-UnitConversion:
files are up to date
wsimport-client-generate:
compile:
run:
Result = 2.54
BUILD SUCCESSFUL (total time: 0 seconds)
```

Exposing EJBs as web services

In our previous web service example, we saw how we can expose a Plain Old Java Object (POJO) as a web service by packaging it in a web application and adding a few annotations to it. This makes it very easy to create web services deployed in a web application.

When working with an EJB module project, we can have stateless session beans exposed as web services. This way, they can be accessed by clients written in languages other than Java. Exposing stateless session beans as web services has the effect of allowing our web services to take advantage of all the features available to EJBs, such as transaction management and aspect oriented programming.

There are two ways of exposing a session bean as a web service. When creating a new web service in an EJB module project, the web service will automatically be implemented as a stateless session bean. Additionally, existing session beans in an EJB module project can be exposed as a web service.

Implementing new web services as EJBs

In order to implement a new web service as an EJB, we simply need to create the web service in an EJB Module or Web Application project by right-clicking on the project and selecting **New | Web Service**.

When using a web application project to create our SOAP-based web service, we are given the option of implementing the web service as a POJO or as a stateless session bean. When using an EJB module project, we can only implement the web service as a stateless session bean.

In the **New Web Service** window, we need to enter the required details as shown in the following screenshot:

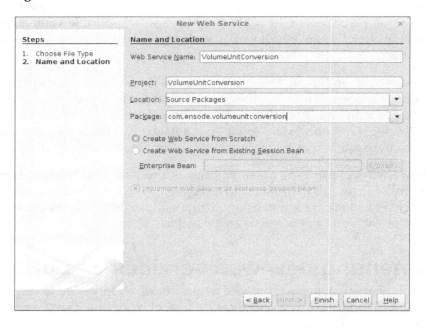

In the web services wizard, we need to enter a name for our web service, a package where our web service implementation code will be created, select the **Create Web Service From Scratch** radio button, and then click on **Finish** to generate our web service. At this point, we should see the web service source code.

```java
package com.ensode.volumeunitconversion;

import javax.jws.WebService;
import javax.jws.WebMethod;
import javax.jws.WebParam;
import javax.ejb.Stateless;

@WebService(serviceName = "VolumeUnitConversion")
@Stateless()
public class VolumeUnitConversion {

    /**
     * This is a sample web service operation
     */
    @WebMethod(operationName = "hello")
    public String hello(@WebParam(name = "name") String txt) {
        return "Hello " + txt + " !";
    }
}
```

As we can see, the generated session bean does not implement a local or remote business interface. It is decorated with the @WebService annotation, its methods are decorated with the @WebMethod annotation, and each parameter is decorated with the @WebParam annotation. The only difference between the generated code for this web service and the one for the previous example is that the generated class is a stateless session bean, and therefore it can take advantage of EJB transaction management, aspect oriented programming, and other EJB features.

Just like with regular web services, a web service implemented as a session bean can be designed using the NetBeans visual web service designer. In our example, after removing the automatically generated operation and adding two operations, our web service visual designer looks like this:

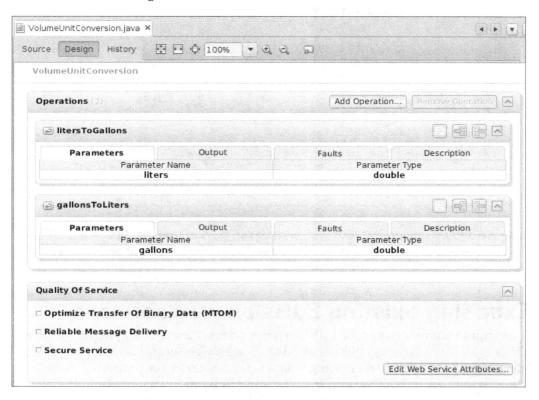

Clicking on the **Source** tab reveals the newly generated methods, along with all the appropriate annotations.

```
VolumeUnitConversion.java ×

Source   Design   History

1      package com.ensode.volumeunitconversion;
2
3    import javax.jws.WebService;
4    import javax.jws.WebMethod;
5    import javax.jws.WebParam;
6    import javax.ejb.Stateless;
7
8      @WebService(serviceName = "VolumeUnitConversion")
9      @Stateless()
10     public class VolumeUnitConversion {
11
12         /**
13          * Web service operation
14          */
15         @WebMethod(operationName = "litersToGallons")
16         public double litersToGallons(@WebParam(name = "liters") double liters) {
17             return liters * 0.26417;
18         }
19
20         /**
21          * Web service operation
22          */
23         @WebMethod(operationName = "gallonsToLiters")
24         public double gallonsToLiters(@WebParam(name = "gallons") double gallons) {
25             return gallons * 3.7854;
26         }
27     }
```

Once we deploy our project, our web service can be accessed by clients just like any other web service. It makes no difference to the client that our web service was implemented as a session bean.

Exposing existing EJBs as web services

The second way we can expose EJBs as web services is to expose an existing EJB as a web service. In order to do this, we need to create a web service as usual by going to **File | New | Web Service**, entering a name and a package for our web service, and selecting the **Create Web Service from Existing Session Bean** radio button. Then, we need to select the session bean to expose as a web service by clicking on the **Browse** button and selecting the appropriate bean.

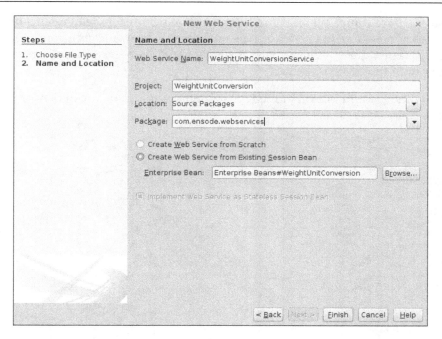

When we click on **Finish,** our new web service is created and its source code is automatically opened.

```
WeightUnitConversionService.java  ×

Source   Design   History

 1    package com.ensode.webservices;
 2
 3  ⊟ import com.ensode.ejb.WeightUnitConversion;
 4    import javax.ejb.EJB;
 5    import javax.jws.WebService;
 6    import javax.ejb.Stateless;
 7    import javax.jws.WebMethod;
 8    import javax.jws.WebParam;
 9
10    @WebService(serviceName = "WeightUnitConversionService")
11    @Stateless()
12    public class WeightUnitConversionService {
13        @EJB
14        private WeightUnitConversion ejbRef;
15        // Add business logic below. (Right-click in editor and choose
16        // "Insert Code > Add Web Service Operation")
17
18        @WebMethod(operationName = "kilosToPounds")
19        public double kilosToPounds(@WebParam(name = "kilos") double kilos) {
20            return ejbRef.kilosToPounds(kilos);
21        }
22
23        @WebMethod(operationName = "poundsToKilos")
24        public double poundsToKilos(@WebParam(name = "pounds") double pounds) {
25            return ejbRef.poundsToKilos(pounds);
26        }
27
28    }
```

As we can see, creating a web service from an existing session bean results on a new stateless session bean being created. This new session bean acts as a client for our existing EJB (as evident by the `ejbRef` instance variable in our example, which is annotated with the `@EJB` annotation).

Clicking on the **Design** button at the top, we can see the visual designer for our newly created web service.

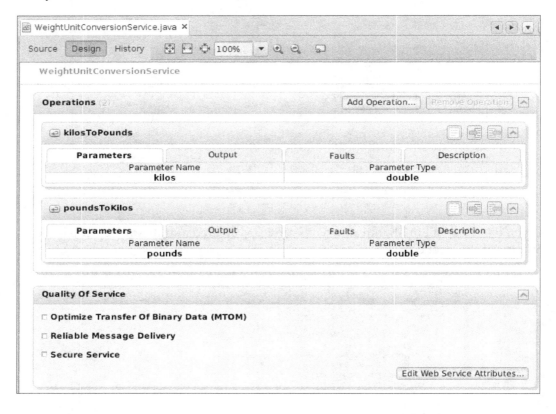

EJBs can also be exposed as web services from a web application project, in which case the generated web service will be a POJO annotated with the `@WebService`, `@WebMethod` and `@WebParam` annotations, with pass-through methods invoking the corresponding methods on the EJB being exposed as a web service.

Creating a web service from an existing WSDL

Normally, creating SOAP web services requires the creation of a WSDL file. The process of creating a WSDL is complex and error-prone, but thankfully Java EE frees us from having to create a WSDL file by hand; it gets generated automatically whenever we deploy a web service into our application server.

However, sometimes we have a WSDL file available and we need to implement its operations in Java code. For these cases, NetBeans provides a wizard that creates a Java class with method stubs from an existing WSDL.

In order to do so, we need to create a new file, select the **Web Services** category, and select **Web Service from WSDL** as the file type.

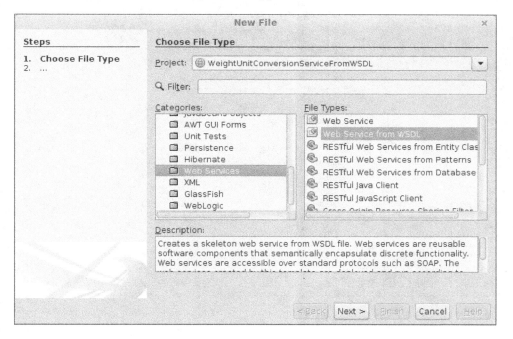

Then, we need to enter a name, package, and the existing WSDL location for our web service.

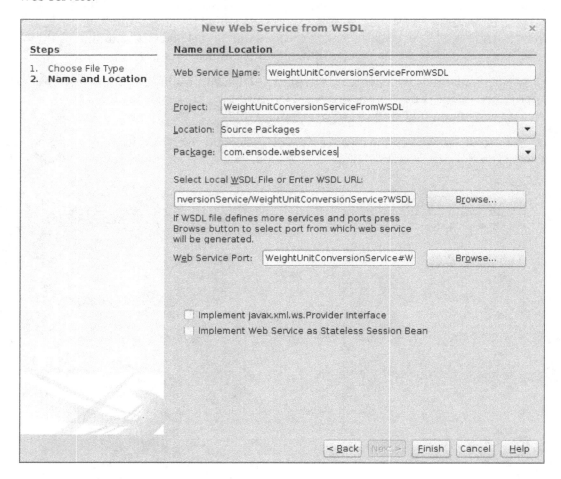

A web service will then be generated with method stubs for all operations defined in the WSDL.

```java
 2      * To change this license header, choose License Headers in Project Properties
 3      * To change this template file, choose Tools | Templates
 4      * and open the template in the editor.
 5      */
 6     package com.ensode.webservices;
 7
 8     import javax.jws.WebService;
 9
10     /**
11      *
12      * @author heffel
13      */
14     @WebService(serviceName = "WeightUnitConversionService",
15             portName = "WeightUnitConversionServicePort",
16             endpointInterface = "com.ensode.webservices.WeightUnitConversionService",
17             targetNamespace = "http://webservices.ensode.com/",
18             wsdlLocation
19             = "WEB-INF/wsdl/WeightUnitConversionServiceFromWSDL/localhost_8080/WeightUnitConversionService/WeightUnitConversionService.wsdl")
20     public class WeightUnitConversionServiceFromWSDL {
21
22         public double kilosToPounds(double kilos) {
23             //TODO implement this method
24             throw new UnsupportedOperationException("Not implemented yet.");
25         }
26
27         public double poundsToKilos(double pounds) {
28             //TODO implement this method
29             throw new UnsupportedOperationException("Not implemented yet.");
30         }
31
32     }
```

At this point, we simply need to add the method bodies for all the generated methods.

In this example, we used the WSDL that was generated from our previous example, which is redundant since we already have implementations for all the operations. However, the procedure described here applies to any WSDL file, either in the local file system or deployed in a server.

Summary

In this chapter, we explored NetBeans support for SOAP-based web service development using JAX-WS, including how to expose POJO methods as web services and how NetBeans automatically adds the required annotations to our web services.

We covered how NetBeans aids us in creating web service clients by generating most of the required boilerplate code; we just need to initialize any parameters to be passed to our web service's operations.

Additionally, we covered how to expose EJB methods as web service operations and how NetBeans supports and makes it easy to expose both new and existing EJBs as web services.

Finally, we saw how NetBeans can help us implement a web service from an existing WSDL file, which is located either on our local file system or deployed on a server by generating method stubs from said WSDL.

Index

Symbols

<ace:pushButton> component 123
<ace:selectMenu> component 123
<ace:sliderEntry> component 123
@ApplicationScoped annotation 211
@ConversationScoped annotation 211
@Dependent annotation 211
@Interceptors annotations
  EJB, decorating with 196, 197
@RequestScoped annotation 211
@Schedule annotation 199
@SessionScoped annotation 211
@TransactionAttribute annotation,
    values 192
@WebMethod annotation 322
@WebParam annotation 322
@WebService annotation 322

A

accelerated HTML5 development
    support 46-51
ACE components 121
activation configuration properties
  acknowledgeMode 247
  clientId 247
  connectionFactoryLookup 247
  destinationLookup 247
  destinationType 247
  messageSelector 247
  subscriptionDurability 248
  subscriptionName 248
add methods
  add(String name, BigDecimal value) 255
  add(String name, BigInteger value) 255

add(String name, boolean value) 255
add(String name, double value) 256
add(String name, int value) 256
add(String name, JsonArrayBuilder
    builder) 256
add(String name, JsonObjectBuilder
    builder) 256
add(String name, JsonValue value) 256
add(String name, long value) 256
add(String name, String value) 256
application
  deploying 30-33
aspect-oriented programming (AOP)
  about 194, 222
  implementing, with interceptors 193
automated generation, JPA entities
  about 149-157
  Bean Validation 159
  entity relationships 159-166
  JPQL 158
  named queries 157

B

bean
  accessing, from client 188-190
Bean Validation 159
BytesMessage interface 251

C

C 10
C++ 10
CDI
  about 30, 207
  typical markup, for JSF page 208-213

V

visual cues 44, 45

W

Web Archive (WAR) 176
web services
  about 319, 320
  EJBs, exposing as 333
Web Services Definition Language
    (WSDL) 320
WebSocket applications
  building 277-279
  user interface, developing 280-282
WebSocket code
  examining, samples included with
    NetBeans used 271, 272
  generated Java code, examining 274

generated JavaScript code,
    examining 275-277
sample Echo application, working 273
WebSocket functionality
  implementing, on client 285-289
WebSocket server endpoint
  developing 282-285
welcomePrimefaces.xhtml file
  generating 111
write() methods
  write(String name, BigDecimal value) 266
  write(String name, BigInteger value) 266
  write(String name, boolean value) 266
  write(String name, double value) 266
  write(String name, int value) 266
  write(String name, JsonValue value) 266
  write(String name, long value) 266
  write(String name, String value) 266

Thank you for buying
Java EE 7 Development with NetBeans 8

About Packt Publishing

Packt, pronounced 'packed', published its first book, *Mastering phpMyAdmin for Effective MySQL Management*, in April 2004, and subsequently continued to specialize in publishing highly focused books on specific technologies and solutions.

Our books and publications share the experiences of your fellow IT professionals in adapting and customizing today's systems, applications, and frameworks. Our solution-based books give you the knowledge and power to customize the software and technologies you're using to get the job done. Packt books are more specific and less general than the IT books you have seen in the past. Our unique business model allows us to bring you more focused information, giving you more of what you need to know, and less of what you don't.

Packt is a modern yet unique publishing company that focuses on producing quality, cutting-edge books for communities of developers, administrators, and newbies alike. For more information, please visit our website at www.packtpub.com.

About Packt Open Source

In 2010, Packt launched two new brands, Packt Open Source and Packt Enterprise, in order to continue its focus on specialization. This book is part of the Packt Open Source brand, home to books published on software built around open source licenses, and offering information to anybody from advanced developers to budding web designers. The Open Source brand also runs Packt's Open Source Royalty Scheme, by which Packt gives a royalty to each open source project about whose software a book is sold.

Writing for Packt

We welcome all inquiries from people who are interested in authoring. Book proposals should be sent to author@packtpub.com. If your book idea is still at an early stage and you would like to discuss it first before writing a formal book proposal, then please contact us; one of our commissioning editors will get in touch with you.

We're not just looking for published authors; if you have strong technical skills but no writing experience, our experienced editors can help you develop a writing career, or simply get some additional reward for your expertise.

NetBeans Platform 6.9
Developer's Guide

ISBN: 978-1-84951-176-6   Paperback: 288 pages

Create professional desktop rich-client Swing applications using the world's only modular Swing application framework

1. Create large, scalable, modular Swing applications from scratch.

2. Master a broad range of topics essential to have in your desktop application development toolkit, right from conceptualization to distribution.

3. Pursue an easy-to-follow sequential and tutorial approach that builds to a complete Swing application.

Java EE 7 with GlassFish 4
Application Server

ISBN: 978-1-78217-688-6   Paperback: 348 pages

A practical guide to install and configure the GlassFish 4 application server and develop Java EE 7 applications to be deployed to this server

1. Install and configure GlassFish 4.

2. Covers all major Java EE 7 APIs and includes new additions such as JSON Processing.

3. Packed with clear, step-by-step instructions, practical examples, and straightforward explanations.

Please check **www.PacktPub.com** for information on our titles